"We evangelicals don't t[   ]
really do. And Matthew [   ]
evangelical world—helps us care, ponder, think, and pray more wisely
as we give our bodies as a living sacrifice to Christ."
    —**Mark Galli,** Senior Managing Editor, *Christianity Today*

"What does Christianity have to say about the body? Much more than
you might think. Matthew Lee Anderson—one of evangelicalism's
brightest young writers—is a serious student of God's Word and
God's world, and in this book he patiently and insightfully explores
a theology of the body from numerous angles. Rightly seeing the
body as a gift from God for our good and his glory, Anderson shows
us what a biblical worldview has to say about the body in relationship
to community, pleasure, sex, sexuality, tattoos, death, prayer, and the
church. Anderson's arguments deserve careful consideration. I suspect
that many of us will think differently—and more biblically—about
the body as a result of this very fine work."
    —**Justin Taylor,** Managing Editor, *ESV Study Bible;* blogger, "Between
    Two Worlds"

"Ours is a befuddling age. We're 'friends' with people we've never met,
we read books that have no material substance, and we store precious
material in something rather ominously termed 'the cloud.' Physicality
is out; incorporeality is in. *Earthen Vessels* is a needed contribution in
such a time. The text is at once an elegant meditation on the body, a
fresh study of Scripture, and a celebration of the Western tradition.
Here is philosophical theology that will foster debate, critical thought,
and praise of the Savior whose physical sacrifice won our salvation."
    —**Owen Strachan,** Instructor of Christian Theology and Church
    History, Boyce College

"Matthew Lee Anderson makes an important contribution to the
evangelical dialogue about the importance and role of the human body
that is both scholarly and accessible. Too often evangelical discourse
on this subject has been either defensive or simply followed cultural
trends. Anderson is both robustly Christian and willing to listen when
other traditions may have something to contribute. Christians will
learn from this book that the body is important, but also that we are
not just computers made out of meat."
    —**John Mark Reynolds,** PhD, Director of Torrey Honors Institute,
    Biola University

"*Earthen Vessels* is a turning point in the evangelical conversation about the meaning of our bodies. If you didn't even know such a conversation was going on, you are lucky to have Matthew Anderson introduce it to you. If you've already been listening in and are as confused as the rest of us, you'll appreciate the way this book sorts things out, settles accounts, debunks myths, digs for sources, raises neglected issues, and points out the way forward. On nearly every page you can find two virtues rarely combined: surprising new insights and good old common sense. Here is good counsel (solid, soulful, scriptural) about how to be human, in a body, under the gospel."

—**Fred Sanders,** Associate Professor of Theology, Torrey Honors
   Institute, Biola University

"Tattoos, cremation, abortion, gay sex, yoga, online church: No subject is off-limits in Matthew Anderson's provocative book on the body. Anderson challenges us to deepen our understanding of what it means to be embodied. When it comes to body matters, the body matters. Though few will agree with all of Anderson's diagnoses and prescriptions, all who read this book will be challenged to consider how our views of the body line up with (or depart from) Scripture and Christian theology. This is a highly ambitious project that deserves careful consideration."

—**Trevin Wax,** author, *Counterfeit Gospels and Holy Subversion*

"I love to think. I love to be challenged. Mission accomplished in reading *Earthen Vessels*. In it, Matthew Anderson takes on prevailing cultural assumptions about the human body that have been uncritically adopted into the church of Jesus Christ. This book is for the church that is in the world. It is a truth-balm for a broken culture addicted to body image. Be challenged to forsake your 'quasi-Gnosticism' and embrace the divine dignity of your body so that you can worship well."

—**Darrin Patrick,** Lead Pastor, The Journey; author, *Church Planter*

"Nearly every strand of theology from postmodern to feminist to Catholic has a robust theology of the body—except evangelicalism. Matt's new book works toward remedying this problem by restarting the conversation about how Christians talk about this fleshly creation into which Jesus himself was incarnated."

—**John Dyer,** Director of Web Development, Dallas Theological
   Seminary; author, *From the Garden to the City*

EARTHEN
VESSELS

WHY OUR BODIES
MATTER TO OUR FAITH

MATTHEW LEE ANDERSON

BETHANYHOUSE
a division of Baker Publishing Group
Minneapolis, Minnesota

Published by Bethany House Publishers
11400 Hampshire Avenue South
Bloomington, Minnesota 55438

Bethany House Publishers is a division of
Baker Publishing Group, Grand Rapids, Michigan.

Printed in the United States of America

Library of Congress Cataloging-in-Publication Data is available for this title.

In keeping with biblical principles of creation stewardship, Baker Publishing Group advocates the responsible use of our natural resources. As a member of the Green Press Initiative, our company uses recycled paper when possible. The text paper of this book is comprised of 30% post-consumer waste.

g green press INITIATIVE

For my wife
"With my body I thee worship."

ACKNOWLEDGMENTS

My journey from graduating university to the publication of this book has taken numerous unexpected turns, some of which I have enjoyed more than others. Yet throughout the past few years I have found myself extraordinarily blessed by the love and support of readers, friends, family, and my church. It is something of a truism among authors that books are communal efforts—it has never been truer than here.

The danger of acknowledging people by name is that I will forget someone. But such dangers should never deter, for the names even of those whom I may have forgotten will be remembered on the day when they receive their crowns in heaven.

With that said, this book would probably not have happened without Sue and Bud Louck, whom I happened to visit during a particularly difficult season of anxiety and writer's block. Their prayer and encouragement revived my spirits and gave me hope for the future. The number of friends who have given similar support over the past decade is almost endless. I am also grateful for the many online friends I have made: Matt Milliner, John Dyer, Rhett Smith, Jonathan Fitzgerald, David Sessions, Trevin Wax, Joe Carter, Justin Taylor, Christopher Benson, Jake Meador, Ben Simpson, and countless others have sharpened my thinking and challenged me to pursue faithfulness. All of them have modeled the sort of thoughtful Christian engagement that I have attempted to undertake here, and have been patient and gracious in their support.

A constant anxiety for me in writing this book was that I would reflect well upon the institution that I consider the finest educational experience in America: the Torrey Honors Institute and Biola University. In particular, Dr. John Mark Reynolds' infectious passion for Jesus and Dr. Fred Sanders' brilliantly creative approach to theology have both been inspirations and models for me. But I am also grateful to Dr. Moyer Hubbard for teaching me to read and love Saint Paul, to Dr. Paul Spears for providing advice and encouragement, and to Dr. Matt Jenson and Dr. Sanders for their comments on an early draft of this manuscript. My hope is that the final version contains something of a glimpse of the good, true, and beautiful.

Additionally, I am grateful to my pastor, Darrin Patrick, for his leadership and support. Few people have been as fortunate in finding church homes as I have been, and his kindness came at a crucial time in my life. Additionally, Simon Yost and the rest of the team at The Journey have been enormously patient with my crazy schedule during this project. The team at Bethany House has been similarly supportive. I am especially grateful to my editor, Andy McGuire, who has encouraged, chastened, and instructed me in the way any author might hope from day one.

Brittany McComb and Matthew Shaw provided crucial last-second support, while Bob Oesch, Isaac Weigman, Benjamin Simpson, Adam Green, Ben Lemery, Timothy Carroll, Jeremy Mann, Eric Manske, Abraham Mohler, and a particular group of sisters in Arizona all read and gave feedback on the manuscript. Additionally, several small groups of people indulged me in having evenings of discussion about the ideas, which were both helpful and instructive.

One final group of readers bears special note, as this project would not exist without them. For everyone who has read, commented, and pushed me to think harder, be more precise, and be more charitable at Mere Orthodoxy, thank you. And to fulfill a promise I made there, here are the readers who took considerable pains to help me on this project: Jonathan Olson, Dan Lower, Christof Meyer, William Bell, Melissa Gutierrez, Eric, Ben Lemery, David Larson, PD Williams, Garrett May, Adam Rabenstein, Steve Robinson, Tyler Wittman, Richard Jones, Ched Spellman, William

Wells, Eddie, Gary, Prufrock, Garrett Jackson, Jane Elmore, Naomi Luce, Chris Leigh, Erin Mann, Kara, Becks, odlaram7, Michael DeBusk, Drew Dyck, SBK, and Kyle Strobel.

Few men have had more loving families than I have had. My siblings have patiently endured my torturous conversations about arcane matters they mostly haven't cared about. My brother, in particular, has sharpened my intellect maybe more than anyone else. And my parents have endured long periods of radio silence during this season. I am grateful for both of them, but especially my mother, who channeled her love and affection into helping me with research. I love you both.

Finally, at the center of the whirlwind has been one whom words fail to describe. She has endured more than any woman should have to endure and has done so with joy, cheerfulness, and above all with the glorious love of Jesus. She read a draft of this book and proved to be one of my very best editors. She has brought me more joy than anyone I know, and it is to her that I dedicate this book.

Sic transit gloria mundi—thus passeth the glory of the world, which is why I wish to live *soli Deo gloria*—for the glory of God alone. The one who made the world and who will make all things new will never fail us nor forsake us. "For from him and through him and to him are all things. To him be glory forever. Amen."

CONTENTS

IN WHICH I CLEAR MY THROAT

The more you look at the body, the more mysterious it becomes.

I once spent a week of my life being entranced by noses. It was my sophomore year of college and I had just finished my first tour through G. K. Chesterton's marvelous *Orthodoxy*. Like many first-timers, I had ignored much of the argument in favor of the prose. And one bit in particular had especially captured me:

> The sense of the miracle of humanity itself should be always more vivid to us than any marvels of power, intellect, art, or civilization. The mere man on two legs, as such, should be felt as something more heartbreaking than any music and more startling than any caricature. Death is more tragic even than death by starvation. Having a nose is more comic even than having a Norman nose.[1]

With the sort of moral seriousness that I felt only Chesterton could understand, I decided to take him at his word, and so spent a week of my life examining—without others noticing, of course— the odd bump between the mouth and the eyes. It was a delightful week, a week full of revelry and realizations that the cutest noses still protrude, and that our obsession with the nose's proper shape makes us forget the startling and remarkable fact that we have noses at all.

I have had a similar experience, I think, in attempting to understand the body. It goes with us everywhere—an unfortunate way of putting it, as we shall see—yet lies beneath the surface of our conscious awareness. When we attend to it directly, we discover that the body shapes our interaction with others and with the world around us in ways we will probably never completely understand.

As in any miracle, chase the causation back far enough and eventually you'll find yourself irrepressibly singing in praise of the marvelous goodness of God's creation. "For you created my inmost being," the psalmist writes, "you knit me together in my mother's womb. I praise you because I am fearfully and wonderfully made" (139:13–14 NIV). But what is a source of praise is also a source of mystery: "Such knowledge is too wonderful for me, too lofty for me to attain" (v. 6).

The more you look the more mysterious and wondrous the body becomes. And as the ancients knew, wonder almost always precedes understanding.

THE CONTEXT FOR THIS BOOK

I grew up in a small church that fit comfortably in the peculiar and frequently maddening tradition we call "evangelicalism." My Catholic and Orthodox friends just scoffed, of course, at my use of the "t" word. But *tradition* it is, and my time in it has shaped me into the person that I am.

Like many young people my age, my relationship with evangelicalism has sometimes taken on an unhappy tone. I have derided its hollowness, mocked its kitschiness, and scoffed at its endless attempts at reform. From the time I began reading the works of A. W. Tozer, C. S. Lewis, and Andrew Murray, I had a vague, yet undeniable sense that contemporary evangelicalism lacked the depth and vitality that previous generations had known.

While there is some truth to the reports about young people feeling disenchanted with evangelicalism's emptiness, it's almost too easy to allow such accounts to dictate our sense of reality. The story of evangelicalism's malaise is an easy one to tell, but there are some indications that the movement isn't quite as unhealthy as we frequently hear. Bradley Wright, a sociologist, even had the temerity to give evangelicals a B grade rating.[2] The problem—and here I implicate myself—is that we writers, pastors, and thinkers often depend upon solving problems for our livelihood, so we have a vested interest in pointing out what's wrong and why our solution is right.

And evangelicals have, if nothing else, been very successful at harnessing energy into those solutions. The worldview and apologetics movement, the emerging church, the Gospel Coalition, Catalyst—these developments don't arise in a vacuum. Their successes stem from a genuine desire to reorient evangelicalism around their respective understandings of the kingdom of God, but also point to a significant number of evangelicals who are open and eager for the message. These could be signs that evangelicalism has a rich store of energy waiting to be directed and not signs that evangelicalism's day is past.

I limit myself, then, to the narrower and decidedly personal claim. When I arrived at college, I began to realize that my life was shallow and that my faith was ill-equipped to handle the challenges of a complex and confusing world. My options were to continue to play among the platitudes and clichés I had adopted, or to do the earnest, serious, and sometimes difficult work of pursuing the deeper Christian life. The path out of the shallows went straight through the body—through wrestling with the fact that our Savior lived in the flesh, died on a cross, and rose again in his body from the grave.

As a lifelong evangelical, I grew up believing we should "invite Jesus into our heart." The phrase is shorthand for a web of theological ideas, but sometimes evangelicals have been tempted to spiritualize our salvation at the expense of our bodies. While it's popular to run from literal readings of anything these days, I propose we take it seriously: The Holy Spirit (of Jesus Christ) can and will dwell in our hearts—the mass of tissue and cells that beats faster every time my wife walks into the room.

This was my path to finding new life for what had become a

broken and arid faith. Our Savior died to save and renew human bodies. Despite brokenness, disease, and decay, he has not nor will he ever forget the frame he knit together in our mother's womb. And the more we embed our minds, our hearts, our bodies, within the uniquely encompassing reality of his love, the more we will see our lives and our worlds transformed. We cannot breathe new life into our broken faith. We can only be breathed into. Like those dry bones in Ezekiel's vision, it is ours to await the one who will make all things new to complete his work in us.

PREFATORY QUALIFICATIONS

It is best not to make excuses for a work before it even begins, but with a project of this scope, a few qualifications are in order.

First, I have already described evangelicalism in ways that will doubtlessly make professional sociologists and ethnographists (a word that should never show up in a book that costs less than twenty dollars) nervous. It is an occupational hazard to say anything about evangelicalism at all, largely because no one can agree on what an evangelical is. I have my own definitions, but my friend Matthew Milliner's is better: "Anyone who perpetually defines what an evangelical is."

It is, at the same time, almost impossible to separate my approach to evangelicalism from my experience of it. The merit of this is that I have seen the movement at its worst—and at its best. I have watched the evangelical church where my father was pastor discard him for not reaching the numbers they wanted, and have also seen my mega-church reach down and support a struggling writer whom they believed in.

The most significant downside of this is that as a white college-educated evangelical from a middle-income home, my focus tends to be on those in the same demographic. Unfortunately, it is a problem that extends beyond me. The media's discussion of young evangelicals has rarely acknowledged that the black evangelical community exists and has young people, or that not all young evangelicals are college-educated. Unfortunately, I am not equipped (yet) to get beyond this problem, which means that I made a conscious decision not to address questions of race and racial identity until I can treat them more fully. Such an omission, given the topic, is obviously problematic, and I hope others will fill in the gaps.

Other omissions are also painful. I do not, for instance, address the body's relationship to art or its role within literature nearly as much as I had hoped when I first set out on this project. The same is true of the sciences and medical literature. While I read a number of books on the brain in preparation for this writing, I found myself constantly turning to other sources. My hope is to continue the work I have begun here through additional writing projects, both at my blog (MereOrthodoxy.com) and elsewhere.

One final note: Rather than attend to every bit of Scripture, I have focused on one author whose works address the physical body more thoroughly and systematically than any other: the apostle Paul. I was first introduced to Paul's emphasis on the body through the work of Dallas Willard, a figure without whom this book would never have been written. But over time, I have become convinced both that Paul and Jesus speak with a remarkable unity on these issues, and that Paul's moral psychology and theological anthropology have brilliance to them that are unparalleled throughout human history.

Such are the self-conscious limitations of the work before you. This is a decidedly personal project, and so a self-consciously egotistical project (to steal again from my hero Chesterton). That is a different thing, I hope, from being a prideful project. This is not the first word, nor the last, on the topic of the body within evangelicalism. But it is *my* word, and I offer it with as much humility and courage as I can muster.

BODIES ON PARADE

In the rest of this book, I want to examine the role the physical body plays in our spiritual, social, and ecclesiastical lives by exploring the shape our bodies should take in response to the love that God demonstrates to us through the person of Jesus Christ. Grace has a shape, and that shape is Jesus. My question is how that grace shapes our arms and legs, our skin, and other organs.

My goal is to explore, to raise questions and provoke the reader, and to propose a path for living in the body in our late-modern world. I have no pretension that I will persuade every reader, but my hope is to engage in a thoughtful, deliberate examination of the body from a distinctly evangelical perspective. My plan is to make much of Jesus and his work for us, and to help those who wish to know him more deeply bring their entire lives under his care and love.

To the structure, then. After an introductory chapter, I'll examine evangelicalism's understanding of the physical body in relationship to the world around it. It is popular to dismiss most of mainstream evangelicalism as gnostic, or as subtly despising the body. I will tentatively propose that evangelical attitudes toward the body are somewhat more complex than that.

In chapter 3, I want to examine what the body is. What the body is shapes what the body does, so a careful treatment of the nature of the body is important for understanding how we should live in it. In the fourth chapter, I examine the body as it relates to other people and to creation.

In chapter 5, I go the other direction and address how the world shapes our bodies. We are, in some sense, products of our environment, and the same is true of the body. My goal is to explore that difficult relationship. In chapter 6, I highlight one dimension of the body that I think signifies a real generational difference in evangelicalism: tattoos. Their enormous popularity among younger people is significant, and my goal is to unpack precisely what makes tattoos in our contemporary world an interesting development.

It is impossible to talk about the body without talking about one of the main areas where our bodies matter—our sexual lives. In chapter 7, I approach the question generally by exploring what a sexuality that takes cues from Jesus might look like. In chapter 8, I raise the difficult and sensitive question of homosexuality within the church. I understand the dangers of blowing the question out of proportion (which I do not want to do) by devoting a whole chapter to it. However, certain questions are unavoidable, and the degree of difficulty merits patience and thoroughness in a way other issues might not.

In chapter 9, I attempt to show how the fact that our bodies will someday die shapes how we live. Death is not a pleasant topic to include in a book, but it seems impossible to discuss the body without addressing the body's end. Finally, I turn to the body as the place where we respond to the presence of God, both in an individual context (chapter 9) and a corporate context (chapter 10).

For whatever imperfections this text may contain (and there are doubtless many) my hope throughout is that you will be confronted by the reality of God's love and its transforming power, to be enraptured by the God who gave himself to us and dwells within us.

John Keble wrote in 1819:

> Lord, we thy presence seek;
> may ours this blessing be;
> give us a pure and lowly heart,
> a temple meet for thee.[3]

Lord, in your mercy, hear my prayer.

CHAPTER ONE

EARTHEN VESSELS

"The Word became flesh."

God took on a human body.

Though Christians have been dwelling on this fact for nearly 2,000 years, it remains among the most impenetrable mysteries of human existence. God, who spoke the world into existence and upholds the heavens by the word of his power, ate and slept as an infant. It was, as T. S. Eliot once put it, "the impossible union of spheres."

If ever there was a question about the goodness of the physical body, the incarnation of Jesus Christ definitively answered it. It was a singularly unique moment in time, an unrepeatable event that altered history so profoundly that we still measure time by our distance from it. God gave himself away to man, dwelling with him not as an angel or an alien, but as a creature formed from the transient weightlessness of dust. But the dust and the clay took on an unparalleled dignity and glory the moment God himself entered it. "The Word became flesh and dwelt among us, and we have seen his glory, glory as of the only Son from the Father, full of grace and truth" (John 1:14).

The goodness of the physical body is inextricable from the

goodness of the world in which our bodies dwell. The creation is, in John Calvin's phrase, the "theater of God's glory." And when the final curtain closes on the play, we shall look back upon it and say with the one who formed the world that it is indeed "very good."

It is joy and goodness for which we have been made, and which God gives to his children in the things of the world. "Man is more himself, man is more manlike," my favorite author has put it, "when joy is the fundamental thing in him and grief the superficial."[1] The rare moments of transcendence that we are given remind us that the world is still good, and that it is a good *for us*: We can sit alone in an ancient church that has fallen silent and hear in the stillness the music of the heavens. We watch a sunset glisten on fall-colored leaves, and play Wiffle ball and other games amidst the frivolity of spring. Our firstborn child smiles at us for the very first time. These moments cause us to forget ourselves and embrace the world around us. We have been made to know and enjoy these things.

In the second chapter of John, Jesus attends a wedding that happens to be insufficiently stocked with wine—a capital offense in some quarters. He solves the problem as only he can—by filling six pots with water and then transforming it all into wine. There is deep significance in Jesus' action. The symbolism of six pots—designated for the Jewish rite of purification—points to the insufficiency of the old covenant. Jesus fulfills the new covenant with the new wine of his blood.

Deep stuff, that. But the more obvious and perhaps more important fact for our purposes is that Jesus enables the party to continue. In a stirring passage in his memoirs, evangelical pastor Adolph Saphir reminds us that God does something more than simply meet our bodily needs. God himself gives the superfluities out of the abundance of his love:

> This is not a case of people starving, as when in the wilderness Jesus fed them, or of disease and suffering when He in love delivered them from it. This was simply a superfluity, a luxury; they had no wine, and what does this mean?—for it is a sign, and must signify something.
>
> That God created man not merely that he should endure

existence, that he should drag through life, but that he should rejoice; that there should be a happiness, a festivity, a gladness within him; not only that he should be reconciled to his existence and have what is needful, but that he should feel within him a music, a rhythm; that he should be able to say, It is a joy to live, He hath crowned me with loving-kindness and tender mercies.

So that in one sense the world is not wrong when it seeks for the ornamental and the beautiful; it is an instinct of what is true, that God created us for brightness and glory.[2]

The divine irruption at the wedding of Cana is an unequivocal affirmation of the goodness of our embodied lives and the creation in which we live. The tapestry of the world is beautiful, and the fabric that composes it is goodness. And our lives, our existence, our bodies, will manifest all the glory and goodness that is revealed in the person of Jesus Christ when we see the creation as it is, given to us for our stewardship by the generous hand of God.

"The Word became flesh and dwelt among us, and we have seen his glory, glory as of the only Son from the Father, full of grace and truth."

THE TECHNOCRATIC BODY

Few stories encapsulate the neuroses of our era like that of Brisa Johnson. In July 2010, she tweeted that she would undergo head-to-toe plastic surgery in order to look exactly like Kim Kardashian—a woman who has managed to become famous based on her looks—so that her husband would not leave her. It might be a comic tale if it were not so believable and so heartrendingly tragic. Whether she got the surgeries is unknown. But that the story itself is news means there's hope yet for our world.

This is where self-expression, technological proficiency, and social fragmentation have led us. The iron law of our age is that our bodies are our own and we can choose to do with them as we please on the single condition that no one else is harmed. While we may think that the Kim Kardashian wannabe has psychological and

marital problems, her proposed solution is simply an extreme manifestation of one of the deepest intuitions of our culture. The combi-
nation of economic prosperity and media saturation has allowed us
to industrialize personal beauty, giving the most physically mediocre
among us the freedom and ability to refashion ourselves into a Brad
Pitt or Angelina Jolie. Where our grandfathers might have turned
to prayer for self-fulfillment, many today prefer plastic surgery.

In *The Cultural Contradictions of Capitalism*, Daniel Bell noted that
in modernism, art and the artistic impulse motivated our humanity. As he put it:

> Traditional modernism sought to substitute for religion
> or morality an aesthetic justification of life; to create a work
> of art, to be a work of art—this alone provided meaning in
> man's effort to transcend himself.[3]

Our postmodern world, Bell argues, replaced this aesthetic justification with an instinctual one that treats "impulse and pleasure as
life-affirming; all else is neurosis and death." The postmodern shift,
in other words, is away from the creation of beauty as the focus of
what it means to be human toward the experience of pleasure itself.

That Bell's "instinctual justification" for life pervades the contemporary ethos is clearly true. Try arguing with your neighbor that
they shouldn't do something that they find pleasurable—like taking
certain banned substances—even when they do not "harm" anyone
else. But the aesthetic justification has not totally disappeared. We
simply take our freedom to "be a work of art" a bit more literally.
The body becomes the canvas, the raw material we can refashion
according to the standards of beauty given to us by Madison Avenue.

The end result is that the decisions we make about the body are
almost always grounded in therapeutic reasons—what makes us
feel fulfilled or complete or happy—rather than through determining whether there are any objective standards that should guide
our decision-making. If a man wants to reshape his nose because
he is desperate to get a woman, we might recommend therapy,
but so long as he isn't hurting anyone else, we have no grounds

to say, "No, you shouldn't do that." After all, it will improve his self-image—and it might help his kissing.

The impulse that we own our bodies and can do with them as we please runs deep. It is one of our tacit, world-shaping beliefs that few of us ever bring to the surface, but nearly everyone affirms. At an open forum my church hosted on body modification, my wife took the premise to its logical conclusion: If a well-adjusted person chops off his arm because he thinks it looks better (or to make a political statement against the repressive nature of our contemporary standards of beauty), what's wrong with that? No one could provide an answer.

The last guardrail against the total dismantling of any cultural morality that is grounded in goodness rather than in not harming others is health. We have become a nation of joggers in our desire to preserve a standard of physical health that the priests in the medical community have handed down to us from the mountain. And the bit about "priests" isn't entirely cheeky. Young people often first learn about sexuality from doctors and trained professionals rather than from their parents—a transition (ironically) that began among the much-maligned Victorians. Apparently, the easiest way to overcome any awkwardness of speaking about sex is to sterilize it and outsource it to the professionals.[4]

Yet even here, the near-obsessive pursuit of physical health that marks our world means that we cannot simply *be* in the body. We cannot embrace it without qualification. It has become a project, a formless lump of clay waiting for us to sculpt it in our own image. It is, as sociologist Chris Shilling put it, an "unfinished entity which is shaped and 'completed' partly as a result of lifestyle choices."[5]

Our bodies are no longer begotten, but are made, constructed by our own individual wills and by the institutions of society that tell us how to act. They are the primary place where we exert our power and domination, which is why we quarantine those who can no longer control their own bodily functions. Because we do not like the inconvenient, uncontrollable, spontaneous interruptions that sometimes characterize the very young and very old, we professionalize their care so we will not be bothered. We have day-care facilities and nursing homes so the young (or middle-aged) can continue jogging.

This industrialized understanding of the body has led some theologians in the twentieth century—George Grant and Jacques Ellul, specifically—to describe our society as a "technological society." Theologian Oliver O'Donovan explains:

> What marks this culture out most importantly is not anything that it does, but what it thinks. It is not "technological" because its instruments of making are extraordinarily sophisticated (though that is evidently the case), *but because it thinks of everything it does as a form of instrumental making*. Politics . . . is talked of as "making a better world"; love is "building a successful relationship." There is no place for simply *doing*. [6]

Whether for aesthetics or health, athletics or business, we treat the body as the raw material out of which we shape our own lives and histories. Our options are to conform to the pattern that has been handed down from Hollywood, or assert our individuality through the "free" expression of our autonomous selves. But even the assertion of our individuality is an inherently self-conscious task, as it inevitably takes shape against the backdrop of our rejection of standards of life that have been prepackaged and sold.

A world dominated by technique is an inherently anti-material world. It does not value the body, but always seeks to turn it into something else. As feminist thinker Susan Bordo writes, "In place of [the materiality of the body] we now have what I call cultural plastic. In place of God the watchmaker, we now have ourselves, the master sculptors of that plastic."[7] Both sexual liberation and the obsessive demands of health have been sold to us under the guise that they affirm the body's intrinsic goodness. But what we have bought simply cannot deliver. The joke is, unfortunately, on us—and it's ultimately not very funny.

A GOSPEL-SHAPED EMBODIED LIFE

Grace is not a technique.

It is not a magical quality that God dispenses like a candy machine, or the power for self-actualization or personal peace and affluence. It is not a lubricant to get the parts inside working properly. And it is not a three-step program for self-improvement. When we treat grace that way, we surrender to the spirit of our age by fashioning ourselves and our bodies through our own efforts. We don't use grace to shape ourselves—it shapes us into the image of the one who gives it.

The grace that God gives, though, is God himself. Theologian Kevin Vanhoozer writes that the gospel is "God's self-giving in his Son through his Spirit."[8] Salvation, the psalmist proclaims, is "from the Lord" (Psalm 3:8 NIV), but the one who comes to save is *the Lord himself.* Ephesians 2:1–10 announces that we have been "raised up with Christ," that God will show us the riches of his grace "in Christ," and that we have been "created in Christ Jesus" for good works. The grace that we receive through faith is nothing less than union with our Savior, Jesus Christ himself.[9]

Our "union with Christ" is the inauguration of a new form of life. When we hear and believe the good news that our sins have been washed away by the redemptive blood of Jesus Christ, the patterns and habits of our lives will never be left alone. That change in our status, wherein we transferred from the kingdom of darkness to the kingdom of God's glorious light, transforms our horizons and reorients our lives. Where our relationships were once marked by the hostility of violence, envy, pride, and anger, our union with Christ opens the possibility for a new mode of being.

Though grace—the presence of God himself in our hearts and lives—is not a technique, it does have a shape. And it looks like Jesus. The love that Jesus' disciples are known by takes the shape of a cross.[10] John writes in 1 John 3:16: "By this we know love, that he laid down his life for us, and we ought to lay down our lives for the brothers." John's subtle move from the reality of God's love for us to the nature of our love for others is not a departure from the gospel, but an affirmation that those who believe the gospel need lives that are shaped by it. As Oliver O'Donovan puts it, "the church can be committed to ethics without moderating the tone of its voice as the bearer of glad tidings."[11]

Christ is not only the pattern for our lives—he is also the power. The union we have with Christ is a union through the Holy Spirit, the third person of the Trinity.[12] The sanctification of our lives and bodies is not disconnected from our salvation, but is the necessary consequence of our life in Christ.[13] The Holy Spirit is both Lord and giver of life—and the life that he gives is the life of conformity to Jesus.

The reduction of our lives and morality to a "technique" is at the root of the malaise within the evangelical world. Sociologists Christian Smith and Melinda Denton introduced the term *moralistic therapeutic deism* to describe the dominant religion among young people in America. It is deistic because its God is not present or active in the world. It is therapeutic because its benefits involve feeling "good, happy, secure, and at peace." And it is moralistic because it teaches that doing the right thing is central to having a "good and happy life." It is technique—the assertion of our wills on the world—applied to morality. As Smith and Denton write, "That means being nice, kind, pleasant, respectful, responsible, at work on self-improvement, taking care of one's health, and doing one's best to be successful."[14]

In contrast, a gospel-ethic of our embodied life is encompassed by the reality that our sins have been forgiven by the one who died for us, and that the proper response to our forgiveness is impossible except through the empowering presence of the Holy Spirit. Paul wrote to the Corinthians: "And because of him you are in Christ Jesus, who became to us wisdom from God, righteousness and sanctification and redemption . . . 'Let the one who boasts, boast in the Lord'" (1 Corinthians 1:30–31).

Unfortunately, evangelicals sometimes suffer from an anemic understanding of how the gospel shapes our lives. We alternate between playing the legalist card when people attempt to draw lines about how Christians should or should not act, and playing the libertine card when others sanction their immoral actions with the gospel. We either have cheap grace or it doesn't exist at all.

A gospel-ethic, though, is a normative account of how our lives conform to the pattern of the life, death, and resurrection of Jesus Christ that is discerned and freely enacted through the power of the Spirit's indwelling presence.[15]

What does this mean for most evangelicals? I would tentatively suggest that three popular ways in which evangelicals talk about ethics need reconsideration and clarification.

First, we need to guard against conflating our understanding of Christian freedom with our culture's premise that freedom is our absolute right to do whatever we want without harming others. I cringe every time I hear St. Augustine's dictum "Love God and do what you will" deployed as a rejection of our responsibility to consider the morality of our actions, or as a denial that as Christians we are obligated to act in certain ways. For Augustine, Christian liberty does not mean spontaneously doing whatever is in our hearts at any given moment—that is a version of Augustine that owes more to Romanticism than to the man himself. Rather, Christian liberty is a reflective, ordered response to the reality of God's love that requires careful discernment and prayer.[16] As O'Donovan puts it, in Christian freedom, "the Spirit forms and brings to expression *the appropriate pattern of free response to objective reality.*"[17]

Second—and I put this forward tentatively—I suspect we need to rethink whether conscience is an adequate guide for how we live in the body. As an evangelical, I grew up believing that our conscience is a moral appendage or organ that tells us how we should or should not act. Specifically, if my conscience did not trouble me and the action in consideration was not explicitly commanded or prohibited in Scripture, then I was "free" to move ahead. But if the conscience is a faculty like the mind or the heart, then it too is fallen—which means that it needs to be brought into conformity with Scripture, the authoritative witness to the reality of Christ's death and resurrection, and is insufficient as a guide to how we should love our neighbors as ourselves.

Third, having lives shaped by the redemption we have in Jesus means that our experiences—whether of our consciences or of the Holy Spirit or of our bodies—are an inadequate guide for determining how we should live in the body. We must listen to our experiences and the experiences of others, as there is no other way to determine whether the gospel will affirm them or reveal them as sin. While the conditions and circumstances of our actions might affect which good we should pursue, they cannot answer that question for us. We must always evaluate our own circumstances and experiences in light of the authoritative Word of God.[18]

This would include the experiences that we have of God within the church. Communion, baptism, and other practices of the church are the proper, God-ordained responses to the historical revelation of God in Jesus Christ as attested to in Scripture. When we respond to God, we should do it in the ways he has set forth for us in his Word. The practices of baptism and Communion are at the heart of our spiritual formation and the church's communal life according to the pattern we have in Jesus. We are, after all, the body of Christ.[19]

EARTHEN VESSELS

The psalmist tells us we are "fearfully and wonderfully made." We were knit together in our mothers' womb by the delicate hands of God. Our bodies are not amorphous lumps that we shape and sculpt into our own self-image—they are divine gifts, given to us by God himself. The body opens the world to us and enables us to experience its goodness and beauty.

Of course, it does not always seem that way. We can't all run like Olympian Eric Liddell or play piano like my sister. Some of us cannot stand on our own two feet or feel the warmth of the sunshine. Some have genetic defects, while others have had their bodies broken through injuries or illness. Some bodies are marked by wounds of rejection; others by scars of self-loathing. Others have been distorted by anxiety or wrecked by the stress of self-aggrandizement. Some of us have chiseled away at our flesh out of a manic desire to maintain appearances, while others have simply quit trying. None of us is in heaven, despite our best efforts to appear otherwise.

"Do you not know," the apostle Paul asks, "that your body is a temple of the Holy Spirit?" (1 Corinthians 6:19). *Do you not know?* It is a question that should haunt us, a question that should force us to revisit every aspect of our lives and every fiber—literally—of our being. I suspect Paul asks it not only for rhetorical effect, but because it is so easy to forget in a world where our lives and our bodies have been altered by sin's presence.[20]

But our body is not simply a gift from God—it is the place where God himself dwells within his people. The physical body was the place of Jesus Christ's presence in the world. And when he was asked for a sign that would demonstrate his authority, he responded: "Destroy this temple, and in three days I will raise it up" (John 2:19). Jesus identifies his own body with the place of worship for the Jewish people, an astonishing association. And after he ascended into heaven, he sent the indwelling Holy Spirit until he returns again.

This is the paradox of the body: The body is a temple, but the temple is in ruins. The incarnation of Jesus affirms the body's original goodness. The death of Jesus reminds us of its need for redemption. And the resurrection of Jesus gives us hope for its restoration.

Our body is a temple, but the temple's beauty is not of our own making. As earthen vessels made from clay and dirt, our glory as humans is that we are free to give ourselves back in gratitude to the one who gave himself for us. Our treasure is what we manifest in and through our lives—that this all-surpassing power is from God and not from us. The God who made the universe, is the one "who will transform our lowly body to be like his glorious body, by the power that enables him even to subject all things to himself."[21] And God transforms our bodies not through technique, the assertion of our own wills, but through giving us himself in the Holy Spirit.

This is the subversive message of Christianity in our late-modern world, which has pursued the gifts of God's created joys without acknowledging the giver: The body is good, but its goodness is not what we expect or anticipate, for it is a goodness that is revealed to us in the life, death, and resurrection of Jesus Christ.

Consider Jesus' teaching in Matthew 6, the Sermon on the Mount: "Is not life more than food, and the body more than clothing?" The answer that Jesus presumes radically relativizes the body's very real demands. We live by bread, but we do not live by bread alone—"but by every word that comes from the mouth of God."[22] The gifts of God, God himself, are no less necessary to our sustenance than physical nourishment.

When Jesus suggests that the body is more than clothing, he shifts from the necessary to the pleasurable, from that which is required for the body's life to that which adorns the body as beautiful. He affirms that the beauty of our bodies is a direct concern of our Father in heaven, a concern that frees us from the anxious demands of style and image that have consumed our time and our money. The lilies of the field neither toil nor spin—they simply live before God for their allotted time, and have no aspirations to be roses. Will he not much more clothe you?

"Seek first the kingdom of God . . . *and all these things* shall be added to you" (Matthew 6:33 NKJV, emphasis added). This is the message of a gospel-ethic. The gifts are given freely, but they are only ours to keep as long as we acknowledge and worship the Giver. Our seeking is a response to the reality of the presence of God in our lives. The presence of the kingdom invades our whole lives, reshaping our interactions with others and the world in the most basic and fundamental ways. The apostle Paul writes in one of the few times he mentions the kingdom: "For the kingdom of God is not a matter of eating and drinking, but of righteousness, peace and joy in the Holy Spirit."[23]

The kingdom is the sphere of the King's authority. Dallas Willard writes, "A person is a 'spiritual person' to the degree that his or her life is correctly integrated into and dominated by God's spiritual Kingdom."[24] The temptation of our postmodern era is to pursue false standards of bodily "perfection" and to be consumed by the anxieties that stem from living in bodies that are marked by sin. But the freedom of the gospel is that we have been bought with a price and that our bodies are no longer ours. As the opening question to *The Heidelberg Catechism* puts it:

QUESTION:
What is thy only comfort in life and death?
Answer: That I with body and soul, both in life and death, am not my own, but belong unto my faithful Saviour Jesus

Christ; who, with his precious blood, has fully satisfied for all my sins, and delivered me from all the power of the devil; and so preserves me that without the will of my heavenly Father, not a hair can fall from my head; yea, that all things must be subservient to my salvation, and therefore, by his Holy Spirit, He also assures me of eternal life, and makes me sincerely willing and ready, henceforth, to live unto him.[25]

I am not my own. The body is for love and for God, not for my own pleasure and not for my own pain. The body is not for me, but for another. The kingdom is not for eating and drinking, but for righteousness, peace, and joy that come from living within the realm of love. God gives himself for us that we might give ourselves to him. And as hymn writer Robert Grant knew, the God who demonstrated his love for us by taking on a body and dying on a cross will be firm and faithful until the end:

> Frail children of dust, and feeble as frail,
> In thee do we trust, nor find thee to fail.
> Thy mercies how tender, how firm to the end!
> Our Maker, Defender, Redeemer, and Friend.[26]

CHAPTER TWO

EVANGELICAL INATTENTION AND THE SECULAR BODY

Donald Miller may have acknowledged the Crusades, but he forgot to mention Precious Moments.

In his provocative and enduringly popular book *Blue Like Jazz*, Miller describes a college ministry that set up a confessional booth with a twist: rather than hear the wrongs done in dorm rooms and frat houses, they would apologize for the grievances Christians have committed throughout history. Clever, yes, but also a missed opportunity. Someone needs to own up for those silly figurines.

Thankfully, their time has started to pass. For a few years, you couldn't walk into a Christian bookstore or a Hallmark store without being overwhelmed by their schmaltzy cuteness. At the company's peak, it was at least a $200 million annual business. It grew so large that the owners ripped a page out of Disney's playbook, creating a "Precious Moments Inspirational Park."[1] The central line of figurines was, at least initially, explicit in its Christian background, featuring infants that had been (literally) angelized in various poses.

But it is a sanitized Christianity, a Christianity that has been domesticated into a religion of niceness and sentimentality. As a result, it gets both infants and angels wrong. Angels in Scripture are messengers, intermediaries between God and men. But they rarely appear as the sort of soft approachable figures that Precious Moments twisted them into. The angel who guards the garden of Eden wields a flaming sword, and nearly every angel who appears in the New Testament has to remind folks not to be afraid.[2]

At the same time, by turning infants into angels, they distort the inescapably messy reality of our humanness. It is a form of what author Chene Heady dubs "baby worship," or the belief that babies are utterly free from sin and worthy of what almost approaches adoration.[3] Not only that, but overly sentimentalized Christianity depends on a vague minimizing of the less pleasant features of the body in favor of an angelic, disembodied faith. Children, as every parent knows, make far too much of a mess to ever be confused with angels.

Yet this vague and general spiritualization of our faith isn't simply at the fringes of evangelicalism, but closer to the center. As I write this book, I routinely have conversations with people in evangelical churches that go something like this:

> Them: "So what's your book about?"
> Me: "The body."
> Them: "You mean, like, the *physical* body?"

The line is often delivered with a slight rise of the eyebrows that betrays either incredulity or incomprehension, and sometimes a little of both. The pattern, which seems to exist among evangelicals of every age, was at first mildly irritating, but has become an endless source of fascination. What's to say about the physical body? More than most evangelicals seem to realize. When we hear the words *the body,* our minds apparently meander over to Paul's great metaphor and the countless sermons we have heard exhorting us to take up our janitorial crosses and assume our place as the pinky toe of Christ's church. We are apparently more comfortable talking about the body of Christ than the body we walk around in.

EVANGELICALS AND THEIR CRITICS

Over the past twenty years, evangelicals have balkanized into several different schools of thought, each of which has their own approach to theology, culture, and church practices. Despite the disagreements, though, almost everyone agrees on this point: Traditional evangelicalism has deeply Gnostic tendencies.

Gnosticism was a second-century movement that has persisted in various forms and places throughout church history. It limited knowledge (gnosis) to only a select few and was frequently associated with an attempt to flee the body for the realm of the "spiritual." Theologian Michael Horton, who is Presbyterian, puts the critique this way:

> It would seem that the critics of modern American religion are basically on target in describing the entire religious landscape, from New Age or liberal, to evangelical and Pentecostal, as essentially Gnostic. Regardless of the denomination, the American Religion is inward, deeply distrustful of institutions, mediated grace, the intellect, theology, creeds, and the demand to look outside of oneself for salvation. . . . If one is to be saved, one must accept the death of individualism, inwardness, emotional and experiential ladders of ecstasy, merit and speculation.

By contrast, Horton suggests that Christianity is a "crude, earthy religion." Though Horton doesn't expound upon evangelicalism's distaste for the body here, he does suggest that certain strands that talk about the "salvation of the soul" are "quasi-Gnostic."[4]

Gregg Allison, a professor of theology at Southern Baptist Theological Seminary, in a recent paper accuses evangelicals of treating the body as a hindrance to our spiritual lives:

> It is my contention that evangelicals at best express ambivalence toward the human body, and at worst manifest a disregard or contempt for it. Many people, often due to tragic experiences with the body (e.g., physical/sexual abuse), abhor their body, and many Christians, due to either poor or nonex-

istent teaching on human embodiment, consider their body to be, at best, a hindrance to spiritual maturity and, at worst, inherently evil or the ultimate source of sin.[5]

The giant of New Testament studies, N. T. Wright, concurs. In *Surprised by Hope,* an excellent book that is justly popular within younger evangelical circles, he criticizes the disembodied notion of "heaven" that he contends most evangelicals believe in. According to Wright, evangelicals are dangerously ignoring the Apostles' Creed's insistent affirmation that "we believe in the resurrection of the body."[6]

Finally, Brian McLaren, the controversial emerging church advocate, aligns himself with this critique as well. In *A New Kind of Christian,* he writes, "Remember, modernity only wants abstract principles, universal concepts, and disembodied absolutes. So we take an expression like 'the kingdom of God' and try to give it meaning without any context. *Postmodern theology has to reincarnate; we have to get back into the flesh and blood and sweat and dirt of the setting, because as I said, all truth is contextual.*"[7]

By my count, that's a Presbyterian, a Baptist, a high-church Anglican, and a member of the emerging church movement all offering some variation on the theme that evangelicals have gone wrong in their understanding of the body. They disagree about the particulars and their preferred solutions, but the unanimity of their diagnosis is striking.

It's not easy or prudent to challenge that many voices, especially when they are from as diverse communities as the four critics above.[8] But evangelicals also have a strong tendency to affirm the worst about ourselves, so we're not very inclined to give ourselves the benefit of the doubt. Is a generous reading of the "evangelical body" possible, or is it really as bad as all that?

A LEGACY OF INATTENTION

Here's the thesis that I want to tentatively put forward: Evangelical understandings of the body are more complex than they have sometimes been presented. Given how strong the critiques of evangelicalism sometimes are, we might expect to find outright denunciations of the body within historical evangelicalism. But such remarks turn out to be very difficult to come by (to the point of being nonexistent). For example, while scathing remarks about alcohol, prostitution, and gambling are easy to find, there is little in the way of an outright rejection of sexuality per se.[9]

Consider preacher D. L. Moody. Moody was one of America's most famous preachers in the early 1900s and a central figure in one of evangelicalism's dominant strands: the revivalist movement. The revivalists have been (often justly) criticized for developing a theology that was inwardly focused and a piety that is wrapped up in spiritual experiences; all the sorts of things that generally accompany distaste for the physical body.

Moody, however, has a more nuanced view of the body than we might expect. Consider what he wrote before dying, a passage that his son would use to open his biography:

> Someday you will read in the papers that D. L. Moody of East Northfield is dead. Don't you believe a word of it! At that moment I shall be more alive than I am now; I shall have gone up higher, that is all, out of this old clay tenement into a house that is immortal—a body that death cannot touch, that sin cannot taint; a body fashioned like unto His glorious body.[10]

It is as clear a statement about the hope of the resurrection as one could possibly hope for.

When it comes to the afterlife, N. T. Wright is correct that Moody's focus is on "heaven," which Moody thinks is "up there," and that it is a place where we will someday "go." But even though Moody reads John's description of "streets of gold" rather literally, heaven is not a glorious place because of the stones or the physical splendor but because of the presence of the triune God. Throughout his sermons, Moody is always focused on the center of theology—God. But the center doesn't consume everything else, and Moody never rejects the resurrection of the body. In fact, in his sermon on the resurrection of Jesus, he suggests that it and the cross are the "chief cornerstones of the religion of Jesus Christ." And that has serious implications for us as believers:

We shall come up from the grave, by and by, with a shout. "He is the first fruits;" he has gone into the vale, and will call us by and by. The voice of the Son of God shall wake up the slumbering dead! Jacob will leave his lameness, and Paul will leave his thorn in the flesh; and we shall come up resurrected bodies, and be forever with the Lord.[11]

Moody clearly isn't bashful speaking about the resurrection of the body, even though he emphasizes the presence of God in the afterlife rather than the resurrection of our physical bodies.

Those emphases have remained in evangelical waters, even down to elder statesman Billy Graham. In an essay for the *Washington Post,* Graham summarized the classic evangelical understanding of the afterlife. After confessing that Scripture is relatively silent about its specific features, Graham moves into the center: "But the most essential truth about Heaven is this: We will be in God's presence forever. And because we will be with God, no harm or evil can ever touch us again." Graham then expands this in the usual directions, namely the absence of war, suffering, and pain, and the presence of family and friends who have trusted in Christ.[12]

Where evangelicals have directly engaged with the body, they have done so primarily through focusing on questions of physical healing and health. John Wesley, one of the originators of the evangelical movement, wrote a book on the methods of healing the body, a work that opens with an unflinching endorsement of the body's original goodness.[13] This emphasis on physical healing has been at the center of charismatic movements in the twentieth century. Yet emphasizing physical healing also carries risks; when it overwhelms our belief in the resurrection from the dead, it can easily slip into the sort of word of faith and prosperity gospel preaching that preys on the worst parts of the charismatic movement.

Additionally, in the early 1900s, social gospel proponents focused on building healthy bodies in order to reform society. There was significant overlap between social gospel advocates and those who argued for a "muscular Christianity," or a Christianity that emphasized the importance of manliness and sports to the Christian faith—a surprising relationship given the layout of contemporary evangelicalism. While I am no fan of the "social gospel," it clearly has had a significant influence on the evangelical world.[14]

Here's my hypothesis: Whatever attitude evangelicals currently have toward the body (and given my feelings about Precious Moments, you can guess I think not all is well), historical evangelicals aren't as negative toward the body as we're often told. There are, of course, problems lurking within the movement. Moody can easily slip into cringe-worthy language about separating from the world around us. But the reaction against these problems has sometimes presented historical evangelicalism in an uncharitable light, finding in their writings a disdain for the body that does not seem to hold up under scrutiny.[15]

The evangelical legacy with respect to the body seems to be more one of inattention than outright rejection or even a conscious ambivalence. If we are uncomfortable with the body, we are so tacitly. When we go on the record about the body, we do so in an orthodox fashion: God created the body as good, it is currently tainted by the presence of sin (but it is not the source of sin per se), and God is going to raise it up again on the last day. In our understanding of heaven and our theological anthropology, we have emphasized the presence of God, which is the right thing to emphasize. But too often we do not spell out the relationship between that presence and our earthen vessels, except when the brokenness of the body pushes it into our consciousness in unavoidable ways.

In that sense, evangelical attempts at understanding the body's role in our spiritual lives seem to have been dominantly reactive rather than proactive. The emphasis on physical healing within the charismatic movement—which is, I think, the strand of evangelicalism that has most consistently focused on the body—certainly takes the body seriously. But it also narrows our attention to God's power to heal the body, rather than God's power to sanctify the body through reforming its habits and dispositions.

41

EVANGELICAL RESPONSES TO MODERN MOVEMENTS

Over the past thirty years, evangelicals have largely continued to be inattentive to the role of the body in our lives. What makes this so surprising is that the dominant intellectual trends during this period have made the physical body their central focus. Many of the most popular intellectual movements have turned to the body in hopes that it would solve the social and philosophical problems of modernity. Unfortunately, these intellectual movements happen to be streams of thought that most conservative evangelicals have been appropriately wary of, which has meant that evangelicals had little to no reason to overcome their inattention to the body in order to meet the challenges.

POSTMODERNISM

During the same period of time, evangelicals have been embroiled in a debate over what has come to be broadly described as postmodernism. The debate has centered on questions of what truth is and how we know it. But swim up the postmodern stream a little, and you'll find yourself in the midst of a strong current of thought that is focused on the body. Jean-Paul Sartre turned Descartes' famous line "I think, therefore I am" on its head, writing: "The body is what I immediately am . . . I am my body to the extent that I *am*."[16] Maurice Merleau-Ponty, the French phenomenologist, wrote several massive and important treatments on the body's role in perception.[17]

Speaking of postmodernism as a monolithic movement is, of course, a gross oversimplification. The movement is as diverse and difficult to pin down as any other cultural phenomenon. But the most famous definition of postmodernism is philosopher Jean-Francois Lyotard's: It is an age characterized by "incredulity toward metanarratives." In other words, our understanding is limited by our finite perspectives. Or, as in the popular slogan, there is no longer a "god's-eye view."[18]

Many of the postmodern thinkers turned to the body to find a unifying story, a way of tying the world together into a coherent whole. But that path has proven to be a dead end. As Sarah Coakley famously put the problem:

> The question that seems to press in a postmodern age is this: if we can no longer count on any universal "grand narrative" to bear the burden of religious and philosophical needs for meaning-making, is it perhaps only resistant fleshliness that we can look to as an Archimedean point of stability—a seemingly unambiguous focus for longings, myths and quasi-religious hopes? Yet on closer reflection this too—the postmodern "body"—becomes subject to infinitely variable social constructions.[19]

The postmodern "body" has been destabilized. In fact, rather than even speaking of *the* body, we must speak of *bodies,* for the postmodern critique is that there can be no single narrative of embodied existence. Gay people have one experience of the body, females another, and white males a third. If postmodernism rejects the possibility of objective truth, it also rejects the possibility of an objective body.

Unfortunately, most evangelical responses to postmodernism have focused almost entirely on the nature of truth, but have ignored the challenge that it poses to our understanding of the body. This has caused us to miss out on potential insights and made us ill-equipped to offer a compelling alternative.

FEMINISM

Judging by the amount of literature on the topic, no corner of Christianity has focused as much on the meaning of our bodies as those engaged in feminist theology—that is, those who are exploring the way our understanding of God both affects and is affected by the unique experience of women. Like every other movement, feminist theology is a moving target, and impossible to easily summarize without turning into a caricature. In its most problematic form, feminist theologians read Scripture through the experience of women, rather than the other way around.[20]

While feminist theology as a discipline has been largely limited to more mainline theological traditions, there are faint signs mainstream evangelicals are becoming more receptive to it. Wheaton professor Beth Felker Jones is one of the leading evangelically minded theologians working in the discipline. Her *Marks of His Wounds* is a careful treatment of the body from a feminist standpoint that includes generous readings of both Calvin and Augustine, but which does not mention the evangelical discussion on the question at all.[21]

Few issues have been as divisive in evangelicalism as the question of feminism. Yet more often than not, the discussion has focused only on questions of church polity, Scripture translations, whether there is submission in the Trinity, and the ever-present question of submission. Those are all vitally important questions. But as "hot button" issues, they have sometimes pushed the work being done on the more basic and fundamental question about the nature of the body to the background.[22] Conservative evangelicals face an important opportunity to clarify a theological account of the body in the context of male-female relationships, but it has largely stayed on the margins of the debate.

PHILOSOPHICAL NATURALISM

Philosophical naturalism, or the idea that only physical things exist, dominated the second half of the twentieth century. While the idea is an ancient one, Charles Darwin's theory of evolution gave it new life in the mid-1800s. In part because of naturalist John Dewey's influence on our educational system, philosophical naturalism's reach has spread so far that it is now one of the most pervasive presuppositions of American life.[23]

Over the past thirty years, evangelical philosophers and theologians have offered strong critiques of the idea and articulated attractive alternatives.[24] Those alternatives have often included arguing for the existence of the soul against the position that humans are only our bodies. Yet this defensive position regarding the soul has in less careful hands sometimes obscured the importance of the body to our human flourishing.[25] As with postmodernism, this is

44

one front where evangelicals have deemphasized the body's role in response to a school of thought that overemphasized it.

ROMAN CATHOLICISM

Between 1979 and 1984, Pope John Paul II spent his weekly radio addresses developing what we now call the *Theology of the Body*. The Pope was by no means the only theologian talking about the theology of the body at the time. But because of his position as the Pope and the depth of his treatment, it is undoubtedly the most well-known theological discussion of embodiment in the world.

While the *Theology of the Body* has played a significant role in Catholic discussions about sexuality—thanks in large part to the efforts of Christopher West, who has been the most prolific expositor of John Paul II's ideas—I suspect that evangelical disagreements with Catholicism have muted the book's impact in our community. Those theological disagreements are incredibly significant. Yet there is a surprising amount of overlap between the Pope's ideas in the *Theology of the Body* and evangelical theology.[26]

Interestingly, however, evangelical inattention to the Pope's massive work may be changing. Professor Craig Carter of Tyndale University College and Seminary in Toronto reported that many of his students were surprisingly receptive to the Pope's book, which he assigned as a text in a class on sexuality.[27] While writing this book, I heard from several friends with stories of how the *Theology of the Body* had impacted them. Neither of these examples prove a trend—but as younger evangelicals continue to search for resources to deepen their understanding of the body, I suspect many of them will make their way through the pope's massive work.

I want to be perfectly clear: I am neither a postmodernist, feminist, philosophical naturalist, nor a Catholic. But those streams of thought have raised important questions and produced valuable insights about the body that evangelicals need to attend to more carefully. At a minimum, if conservative evangelicals want to offer careful, gospel-centered responses to these various "isms," then we must overcome our inattention to the body and engage these communities on this ground in distinctly evangelical ways. It is not enough to just show that how they think about human bodies is wrong. We must also show them a more excellent way of thinking about—and of living in—these human bodies.

THE SPIRITUAL DISCIPLINES UNDERCURRENT

While evangelical theologians have been largely inattentive to the body over the past thirty years, a small but influential groundswell of pastors and lay theologians has worked to reincorporate the body into the evangelical spiritual life.

The most influential voice in the movement belongs to Dallas Willard, who articulates in both *Spirit of the Disciplines* and *Renovation of the Heart* a robust and well-reasoned understanding of the human body and its importance for our spiritual lives. Willard bluntly made the case in *Renovation of the Heart*: "For good or evil, *the body lies right at the center of the spiritual life.*"[28] His contributions and Richard Foster's *Celebration of Discipline* have slowly gained institutional support for their central teaching that the body and the spiritual disciplines are central to Christianity. From Biola University's *Institute for Spiritual Formation* to *Renovare,* organizations devoted to recovering and teaching the historical spiritual disciplines have found audiences hungry for a deeper experience of their faith.

Not surprisingly, the wing of evangelicalism most sympathetic to postmodernism and feminism, the ever-elusive "emerging church," has attempted not only to reintegrate the body into our Christian spirituality and practices but also to move the body closer to the very center of our theology. Like the "isms" above, generalizing about the emerging church is like driving a steamroller through a minefield. But once underway, it's probably wise to simply proceed forward and hope for the best.

In addition to Brian McLaren, the most consistent advocate for the body's role in Christian theology is Doug Pagitt, pastor of Solomon's Porch in Minneapolis. He writes, "At Solomon's Porch, the physical nature of the incarnation and resurrection spurs us to create practices in which our bodies help us to follow Jesus."[29] For Pagitt, the life of faith is tied up with the body and its role in our lives, a position that he has implemented consistently in his writings.[30]

At the heart of this emphasis on the body is the notion that right belief is an extension of having right practices. As has been frequently noted, the emerging church movement has shifted the focus from orthodoxy to *orthopraxy*—or at least has sought to make them mutually dependent. In their understanding, Christianity is less about a normative system of beliefs regarding a historical person, communicated in the Bible and mediated and made effective by the Holy Spirit; instead, it is a system of practices that Christians do in order to bear witness to the historical person as communicated in the Bible. Tony Jones writes in *The New Christians*, "The emergent movement is robustly theological; the conviction is that theology and practice are inextricably related, and each invariably informs the other."[31]

While there are good ways of reincorporating the body into Christian spirituality, other ways are fraught with danger. While I am thankful that many emerging church leaders have recognized the need to pay attention to our bodies, I'm less convinced their solution of intertwining theology with church practices is the best. For one, I suspect their understanding of the nature of the body is wrong, and because of that their theological method is mistaken—a claim I'll unpack in the next chapter. But there is also an inherent ambiguity in church practices.[32] The act of taking Communion looks functionally the same in Presbyterian, Roman Catholic, and Episcopalian churches—but what is happening in those practices, according to those who receive it, is very different. In other words, everyone doing the same practices isn't enough to nail down the meaning of them in the world.[33]

EVANGELICAL INATTENTION AND A TACIT SECULARISM

In 2 Corinthians 10, Paul uses warfare imagery to describe the conflict that Christians have with the world. The analogy suggests that our relationship with the world must sometimes take a critical posture. Yet he underscores that Christians do not fight with the "weapons of the world," but have the power of God to "demolish arguments and every pretension that sets itself up against the knowledge of God" (v. 4). The verse is popular in circles devoted to Christian worldview training, and for good reason: Bad arguments and false understandings about the nature of reality enslave the person who believes them.

47

But more often than not, we don't know which lies and bad arguments we have formed our lives around.[34] After all, the ideas that are deepest in us are almost never learned in books, but are forged and engrained through the habitual patterns of life that make up our embodied existence—or what theologian James K. A. Smith refers to as "liturgies." He writes, "Every liturgy constitutes a pedagogy that teaches us, in all sorts of precognitive ways, to be a certain kind of person . . . implicit in [liturgies] is an understanding of the world that is pre-theoretical, that is on a different register than ideas."[35] And for Smith, it is specifically the body—rather than the mind or our conscious awareness—through which we integrate these pre-theoretical understandings into our lives.

It is my suggestion that Paul and the other writers of Scripture want us to "take captive" these "pre-theoretical understandings" that we gain through our embodied lives and bring them into conformity with the revelation of God in Scripture.[36] David writes in Psalm 51, "Behold, you delight in truth in the inward being, and you teach me wisdom in the secret heart" (v. 6). In Psalm 139, David confesses that God knows his inner workings better than he knows himself, and concludes by pleading with God to search him and try his thoughts. It is those preconscious depths that David asks to have God search out. It is an anthropology not so different from Paul's in Romans 8, where he suggests that the "Spirit himself bears witness with our spirit that we are children of God," and that he "intercedes for us with groanings too deep for words" (Romans 8:16, 26). The empowering presence of the Holy Spirit brings the tacit beliefs and dispositions of our hearts to the surface so that they can be brought into conformity with the love and truth of God.

To put a sharper edge on it, evangelical inattention to the body is not a virtue. If we are not attentive to the ways in which the habits, practices, and rhythms of our bodies are shaped by the world in which we live, then we will be susceptible to living according to false understandings of reality. If we do not cultivate a strong and thoughtful evangelical understanding of the body and enact practices that integrate this understanding into every part of our lives, then we will end up incorporating ideas and beliefs into our systems that are contrary to what we would consciously affirm.

Of course, discerning which practices and beliefs within evangelicalism are faithful to Scripture and which are driven by the culture is precisely the question. One man's syncretism is another man's baptism. Where emerging church proponents would argue that they have learned from the Bible and are attempting to express the truth in the language of postmodern thought, critics contend that they have been co-opted by ideas that undermine the truth of the Christian faith. The argument can be reversed, too. Emerging church advocates contend that traditional evangelicalism is captive to the trappings of individualism, consumerism, and modernism. Our tendency is to think that those whom we disagree with have fallen in with the "spirit of this age," while we have not.

But just because these are tricky waters to navigate does not mean we should ignore these questions altogether. We have a responsibility to receive with grace the tradition most of us were raised in, and a charitable reading of the evangelical movement should give priority to the conscious affirmations of the body's goodness. But we also need to acknowledge that the body currently does not stand at the center of our understanding of what it means to be human, but is at the edges, and as such we are more susceptible to tacitly adopting secular practices and habits. From what I can tell, when evangelicals talk about the body, we say all the right things—but we simply have not thought about the body enough to ensure that our account of its goodness takes its cues from Scripture rather than the broken world around us.

I am confident that we as evangelicals can recover a rich understanding of the body without shifting our emphases away from what has historically marked us as a movement. In his important book *The Deep Things of God,* theologian and friend Dr. Fred Sanders suggests that the four historical evangelical concerns of Bible, cross, conversion, and heaven can only be emphasized properly when they are placed against the broader backdrop of a robust Trinitarian theology. When we lose that backdrop, our theology becomes reductionistic. We simply shout those four emphases over and over, without understanding why they are important or how they fit together. As he puts it, "What is needed is not a change of emphasis but a restoration of the background, of the big picture from which the emphasized elements have been selected."[37]

Sanders's solution to the problem is to recover the doctrine of the Trinity as the heartbeat of Christian theology and spirituality. While he contends that evangelicals are tacitly Trinitarian—that is, we have been brought into the inner life of the Father through the working of the Son by the Holy Spirit—we have forgotten our Trinitarian heritage, which has undermined the vibrancy of our faith and created a widespread sense of shallowness.

I agree that evangelicals need to recover the broad backdrop of Trinitarian theology. But if we are going to "take every thought captive," we also need to recover a thorough understanding of what it means to be human and how the body fits into that. In the opening of John Calvin's *Institutes of the Christian Religion,* he argues that while the knowledge of God precedes the knowledge of ourselves, we cannot know who God is without reinterpreting what it means to be his creatures in light of that knowledge. The God of the universe is God with us, Immanuel. He is God for himself and with himself before the world began. But Calvin is right: Our knowledge of God is inseparable from knowing what it means that he is with *us,* from understanding what it means that we are made in his image.

This knowledge of our humanity is given to us in the person and work of Jesus Christ, which Scripture attests to. His historical life, death, and resurrection are the center of our theological reflection—not the body per se or our experience of the body in the church. Church practices are important for our formation in the life we have in Christ, but the pattern for that life is not taken from practices but from Scripture.

The gift of God in Jesus Christ is a gift for and to human bodies, and as evangelicals, we need to attend carefully to the ways in which the Holy Spirit shapes our flesh. In a world where the body's status is in question, we have an opportunity to proclaim that the God who saved our souls will also remake our bodies; that the body is nothing less than the place where God dwells on earth. It means moving the body to the center of our understanding of what it means to be human, but it is a move that is justified when we remember that the Word himself became flesh.

CHAPTER THREE

WHAT IS THE BODY?

My sister reminded me that my grandfather would have been ninety yesterday.

He died just over five years ago, a few weeks before I married my wife. It was a painful loss for my family—we had moved an hour south of him when I was in the third grade, and had spent more time with him than any other member of our extended family. He was a loveable curmudgeon. Fiercely independent, he took great joy in spoiling his grandchildren.

When he died, my brother and I both wrote eulogies on our blogs. My brother's was better—so good, in fact, that they read it at his funeral. I occasionally go read it when I think about him: "Grandpa—for he was always Grandpa, not Victor or Vic or Granddad or Pa-Pa—was genial with a charming touch of the curmudgeon—in short, a model patriarch. He must have marveled at his progeny; we are deep, intellectual types, teachers, preachers, writers, musicians. Grandpa was a tradesman, a craftsman, a tinkerer."[1]

He had also had polio, a disease that has been all but eradicated from the United States because of vaccines. He contracted it as a child, and though it didn't kill him, it left him with the use of only one arm for the rest of his life. He worked in a Ford shop and did much of his own woodworking and carpentry. He was married as a young man, but spent the last twenty years of his life alone, after my grandmother—whom I never knew—passed away. As my brother put it, Grandpa "was a survivor."

My favorite moment with my grandfather happened when I was in high school. We lived in western Washington, and had just suffered a heavy dose of snow, followed by some light rain, followed by a spell of sub-freezing temperatures that left the trees loaded with ice. This brought down branches and trees everywhere, including at Grandpa's house. The electric company later came through and finished the job to protect the lines, leaving several trees cut up into eighteen-inch segments lying on Grandpa's lawn.

My job was to turn those ancient cylinders into firewood, a job that I decided to take on over my spring break. It proved more difficult than I'd imagined. I used a nine-pound maul to split the logs, and was spent after only a few hours of the first day.

My grandfather, ever the observant one, watched me for a little while one morning and then stepped in to offer a few tips. When I didn't quite get it, he grabbed the maul from me with his good arm, raised it above his head, and dropped it on the unsuspecting log. That process repeated itself several times, and would have continued had I not recovered my dignity enough to grab the maul back. I've never been a terribly muscular fellow, but I do have my limits, and being outdone at chopping wood by a one-armed seventy-year-old man goes way beyond them.

Naturally, when he went back into the house, I tried it. I grabbed the maul in my right hand and . . . I failed. Miserably. The maul had gained an additional ten pounds (it seemed) and I could barely get it up, much less pull it down with any force. It weakly glanced off the wood, and I hurriedly looked around to make sure no one had seen me. I was alone, so I tried again to the same effect before embracing my weakness and swinging the axe with both hands.

THE BODY UNDER SCRUTINY

My grandfather's polio shaped his life in ways I will never understand. He couldn't serve in World War II because of it, and must have faced incredible social obstacles. I have sometimes thought that his stubborn belligerence to take care of himself was forged in response to a world that treated him as less valuable because of his paralyzed arm. His body—and what happened to it—shaped his understanding of himself and the world.

What the body is shapes what the body does. It sets the context for our actions—it establishes the options for our lives, making some actions and forms of life more plausible than others. As a child, I spent hours dribbling a basketball, dreaming of game-winning fadeaway three-pointers to win the NBA finals. But as I grew older, the scenario I longed for as a child would almost certainly never come to pass. The body I have been given and the way I trained it growing up made that option all but impossible.

I'm not sure why anyone would read it—I was forced to in high school—but the odd short story "Rain, Rain, Go Away" by Isaac Asimov makes the point well.[2] The story is about a family who only goes outside when the sun is out, and constantly examines the weather. While out with their neighbors at the fair, they gorge themselves on cotton candy until a storm rolls in and they race home. The story ends with the family dissolving in the rain as they race to their house because they're *sugar*, not humans.

In a less fanciful world, the same principle applies. The decisions we make about whether to pursue the NBA or become a writer, to play piano or play football, will presuppose our understanding of what our bodies are—and are not—capable of. Despite my best efforts to the contrary, I will never be a concert pianist. I simply don't have the fingers for it. As humans we may not be made of sugar and so do not have to fear inclement weather. But we're also not made of steel, and our pretensions to be supermen should be tempered accordingly. We have been made from the dust, and to dust we shall return, a reality we need to understand properly if we want to experience a revitalized faith.

But before I point toward what the body is, let me address what the body is not.

THE PRISON

To call the body a prison has been enough to doom Plato to the wastebin for most contemporary evangelicals (regardless of whether they've read him or not). It suggests that the body is evil and that the goal of our lives is to escape the material world for the purer, less tainted world of the spiritual. But Plato's reputation as someone who hates the material world might be overstated.[3]

Regardless of whether Plato is to blame for the idea, this overtly negative approach to the body in favor of the soul is certainly a feature of Gnosticism. And while criticizing the Greek influences on early Christianity and suggesting the early church hated the body have become something of a cottage industry, here too the reputation may be more of a distortion than deserved. Augustine, who is probably accused of despising the body more frequently than anyone else, repeatedly affirms its goodness and rejects the Gnostic tendency of the Neoplatonism he inherited.[4] Whether Augustine's views are consistent is a separate question, but his most mature writings make it abundantly clear that he affirms the goodness of the physical world and the bodily resurrection from the dead.

But the idea that the body is a prison of the soul has made its way into the Christian consciousness in various places and times. Most prominently, the Reformer John Calvin uses the phrase several times in his most enduring work, *The Institutes of the Christian Religion*. Calvin's understanding of what it means to be human is orthodox, and he does not disparage the body as intrinsically evil. But the strength of Calvin's language and his frustration with the body is certainly jarring when contrasted to our contemporary sentiments.[5]

The notion that the body is a prison for the purer, more refined soul is a distortion of orthodox Christian teaching about the nature of the human person. Where it has lingered in Christian theology, it has done so as a houseguest who has overstayed his welcome.

THE MACHINE

Most people would not consciously acknowledge that the body is a prison, but they might affirm it is a machine. The metaphor is often traced to Descartes, the seventeenth-century philosopher and mathematician. For Descartes, the soul is only tied to the body through a certain gland in the brain. The body, then, is simply an object that is extended through time and space, a tool that the soul—which is who we *really* are—uses to get around in the world.[6] This has led some philosophers to describe Descartes' position as the "ghost in the machine."[7]

This notion that the body is a machine pervades the intellectual period known as modernity. Noam Chomsky, the linguist and philosopher, argues that the astronomer Galileo thought we could only make sense of things if we described them as machines. Yet there was pressure on this approach even at the very beginning. Isaac Newton, who adopted it, was accused of introducing occult practices into science because he found himself unable to provide mechanical explanations for every aspect of human existence.[8]

This divide between the body-as-machine and the body-as-mystery has continued into our own era. The scientific and medical communities tend to presume that explanations of how the body works are only allowable if they fit within mechanistic presuppositions. Hans Jonas wrote in 1966, "It is the existence of life within a mechanical universe which now calls for an explanation, and explanation has to be in terms of the lifeless. . . . That there is life at all, and how such a thing is possible in a world of mere matter, is now the problem posed to thought."[9]

It's important to underscore that the phenomenal successes of science are a testament to the rational ordering of the created world. In reality, the machines that we create are only approximations of the marvelous complexities of the human body.[10] That the world and our bodies can be understood in terms of machines is a marvel in itself.

The downside, though, to this vision of the universe is that it has left many of us with a stunted understanding of the nature of the human body. We can and should study how the body works.

But we must also realize that there are limits to what science and medicine can tell us, and an approach that only allows scientific or medical explanations is a watered-down understanding of what it means to be human. In his book *Begotten or Made*, theologian Oliver O'Donovan highlights the paradox that arises when humans study themselves. He writes:

> But in order to study himself, man must be differentiated, spirit and matter. . . . We confront a paradox: we cannot pin ourselves down *in toto*, spirit and matter; we cannot see ourselves whole, because in the very act of seeing ourselves, a part of us is withdrawn from the study. . . . How can we corner the elusive spirit, which declines to be an object of scientific enquiry as such? Only, perhaps, by studying a material correlate of spirit in man's physical constitution, by tying spirit down to its material substrate where we can examine it in a way that will assert our transcendence over it. This, I suppose, is the fascination of investigating the brain.[11]

O'Donovan's critique isn't against studying the material composition of our bodies. But it does, I think, establish limits around what we study scientifically. Transgressing those limits, though, is at the heart of the modern project of self-transcendence through technological mastery.[12]

The notion that the body is a machine turns scientists and doctors into priests, as they become the only ones who can tell us what the human body is. Yet the body is something more than the genes, bones, muscles, blood, and other parts that compose it. Those things are necessary for understanding how the body "works," but that is not enough to explain the body's role in our human existence. We are embodied creatures, creatures whose experience of the world is affected by the structures not just of our brains but of our entire bodies.[13]

There is, as O'Donovan puts it, a "biology that we *live.*"[14] When we go about our day, we have a very different relationship to our bodies than we do when we enter the lab. Whether we are riding horses or writing books, our awareness is rarely on the body itself, but is directed toward the goals we are pursuing. When driving the car to the store, we don't think about the muscles moving our hands, but the road, the cars around us, and Counting Crows blaring on the radio. When we move toward certain ends or goals, we don't tend to reflect about *how* the body is going to get us there—until, that is, something goes wrong and the body intrudes into our consciousness.

How is the question of what the body is made of related to what the body is for? Philosopher Alasdair MacIntyre points out the difficulty of this question:

> Medieval philosophers were not sufficiently puzzled by this question, because they knew too little about the materials of which the human body is composed. Modern philosophers have not been sufficiently puzzled by this question, because, from . . . [artificial intelligence] programs to the theorizing of philosophers recently engrossed by the findings of neurophysiology and biochemistry, they have tended to suppose that, if only we knew enough about the materials of which the body is composed, the problem of how we find application for teleological concepts would somehow be solved or disappear.[15]

MacIntyre doesn't really provide an answer for the relationship between our material composition and how we live in the world. But his point is suggestive: Scientific advances in understanding how the body works are insufficient to inform us about what the body is or how it relates to our understanding of the world.

Over the past twenty years, the closest evangelicals have gotten to reflecting on the nature of the physical body is in their ongoing debate about the soul. There are numerous positions in the debate, but the most popular seems to be the idea that humans are composed of a union of soul and matter, or a position that is frequently called "substance dualism."[16] Others would classify themselves as "non-reductive physicalists," which is the idea that humans are only physical creatures but that we cannot explain every feature of human existence through physical categories.[17]

But within this debate, it seems that all the attention has been on how our consciousness (or the soul) relates to the body's parts, whereas there has been relatively little reflection about the nature of the body itself in our lived experience. As a result, both sides have struggled with the tendencies of modern science to reduce the body to a machine. Philosopher Calvin Schrag writes, "A curious consequence of the intensified theory construction of the mind-body relation in modern and recent philosophy is the concentrated attention given to the meaning of *mind* and the virtual inattention given to the meaning of *body*. The assumption appears to be that everybody in the philosophical neighborhood knows what it means to be a human body, leaving the central task that of getting things straight on the peculiar marks of the mental."[18] In other words, within the discussion about bodies and souls, the nature of the body has again been forgotten.

WHAT THE BIBLE SAYS THE BODY IS

It is difficult to articulate Scripture's teaching about anything, let alone the nature of the human person. Theologian John Cooper summarizes the problem: "The Bible is neither theoretically clear in its mode of expression nor is it interested in addressing such philosophical issues as the number of substances of which human beings are composed."[19] Because of the extensive nature of the debate, and the vast literature elsewhere, I see no need to repeat what has been written. Instead, my goal is to provide a rough outline of a scriptural understanding of the human body so that we can begin to see how this might shape our lives.[20]

The place to begin, of course, is at the beginning. The crucial text is from the early pages of Genesis: "The Lord God formed man of the dust of the ground, and breathed into his nostrils the breath of life; and man became a living being" (2:7 NKJV).

While the line has been a source of endless speculation, I think there are two conclusions that we can safely draw from it: first, matter needs organization, and in the original creation that organization happens through specifically divine action.[21] The dust of the ground doesn't make itself, but is formed into a particular shape. As scholar Gordon Wenham points out, the language of God "forming" is that of a potter shaping clay. It is an "artistic, inventive activity that requires skill and planning." God's creative activity is intentional—he is intimately involved in how our human bodies work.[22]

Second, the organized whole needs animation, or the ability to decide on and direct itself to its own ends and goals. The body has life—it is something more than "an interesting collection of chemicals and electrical impulses." Unlike machines, humans are self-directed. We act for our own ends, under our own motivation and power. Even within the Old Testament, though, this "life" is a gift from God, and it is to be fundamentally directed toward God. Job used similar language to Genesis: "If [God] should set his heart to it and gather to himself his spirit and his breath, all flesh would perish together, and man would return to dust" (Job 34:14–15).[23] But this life is also not something that is separate from the body, but is within the body, permeating every part and allowing us to move as a unified, organized whole.

As human persons, we have a unique place and role within the order of creation. As the first creation narrative states, male and female are made "in the image of God." That phrase has been a veritable theological playground throughout church history. Christians have demonstrated a tendency to project onto the phrase whatever we already care about; for example, to see the image of God as our reasoning abilities, if those are in vogue, or our relational capacities, if those are more fashionable.[24] Perhaps the most intriguing suggestion comes from Eastern Orthodox theologians: God is a mystery, and therefore so are humans.[25]

But the language of the "image of God" does mark humans off as distinct from anything else in the universe—which also means we stand in a unique relationship to the Creator. This relationship presents possibilities for human life that no other aspect of creation will ever know. This radical uniqueness of our lives before God cannot be separated from our status as embodied creatures. After Adam and Eve sin, God reminds them, "For you are dust, and to dust you shall return" (Genesis 3:19). Our relationship with God is inextricable from the body.

The close identification of the human person with the bodily form in our original creation suggests that the best understanding of the body may be Gilbert Meilaender's striking phrase: it is the "place of our personal presence."[26] As human persons, we live, communicate, and move in the flesh and bones that we indwell. Our bodies are not instruments for us to operate, as though we were driving them about like captains of a ship.[27] They are not tools for us to communicate with others, or pieces of property to dispose of as we wish. What our bodies do, *we* do. What we do to other animated bodies, we do to other persons.

THE GOODNESS OF THE BODY

As discussed in the previous chapter, the history of Christianity and the physical body is far too complex to fit the generalization that Christians have thought the body is evil, but the fact that we continue to distance ourselves from that perception means the message still hasn't gotten through.[28] There have doubtless been abuses and distortions of biblical teaching throughout the centuries, but the consensus, orthodox Christian position has been that the material substance that is the human body is "very good" (Genesis 1:31).

Yet the narrative of "the fall" does pose a question about our embodied lives. The rebellion of Adam and Eve against God reshapes not only their relationships with him, but their understanding of each other and their own bodies. Their decision to clothe themselves after "their eyes were opened" suggests the presence of shame, which introduced a new self-consciousness about the body and prompted them to cover it. Adam and Eve's personal relations were inextricable from their bodily presence, and the sin that broke the former inevitably forced them to alter the latter.

Yet the Bible's proclamation that sin entered the world is not the final word—or even the first word. "The Word became flesh and dwelt among us" (John 1:14). I said it in the opening, but it cannot be repeated enough: The God in whose image we are made took on human form. The incarnation established that God is *with* us in all the dust, the sweat, and the tears of our physicality.

Though the incarnation leaves no question about the goodness of our corporeality, the bodily resurrection of Jesus adds additional evidence. The resurrection of the body means that to be human with God is to be with him not as disembodied souls, but as people with noses, faces, arms, and legs that are similar to those we currently have. In Paul's loftiest treatment of Christ's resurrection and its implications for our own embodied lives, he writes:

> What is sown is perishable; what is raised is imperishable. It is sown in dishonor; it is raised in glory. It is sown in weakness; it is raised in power. It is sown a natural body; it is raised a spiritual body. . . . For the trumpet will sound, and the dead will be raised imperishable, and we shall be changed. For this perishable body must put on the imperishable, and this mortal body must put on immortality. (1 Corinthians 15:42–44, 52–53)

We don't know that much about the precise nature of our physical bodies when they are raised from the dead, but the fact that we will have physical bodies is not in question for Paul. The language of the "spiritual body" does not mean that we will be shadows or insubstantial spirits. Rather, "spiritual" is a suggestion about what will be animating our bodies—namely, the Holy Spirit. In the gospel of John, the apostle depicts the risen Jesus sharing bread and fish with his disciples for breakfast, as though to make a point that the body isn't going to simply go away in the resurrection from the dead (John 21:9–14).

In addition, Paul's point is clear that our resurrected bodies will no longer be corruptible or perishable. That doesn't mean that we won't *do* things or learn or grow, but as we act, we will not need to fear the breakdown of the body's organization or the loss of the body's life. In an evocative phrase, Rodney Clapp muses that "resurrection and transformation into a spiritual body . . . is the divine equivalent of inventing the internal combustion engine."[29] N. T. Wright wrote in a famous passage:

> [The future resurrection body] will be incapable of dying or decaying, thus requiring a transformation not only for those already dead but for those still alive. This new mode of embodiment is hard to describe, but we can at least propose a label for it. The word *transphysical* seems not to exist . . . and I proffer it

for inclusion between *transphosphorylation and transpicuous* in the *Oxford English Dictionary* . . . *[Transphysical]* merely, but I hope usefully, puts a label on the demonstrable fact that the early Christians envisaged a body which was still robustly physical but also significantly different from the present one. If anything—since the main difference they seem to have envisaged is that the new body will not be corruptible—we might say not that it will be *less* physical, as though it were some kind of ghost or apparition, but more. "Not unclothed, but more fully clothed."[30]

THE BODY'S HABITS

I was never a very good basketball player, but I enjoyed the game. My coaches always appreciated me because despite my minimal talent, I worked hard in practice. But that hard work rarely translated into success on the court for one main reason: I thought too much.

Basketball is a game of immediate, intentional reactions that are shaped by the habits acquired on the practice floor. Players aren't supposed to think about how their arms look when they're shooting, or where they're supposed to go next during a play. When they shoot, they focus on the rim, and when running plays they try to see the whole floor so they can spontaneously adjust.

The paradox of contemporary culture is that while many of us are obsessive about how our bodies *look,* we are not conscious of the habits of the body we've picked up through our practices of life. We look in the mirror, but we fail to notice the way our body responds involuntarily to the world around us. We smile when we see children playing in part because we have trained ourselves in such a way that our faces inevitably react. Some people will utter swear words ("Christian" or otherwise) when caught off guard without realizing it because they have habituated their tongues and lips to respond that way. Even though most of us are not aware of these responses, they are embedded into the structure of our bodies.[31]

Under normal circumstances, it is actually best *not* to attend to how our bodies are acting, but instead to keep our minds on what we're doing. The race is not necessarily the best time to work on your running form. While a runner might make small adjustments based on the terrain, discomfort, or other contingencies, most of the time his attention should be directed toward the runner in front, or the finish line. We race like we practice, with the habits that we have taught ourselves (and unfortunately with those we have yet to un-teach ourselves).

J.P. Moreland and Klaus Issler define *habit* this way:

> A *habit* is an ingrained tendency to act, think, or feel a certain way without needing to choose to do so. The way you write the letters of the alphabet is not something you need to think about. It is a habit learned years earlier, and you concentrate on what you are writing, not on the style of handwriting. *Character* is the sum total of your habits, good and bad.[32]

Our bodies are organized by the ends and goals we pursue. We can play basketball, or we can break-dance, and our body will move accordingly. But as we make those decisions, we slowly build habits and patterns that affect the way we reach our goals. If we never play scales, it is unlikely we'll ever play Beethoven's *Moonlight Sonata*. The body is organized by what we pursue, but how we get there—if at all—depends considerably on the habits we have adopted.

Our body's habits also affect our relationships. When we were newly married, my wife pointed out that when I am passionate about an idea I sometimes look angry because I do not smile—and my eyebrows, which tend to be overly tense, are often furrowed in such a way that people who don't know me would think I was angry. That habitual face—which I do not remember choosing—has subtly shaped my relationships with others, as they have thought that I was angry even when I wasn't, and guarded themselves accordingly. My wife, however, has a much more cheerful face, which makes her appear more warm and inviting than I am and so opens up different possibilities in her relationships.

These habits are pre-reflective. We don't plan them out ahead of time. We don't consciously decide to scowl when people cut us off in line. For many of us, the response is ingrained through years of practice, such that we may not even realize we are doing it and deny it if accused. This lack of attention to the habits of our face, our arms, and our shoulders, and how they affect others subtly affects our relationships in ways we might not desire.

Biblically—and I will return to unpacking this dimension of the body's responses to the world in chapter 10—I would note that when God calls his people "stiff-necked" and "hardhearted" in their rebellion, he is not only speaking metaphorically. The body is not sinful, but sin can dwell within it and transform our habitual responses to others in ways that do not manifest the love and grace of God in our lives. The next time you get angry, note the tension in your neck and shoulders and what happens in your chest, and the description will start to make sense. As Dallas Willard writes:

> [The inclinations toward temptation] are actually present in those parts [of the body] and can even *be felt* there by those who are attentive to their body and who are informed, thoughtful, and willing to admit what they find upon careful reflection. . . . These various tendencies actually present in our bodily parts can *move* our body into action independently of our overall intentions to the contrary—often quite genuine—and of our conscious thoughts.[33]

THE BODY AND THE INNER LIFE

Critics of evangelicalism who have argued for a more embodied approach to Christianity have often objected to the existence of the soul in part because it ostensibly devalues the physical world. While criticizing the dualism of the early church, Nancey Murphy puts the charge this way: "If souls are saved *out of* this world, then nothing here matters ultimately. If it is our bodily selves that are saved and transformed, then bodies and all that go with them matter—families, history, and all of nature."[34]

While the inward (and upward) focus of evangelicalism does deserve some of the criticism it has received, it's important not to reject the parts that fit with the language of the Bible. Even if we ultimately determine that humans are only physical, Paul speaks of two dimensions or aspects of the same human person.

When I look at my wife and smile—which is the only appropriate response when looking at my wife—she may have some understanding of what I am thinking about, but clearly would not know for sure. I could be remembering our wedding or thinking about *cockatoos*, which is a word that simply makes me smile. We have, in other words, an inner life that is reserved for us—and God—alone. Where the early Christians spoke of the soul to explain this phenomenon, today we speak of "consciousness," which from what I can tell remains very much a mystery. In fact, some philosophers have suggested that there is no possible explanation for consciousness.

Second Corinthians 4:16–18 contains one of Paul's clearest statements about the distinction between our inner and outer lives. He writes:

> Though our outer self is wasting away, our inner self is being renewed day by day. For this light momentary affliction is preparing us for an eternal weight of glory beyond all comparison, as we look not to things that are seen but to the things that are unseen. For the things that are seen are transient, but the things that are unseen are eternal.

Just before this, Paul highlighted the persecution that he and his compatriots experienced for the sake of the gospel. According to him, they "carry about in their body the dying of Jesus so that the life of Jesus may be manifested in the body." In other words, Paul's inner life is shaped by the presence of the Holy Spirit, who lives in the temple of Paul's body and forms it according to the pattern of Jesus on the cross.

Paul keeps this distinction between his inner life and his visible body throughout his writings. In Romans 7:22–23, he writes, "For I delight in the law of God, in my inner being, but I see in my members another law waging war against the law of my mind and making me captive to the law of sin that dwells in my members." In Romans 8:10, 16, he writes, "But if Christ is in you, although the body is dead because of sin, the Spirit is life because of righteousness. . . . The Spirit himself bears witness with our spirit that we are children of God."

It is tempting to build more into Paul's understanding of the human person than the text allows. But at a minimum, it seems clear that Paul is capable of distinguishing between our inner and outer lives, between what is invisible to us and to others, and that which is made visible. For Paul, the body is our external dimension, facing others and acting in the world—but we are responsible before God for both dimensions.

I don't think Paul is falling prey to some sort of Hellenistic dualism. Rather, he seems to be faithfully transmitting (if modifying slightly around the revelation of Jesus) the Old Testament understanding of humanity. While the Old Testament's anthropology is unquestionably focused on the unity of the human person, it seems there is an ability to distinguish between various dimensions of that unity. The Hebrew term for *flesh* sometimes means simply the material stuff that makes up the body—but according to theologian Hans Walter Wolff, it can also mean "man in his bodily aspect," as in Psalm 38:3: "Because of your wrath there is no health in my body; there is no soundness in my bones because of my sin."[35]

The distinction between our inner and outer dimensions is not in itself a problem. There is a basic human subjectivity that distinguishes my experience that would have been in place prior to the fall. There's nothing immoral or wrong with my wife not having the ability to read my thoughts—if anything, the speaking and listening necessary to overcome this inability is at the heart of our humanity and relationships. I think Paul's suggestion, though, is that what was a normal distinction has been widened not only into a division, but an opposition. There is a gap between our subjective awareness and what our bodies do—"I do not do what I want to do" (Romans 7)—that is the result of living in a fallen world. Even when our inner life is regenerate—though itself not fully sanctified—the habits of our bodies are still under the domain of sin and in need of reforming according to our new life in Christ.

In other words, when our original parents sinned, they did not simply destroy our relationship with God, with each other, and with the creation around us. They also destroyed our integrity as human persons so that our internal and external dimensions no longer work in harmony. In our late-modern world, where this gap is especially wide, Christians have oscillated back and forth between an inwardly oriented devotional piety that tends to slip into a withdrawal from the world, or an emphasis on social action that is constantly in danger of minimizing the specific revelation of Jesus Christ and the empowering presence of the Holy Spirit in its pursuit of public justice. It is for this reason that the church looks forward to the resurrection of the dead, when the Savior will return and restore the harmony both within us and all around us.[36]

An evangelical theology of the body, then, preserves an inner life without preserving an *inward* life. Martin Luther, the Protestant theologian, described sin as *incurvatus in se,* or humans being curved in on themselves and away from God.[37] That is not what I am advocating. The inward focus of the sinful heart is a cheap imitation of the rich inner life of communion with the Holy Spirit, whose life extends outward through our bodies into the worlds we inhabit. Dallas Willard has, perhaps, put it best:

> The outcome of spiritual formation is, indeed, the transformation of the inner reality of the self in such a way that the deeds and works of Jesus become a natural expression of who we are. But it is the nature of the human being that the "inner reality of the self" settles into our body, from which that inner reality operates in *practice.*[38]

LIMITS

To speak of the body means speaking of *limits.*

If there is an aspect of embodied life that I struggle with the most, this is it. I inherited an overly healthy dose of stubbornness from my grandfather, who refused to let his disability or his age hinder his independence. Like him, I do not like being told that I am incapable of doing things. To acknowledge that is to acknowledge my own limitations, to confess that I am not capable of doing everything I want to do in this world.

Yet to have a body means having boundaries. While some limitations may be repressive distortions that are grounded in sin—as, for instance, slavery was—others are natural limitations based on who we are as humans. We need to eat food for our survival because our bodies need energy. We sleep because our bodies need renewal.

Other limitations, of course, are rooted in the particularities of our bodies and their specific capabilities. To return to my dream of playing in the NBA, as I matured I realized that my physical abilities would prevent that dream from becoming a reality, and that never playing in the NBA would not prevent me from leading a full, joyful, fulfilled life. Part of our development as adults is discerning which limits we should push through, and which we should respect. But there is no escaping the fact that if we are going to live in the body we have to embrace some of the limits that it entails.[39]

Yet the body's limits are not simply in what we can or cannot do. Our bodies also locate us in particular places and times. While technology has increased our mobility and the sense of rootlessness that many people feel, the more we attend to the body, the more we will be tied to the places where we dwell. We are not abstract souls, floating above the clouds, but have histories, languages, and understandings that are unique and are based on the local circumstances in which we were raised and live.

According to advocates in the emerging church, part of having a theology that is "embodied" means acknowledging the limitations of the local context in which God became man and the Scriptures were written. In *Listening to the Beliefs of Emerging Churches,* Doug Pagitt writes:

> The gospel of Jesus is meant to be good news in its particulars. We are always living in particular situations and the gospel must meet those situations. This has been one of the most compelling parts of Christianity—Jesus was not a generic Messiah but was embedded in the life and dirt of culture, and was the fulfillment of particular promises. Christianity does not mandate a singular culture, nor a single cultural worldview.[40]

That our world is different from the "dirt" of the first-century Judeo-Hellenistic culture is indisputable. Yet there is a temptation to allow the differences between Jesus' time and ours to overwhelm the more fundamental unity that lies beneath: We are all humans, made by the same Creator and walking before the face of the same God. As we pay attention to the flesh, which the Word assumed, we will discern the ways in which that culture contained universal, timeless truths.

In fact, the church's traditional understanding of Christ depends on the universality of human nature. As the second Adam, Jesus' human body stands in for all humanity. "One died for all, therefore all died," Paul tells us. Jesus' particularity, in fact, is a specific feature of his divinity. "Who is like the Lord our God?" No one. Which means the incarnation is unrepeatable not because of the culture in which Christ entered, but because of the one who entered it.

An embodied theology is a theology that acknowledges the radical uniqueness of Christmas, the cross, and Easter. Only there did the one who transcends creation enter it, die for us, and rise again. But in taking the form of a human, Jesus opened the possibility of redemption for everyone and established the pattern for human flourishing. He is not only the revelation of God to us, but the revelation of man to us. Even as we acknowledge the particularities of the cultural context of Scripture, our theology and our theological understanding of mankind will be for all people, in all places, at all times.[41]

THE GOD WHO SHAPES THE BODY BY HIS GRACE

"For you are dust, and to dust you shall return."

It is my favorite line in the church calendar, for it reminds me of the frailty of my existence. Said during the imposition of ashes on Ash Wednesday, the line reminds us that we grow old and die. Yet death is tragic precisely because life is fundamentally good. "From dust to dust" is the judgment God passes on Adam and Eve before exiling them from the garden, where they lost their original goodness.

The good news of the gospel is that the God of the universe took on a body, died on our behalf, rose again on the third day, and now lives in our hearts and our limbs. We have been set free from sin's power (though not necessarily its presence) by grace through faith. Yet the faith that saves is not an abstract commitment to a vague deity who offers generic blessings and requires moral obedience. It is a trust in the historical figure of Jesus Christ as attested to by the Scriptures. Fred Sanders puts it this way: "The gospel is that God is God for us, that he gives himself to be our salvation."[42]

The God who gives himself to us in Jesus Christ is the God who fashioned the universe, and our trust in his salvation is our confidence that even the material conditions of this world cannot prevent him from fulfilling his promises to his people. This is Paul's point in Romans 4:18–21, where he examines the faith that was counted as righteousness to Abraham. He writes:

> In hope he believed against hope, that he should become the father of many nations, as he had been told, "So shall your offspring be." He did not weaken in faith when he considered his own body, which was as good as dead (since he was about a hundred years old), or when he considered the barrenness of Sarah's womb. No distrust made him waver concerning the promise of God, but he grew strong in his faith as he gave glory to God, fully convinced that God was able to do what he had promised.

God had promised Abraham that he would be a blessing to the world and the heir of many nations. Yet to fulfill this promise God had to overcome the frailty of the body. Abraham's body was "as good as dead," and Sarah's womb was barren. Yet rather than doubt God's faithfulness, Abraham rested in the fact that God "gives life to the dead and calls into existence the things that do not exist" (4:17), a fact that makes God worthy of all our worship and adoration.

The same God who forgives sin shapes and reshapes human bodies. In Matthew 9, Jesus forgives the sins of a paralytic, and the scribes and Pharisees grumble. In response, Jesus reveals the fullness of authority: " 'But that you may know that the Son of Man has authority on earth to forgive sins'—he then said to the paralytic—'Rise, pick up your bed and go home' " (v. 6). Jesus does not associate paralysis with sinning, nor should we. But his authority to forgive sins is connected to his authority over our human bodies.

CHAPTER FOUR

THE BODY TOWARD OTHERS

We are social even in the womb.

Though most critics lambasted the film for being a glorified home video, I thought *Babies* was one of the most interesting films of 2010—a year that included *The Social Network*, *True Grit*, and *Inception*. The documentary-style film follows four infants on four different continents from their birth through their first birthday. Though most critics could only see "cute," the film is an interesting meditation on the joys and dangers of human exploration and relationships.

It's also an interesting bit of social commentary. In one particularly nauseating scene, Hattie—the infant from San Francisco—attends a New Age sing-along with her mom. She wisely scoots toward the door while the circle of mothers and infants sing, "The Earth is our mother/We must take care of her/Hey yana, ho yana, hey yan . . ."[1] It's an ironic moment, as Ponijao—who lives in Namibia—sits in the dirt, plays in the mud, and has his feces wiped away by his mother's hand. I'm not a New Ager, but given how much time Ponijao spends playing and examining the earth, he actually has a plausible case for Hattie's little song.

Babies are social creatures—as the film amply demonstrates.

And their sociability is not something they grow into, but something they come out of the womb with. Studies have concluded that infants are able to recognize and imitate facial expressions within the first hour out of the womb, and to adapt their own facial muscles when the other's changes. Philosopher Shaun Gallagher points out that this "indicates a rudimentary differentiation between self and non-self."[2] This differentiation depends upon infants' awareness of their own bodies, and their recognition that their parents are similar to them. As persons they are capable of acting and reacting in relationship to others from the moment they are born.

What's more, researchers have started to conclude that our directedness toward others actually begins *before* we're born. In October 2010, a group of psychologists in Italy studied twins in the womb and concluded that "by the 14th week of gestation, unborn twins are already directing arm movements at each other, and by the 18th week these 'social' gestures have increased to 29 percent of all observed movements. In contrast, the proportion of self-directed actions reduced over the same period." Of course, Christians already knew this. The fact that Jacob was holding Esau's heel during their entrance into the world is evidence they had already spent nine months fighting (Genesis 25:26).

Our sociability as humans is inextricable from the structure of our bodies. "It is not good," the Lord said of Adam, "for the man to be alone." Adam spends the next bit of his life naming the animals, during which time he was undoubtedly confronted with their differences from him. Unlike infants who imitate their parents, he did not recognize any animal of his own kind—a recognition initially based on the body's form. While our human interactions (hopefully) mature as we grow older, they are invariably shaped, for good or evil, by the habits and structures of the human body.

CONSUMERS AND CONSUMERISM

I had never been so relieved to hear running water.

My wife and I are strong-willed people who like our sleep, and we were paying a steep price for it. We were hiking into the Grand Canyon in early July, when temperatures can reach well over 100 degrees. Rather than leaving at four or five AM, as sane people would do to avoid the heat, we had overslept and left at ten. We were in the middle of our eight-mile hike during the hottest part of the day.

The longer our journey took, the more our ample supply of water seemed insufficient. My wife tends to be a worrier, and her vocal concerns had started to rattle my otherwise cheerful optimism. As the temperature climbed and our water levels dropped, it was easy to imagine the worst.

And then we turned a corner and heard the gurgling of a stream, a sound that brought a rush of relief. We knew that our final destination must be close. For the first time, I understood the biblical metaphors of God being like water in dry land. We rejoiced and played in the stream, delighted that the end of the trail was near.

I don't think very often about how my human body needs water to survive. As a resource, its ready availability is something that I usually take for granted. When I feel thirsty, I simply walk over to the sink and turn on the spigot. Relief flows like . . . water. But for many people in the world, the body's dependency upon food and water pervades their conscious awareness far more than mine. Whether they go to bed hungry or walk a mile for clean water, like Ponijao, the baby from Namibia, they are closely connected to the earth and their body's dependency upon its resources.

In fact, this dependency is at the heart of our lives together with other people. Growing up, before every meal we would close our eyes, grab our parent's or sibling's hand, and plunge together into prayer. Our saying grace was an acknowledgment that we lived only as the providence and care of God continued to provide for us. When we thank God for our food, we confess our shared humanity before him. We are "frail children of dust" who are as "feeble as frail," and our acknowledged dependency upon the Creator for our life is at the heart of a flourishing human community.

The social dimension of our embodied life is tied to our experience of pleasures as well. The sacred celebrations of this life, the ones that are at the heart of human community, almost always involve meals. Growing up, I knew that there was at least one day every year—my birthday—where the threat of Brussels sprouts would be suspended. We always got to choose what we wanted to eat in celebration of our existence. As the poet W. H. Auden put it: "Only man, supererogatory beast, Dame Kind's thoroughbred lunatic, can do the honors of a feast . . ."[3] Sharing an excellent meal does not simply curb our loneliness, but is a manifestation of our gratitude for the goodness of the created order that God has placed us in.

Yet in our late-modern world, the body's basic dependency upon the world for both its sustenance and its pleasures has been distorted to the extent that what we consume has become central to our identity as persons. What we wear, what we eat (or don't eat), what we endorse—these become the means by which we construct ourselves. Probably the best example is the war between Apple and Microsoft. The "I'm a Mac" campaign is not just about how Apple's products are better than Microsoft's—it is about how Apple *people* are cooler, savvier, and trendier than Microsoft people. Microsoft eventually countered this campaign with a version of its own, but the damage had been done. Tyler Wigg Stevenson sums up consumerism: "We buy to be; we are what we buy; we are what we consume."[4]

Because consumerism is a form of identity construction—my consumption makes me who I am—it is a form of *technique,* or the idea that everything we do is a form of "instrumental making." But the corollary of that principle is that "everything around us is raw material for our use"—or what is sometimes called commodification. Skye Jethanie's definition of the phenomenon is helpful: "The act of assigning an exchange value to something converts it into a commodity. As a result, an object's value is not linked directly to what it *is* but what it can be exchanged *for.*"[5]

In a consumerist society, the world is flattened out as everything becomes an instrument for the individual's well-being. Things only have value when a consumer desires them, which means that there is no order of goods to which our desires should conform. When God looked at creation and said it was "very good," he was acknowledging the goodness that is intrinsic to it rather than adding something on top of it. But in a consumerist world, the only goodness things have is what we assign to them. For Augustine, desires are sinful when they are "disordered"—when we love, for instance, cheesecake more than God. But the modern world believes there is no order at all, since that might impose obligations on us. As Rodney Clapp puts it, consumerism "does not specify desires according to the substantive, actual objects of those desires. It promotes desire for desire's sake."[6]

The tentacles of consumerism and commodification have reached into every realm of human life, destroying human relationships. To choose one prominent example among a range of options, a commodified sexuality treats other human bodies as instruments for one's own pleasure and self-identity. Sex trafficking and prostitution—which have increasingly been recognized as the moral evils that they are—are the most obvious and destructive forms of this. Sexual pleasure that comes from a financial transaction is wholly and utterly dehumanizing for both parties, as it treats the other as an instrument for one's own personal gain and well-being.

INDIVIDUALISM: KISSING COUSINS WITH CONSUMERISM

As a boy, some of my favorite books were from a series detailing the lives of many American legends and heroes. Though I've forgotten many of the details, the story of Jim Thorpe has stayed with me. Thorpe was a multi-sport athlete and Olympian from the first half of the twentieth century, who rose from the margins of society to the center through talent and hard work, overcoming opposition and challenges along the way. Like many of the tales in the series, Thorpe's story perpetuated a can-do spirit and a healthy resistance to artificial limits.

The series had a strong undercurrent of the American individualism that has received so much attention in recent years. From the myth of the American cowboy to the iconic hipster James Dean, Americans love those who stand out from the crowd, who make their own way without outside help.

This emphasis on self-sufficiency goes to the heart of modern liberalism, a political philosophy that starts from the basic rights and liberties of the individual.[7] In its degraded contemporary form, liberalism isolates individuals from social ties or obligations, except those that we enter contractually. The problem with this idea—which is so deeply ingrained that it is almost impossible to examine properly—is that it pushes to the background the bonds that we have with others by virtue of our human bodies. Gilbert Meilaender describes the position of Thomas Hobbes, an early advocate of this view, this way:

> Hobbes's human beings are all will and choice—and no body. Children, as he imagines them, are not born into any institution which corresponds to our concept of the family nor under the care of any person who is father or mother according to our traditional understanding of those roles. Indeed, there is nothing in his picture that could quite be described as a relation between the generations; for there are only sovereigns and subjects.[8]

By reducing human relationships to "all will and choice—and no body," this sort of modern American individualism becomes a close cousin of consumerism. Liberalism reduces the human person to a naked individual, eliminating any social relationships except those we choose. But the void cannot stay empty for too long, and consumerism has stepped in to complete our understanding of what it means to be human. Both treat the body's relationship with others as only having value when we make conscious decisions to enter into them. Our bodies are hollow, waiting to be filled out by the products and relationships we choose to enter.

THE BODY IN THE ORDER OF CREATION

Consumerism and individualism are the twin towers, the two massive ideologies that are embedded in our cultural practices and our beliefs. But they also undermine the fullness of Christian faith and practice, which in its orientation around the God who created the world has a different understanding of how humans are related to each other and the creation. My goal in what follows is not to articulate every aspect of a biblical understanding of creation, but to highlight three points of emphasis that put Christians in tension with both consumerism and individualism.

The most obvious fact about the biblical doctrine of creation is that the world is *created*. God is the one who "calls into existence the things that did not exist." Or as John puts it, "All things were made through him, and without him was not any thing made that was made" (John 1:3). As the old hymn puts it, "This is our Father's world." Leaving aside the thorny question of how he made it, that God is responsible for the world and governs it by his providence pervades both the Old and New Testaments. As the psalmist writes, "The earth is the Lord's and the fullness thereof, the world and those who dwell therein, for he has founded it upon the seas and established it upon the rivers."[9]

But in the first pages of Genesis, we discern that *creation* means God dividing the world and arranging it into various kinds or species. He separates the light from the darkness (1:4), the waters of earth from those of heaven (1:7), the seas from the dry land (1:9), and then makes living things spring forth according to their kind (1:11, 12, 21, 24). In other words, God gives structure to a world that had been formless and void. His creation is orderly—it has a variety of creatures, each with their own unique dignity and value. Gordon Wenham puts it this way: "God is more than creator, he is lawgiver. . . . [He] sets bounds for the natural order and specifies the role of the species within it. With this goes the corollary that all creatures will fulfill their divinely appointed role only if they adhere to God's directive."[10]

With its emphasis on our choices as the arbiter of our values, consumerism undermines this order. The "heavens declare the glory of God" (Psalm 19:1), regardless of whether we ever colonize them. And when humans relinquish their seat in the choir of worship, the rocks are prepared to stand in as substitutes (Luke 19:39–40).

Within the creation narrative, humans are the high point. We are made in the "image of God" and are instructed to "be fruitful and multiply and fill the earth and subdue it and have dominion over the fish of the sea and over the birds of the heavens and over every living thing that moves on the earth."[11] Unlike the animals, who are also commanded to "be fruitful and multiply," humans are given authority over the earth. Yet that authority is grounded in their personal relationship with God. The author of Genesis emphasizes that God gives the commandment *to* the humans, denoting their unique relationship with him.

The idea that humans are at the center of creation continues even in the New Testament.[12] Jesus says in the Sermon on the Mount: "Look at the birds of the air: they neither sow nor reap nor gather into barns, and yet your heavenly Father feeds them. *Are you not of more value than they?*"[13] The twofold suggestion in Jesus' line is that God cares deeply about the nonhuman creation. He feeds the birds of the air through his providential kindness. Yet humans are also "of more value"—not because God arbitrarily chose humans to have more value, but because of the sort of things we are.

Humans, then, are at the center of creation—at least when we put them in relationship to the other animals. Looked at in relationship to God, he is at the center of creation, for he made everything for his own glory. These two axes—our authority over creation and God's glory—meet in the person of Jesus Christ, who affirms the goodness of creation and our position as stewards within it.[14]

I want to emphasize, though, the fact that our authority is relative to our relationship with Jesus. We have no authority to exploit creation for our own (broken) ends. Steven Bouma-Prediger points out in *For the Beauty of the Earth* that the final chapters of the book of Job are a blistering assault on Job's arrogance, during which God reminds him of his insignificance—and God's own majestic and glorious providence—in creation.[15] When humans forget that their authority over creation is divinely commissioned, the temptation to exploit the natural world will overwhelm us. Gordon Wenham comments, "Mankind is commissioned to rule nature as a benevolent king, acting as God's representative over [it] and therefore treating [it] as does the God who created [it]."[16]

Finally, a biblical understanding of creation emphasizes that our consumption should be ordered toward cultivating and creating—for it is in the latter aspect that the distinctness of our humanity lies, as Andy Crouch argues in his excellent book *Culture Making*.[17] The first creation story points to humanity's position over the creation. But the second creation story emphasizes humanity's position *for* the rest of creation, a position that takes shape specifically through our human works. The author writes: "The Lord God took the man and put him in the garden to work it and keep it." The language of "work and keep" is religious language that was used later of the Levites—the priests—suggesting that later writers saw a sanctity and holiness to human work even in the original creation.[18]

Rather than subverting this, the New Testament reinforces humanity's fundamental status as creators. Our dependence on the world's resources—the fact that we need food, clothing, and shelter—which in its most raw form drives our consumption and the problems that arise through overconsumption, is ended in the new creation. In 1 Corinthians 6:13, Paul points out, "Food is meant for the stomach, and the stomach for food—and God will destroy both." As Augustine writes, "We restore the daily decay of the body by eating and drinking, until in time you destroy both food and stomach, when you will kill need with a wonderful satiety and when you clothe this corruptible body with everlasting incorruption."[19]

In the resurrection, our bodies will no longer be dependent upon resources for their ongoing existence, suggesting that when we consume, it will be for the purposes of pleasure. But in putting it that way, we also need to remember that there are few pleasures more fulfilling or enriching than creating good things.

THE BODY, THE WORLD, AND BABIES

Over the past thirty years, evangelical awareness about the intrinsic goodness of creation has grown considerably and has recently coalesced around the idea of *creation care*.[20] In 1993, the Evangelical Environmental Network was founded to draw attention to environmental issues. In 2000, a number of conservative evangelicals formed the Cornwall Alliance to do the same thing. Six years later, eighty-six evangelical leaders signed the Evangelical Climate Initiative, and in 2008, the Southern Baptists got into the act by passing a Declaration on Environment and Climate Change.[21]

The popular perception of young evangelicals is that we are more invested in environmental activism and creation care than our parents' generation. While there are certainly young evangelicals writing and speaking about the topic, the perception may be more wishful thinking than factual analysis.[22] Some research indicates that people under thirty-five are actually less concerned about global warming than their parents, and that young evangelicals aren't particularly different from their parents on these issues.[23] Other studies point to a greater concern about environmentalism among evangelical youth.[24] The judgment of Jess Rainer, coauthor of *The Millennials,* seems right: "Millennials will do our part to protect and restore the environment. We are green, but not that green."[25]

Whether or not young evangelicals are leading the charge, the increased attention to the idea of creation care is a welcome development. As people who are oriented to the God who made the world, we need to steward his creation well. And that means recovering an understanding of its intrinsic goodness (beneath the reality of sin's presence) and shifting our practices accordingly.

Yet there is a danger—and I register this only as a caution— that in recovering the intrinsic goodness of the created order we will relegate humans to the margins rather than keeping them in the center. I was stunned when one particularly bright young woman told me that she would give her life for a dolphin if it were threatened. I understand that some species of dolphins are on the endangered species list, and that preserving them is a noble and worthwhile good. But for some reason I suspect that sort of death wasn't quite what Tertullian had in mind when he suggested "the blood of the martyrs is the seed of the church."

For our creation care to be authentically *creation* care, we must respect the biblical order of keeping humanity at the center. Because of the incarnation, our ecology flows from our theological anthropology—and not the other way around. All sin separates us from God and ruins our relationship with each other and with creation. But not all sins have the same effect or corrupt the world in the same way. The moral evil of directly killing an infant (or experimenting on one) is of a different—and more serious—kind than the ostensible indirect killing of generations of children yet to be born through environmental destruction.[26]

In fact, abortion is the clearest example of how our consumerism and individualism have collided to distort our relationship with the world and others. Children are among the most dependent on others for their existence—they can, literally, do nothing on their own and require constant attention from parents and other loved ones. At the heart of the biblical command to care for the poor, the orphan, and the widow is an exhortation to protect the defenseless, to supply the needs of those who cannot feed themselves. Even where injustice flourishes and the poor are exploited, there is no one who fits that category more than an infant. The infant body reminds us that we are not, in the first moments of our lives, individuals who live at our own pleasure.

What's more, infants restrict our freedom of choice. Like our own bodies, they are given to us to care for, and they limit our range of options in ways that repel hearts and minds shaped by consumerism. This commodification of the infant, which is intrinsic to the pro-choice position, was on display in the film *Juno*. After Juno has the baby and gives it up for adoption, her dad makes the point clear: "Someday, you'll be back here, only on your own terms." I'm all for adoption—but not if it means that infants have a status within the family *only* when they are chosen in advance. She had tried the baby on for size, but wasn't quite ready to buy.

Even if we were to grant that the woman has rights over her own body in the way abortion advocates claim, as Christians we would still point out that "greater love hath no [woman] than this, that [she] lay down [her] life for [her] friends" (John 15:13 KJV). Here too Jesus and Paul stand in agreement. In a surprising moment, Paul suggests that women "will be saved through childbearing—if they continue in faith and love and holiness, with self-control" (1 Timothy 2:15). The line has confused the church ever since Paul penned it. But it's worth pointing out that women give up their bodies when they bear children in ways that men will never understand. If I ever give up my body for my children, it will be through death—not in life, as my wife will. The woman's hospitality imitates the sacrificial love of Jesus, who draws all people to himself when he is lifted up on the cross.[27]

The treatment of other human bodies—including and especially the bodies of infants—is the heartbeat of our theological ethics. While we must treat the entire created order as God intended us to, we cannot let our renewed emphasis on these issues minimize our work to restore the value of human life within the church and society. The body is the seat of our personal presence, which means it has an inherent dignity from the moment of conception by virtue of being a human body. We cannot ignore the profound and horrendous injustice that is the direct taking of human life even as we seek to remove the social and environmental factors that prompt people to do so.

A CONCLUDING THEOLOGICAL POSTSCRIPT

Creation care is human care, and human care is creation care. Because our bodies connect us to others and the world, the resurrection of the body is inextricably linked to the restoration of the cosmos. "For the creation waits with eager longing for the revealing of the sons of God," Paul writes in Romans 8:19. It was subjected to "futility," but will someday be "set free from its bondage to corruption and obtain the freedom of the glory of the children of God" (vv. 20–21).

But the ordering and means of restoration matters as well. The whole creation groans, but it is humans (who groan inwardly) who have the "firstfruits of the Spirit." While the Spirit goes where he wills, his primary place of dwelling is the temple, the human body. He brings us, our bodies, and our desires into conformity with the will of God and radiates outward through us into the cosmos. David Van Drunen writes in *Living in God's Two Kingdoms:* "Believers themselves are the point of continuity between the creation and the new creation."[28]

The gospel redeems sinners from their sin and opens up the possibility for a restored human flourishing—flourishing that necessarily involves caring for other people and the created world. Our bodies are the fulcrum, the place where we live toward others and for others. And as the stewards of creation, how we treat each other reverberates through the farthest corners of the cosmos. When our bodies are at last made incorruptible in the resurrection from the dead, so too shall creation finally be "set free from its bondage" and the music of the spheres will once again be in tune with the choirs of heaven.

CHAPTER FIVE

THE BODY AS SHAPED
BY THE WORLD

Gothic has been given a bad name.

The word has come to designate a small subculture that thrives on a particularly dark sort of rock music and an alternative way of dressing. They often dye their hair black and wear white makeup to make their skin more pale. I don't understand the nuances of the culture or why they take up this identity, but from a distance, it all seems decidedly depressing.

Unfortunately, most people today know more about goth culture than Gothic architecture, the latter of which I occasionally like to argue (to pick a good nerdy fight) was the high point of Western architecture. Like most cultural shifts, the style was made possible by new technologies that were incorporated into existing structures. In the early twelfth century at Saint-Denis, France, Abbot Suger applied medieval theologies of light to architecture and designed what is generally considered the first Gothic cathedral. Where the Romanesque style had an arch that was rounded (like a half circle), the Gothic arch came to a point at the top, redirecting the weight of the ceiling down the sides of the arch and thereby enabling taller buildings with bigger windows.

The extraordinary effect of Gothic architecture has, unfortunately, been muted by decay. In most of the Gothic cathedrals I have visited, the windows are dirty from pollution, making the insides damp and dark. The walls are frequently an ugly gray rather than the brilliant white they would have been—like Chartres Cathedral, the best-preserved Gothic cathedral in the world. While it is popular in some circles to refer to the medieval period as the Dark Ages, applied to Gothic architecture, the distortion couldn't be more ironic. *Dark* was precisely what Gothic architecture was *not* supposed to be.

The technological developments of the eleventh and twelfth centuries allowed medieval Christians to shape their buildings in remarkable ways. It was akin to discovering a new palette of colors—it opened up an intellectual and aesthetic horizon that had previously been closed. But where contemporary developers might apply the newest technologies to shopping malls or civic centers, the theologically saturated medievals decided to apply their technologies in the service of the church in ways that fit and reinforced their theology. Because God is light and has filled his world with different sorts of light, they seized the opportunity for more natural luminosity in their places of worship.

In the middle of World War II, the House of Commons—Britain's most powerful legislative body—had its historic meeting place bombed. As it deliberated how and when it would rebuild, Prime Minister Winston Churchill rose and defended rebuilding it in the exact style and layout as the previous version. He opened his speech with what is now a classic statement of the importance of architecture: "We shape our buildings, and afterwards our buildings shape us." He goes on to argue that the shape and size of the room were integral to how the House of Commons functioned. Among other reasons, he pointed out that the small room is necessary for having a conversational way of getting things done, as it makes it feel full even with fewer people in it.[1]

Churchill's basic insight is that our environments change how we act in ways that we usually do not realize. We act differently in a medieval cathedral than in a converted warehouse. Vaulted ceilings and arched windows inevitably draw our eyes upward and make us feel smaller than we are, while the hard tile floors reverberate sound and make speaking loudly inherently more intimidating. The building itself engenders a sense of reverence and awe that the low ceilings and carpeted floors of a converted warehouse simply cannot.

That is not to say that one architectural style is better than the other for churches. That is a separate conversation. My limited point is simply that the world in which we live has a profound effect on our inner lives—that architecture matters for our spirituality. As G. K. Chesterton put it:

> Architecture is the most practical and dangerous of the arts. All the other arts we have to live with. They are things we have to live with, and some have even said, with regard to some kinds of music and paintings, that they are things they could live without. But architecture is not a thing that we only have to live with—it is a thing we have to *live in*. We live with it as Jonah lived with a whale. Jonah could not see the monster, and there is a great deal to be said for living in the most hideous house you can see in the landscape. That is the one place you will be unable to see it.[2]

As I argued in the first chapter, God gives the superfluities. A beautiful building can be a sign of God's lavish and profligate generosity to his people. And, as it was for the medieval, a building can serve as a tutor in the faith for those who are illiterate or cognitively impaired.

There is, of course, the pragmatic problem of how to allocate limited resources within the church—especially when the needs of the hurting and poor are so vast. But as a general rule of thumb, it's not good to be on the same side as Judas, who criticized Mary's decision to break an extraordinarily expensive perfume flask on Jesus' feet.

What's more, the pragmatic objection almost always ignores the decisions church members make to adorn their own living spaces. To put it bluntly, a Christianity that spends more money improving and beautifying the homes of its members than it does its places of corporate worship is a Christianity that has forgotten the profligate lavishness of God's mercy.[3]

In Matthew 15, Jesus reminds us that it is not what we eat or do not eat that defiles us, but what comes out of the overflow of our hearts. But whether we like it or not, the raw material the heart works with comes from the environments in which we place ourselves. If we wish to be "in the world" without being "of the world," then we must root ourselves even more deeply in the Word and person of Christ. Our transformation happens from the inside out. But the kindling for the refining fire of the Holy Spirit comes into our hearts from the outside in.

What is true of architecture, then, is true of everything else in our world. The tools we use, the words we hear, the images we see—each of them shapes our inner lives in ways that we do not always understand. Churchill's important line has a broader application: We shape our worlds, and afterwards our worlds shape us.[4]

THE MEDIATED BODY

I remember only a few stories from Mr. Hatch's kindergarten class. One of the most vivid involves a girl. (Come to think of it, they all involve girls.) I wasn't particularly self-conscious as a kid, but when the cutest girl in the class teased me because my ears stuck out, I felt the blood rising as my face burned with shame. She wasn't malicious, but she made it clear that they weren't very attractive.

Prior to that moment, I don't remember ever thinking about the shape of my ears. In fact, to my mother's chagrin, I could barely be bothered to look in a mirror—a tradition that like any good conservatively minded fellow I have belligerently clung to. Even if I had paid attention to my looks, I doubt I would have noticed anything unusual. I didn't have the subtle, discriminating eye that my female classmate had. But then, women are always ahead of men at this sort of thing.

I have, though, thought about my ears many times since then. From my hats to my sunglasses, I take note of whether they push my ears out. I even went through a period where I sat at my desk alternately leaning on each ear in a desperate attempt to pin them closer to my head. I would like to say I am joking about this, but I'm not.

Do my ears stick out? I don't know and I don't care (much) anymore. I spent a season looking at everyone else's ears, and while some stick out more than others, the only firm conclusion I was able to draw was that if you stare at ears long enough they all (like noses) look kind of funny. But for years of my life I was particularly sensitive to them, sometimes even wishing that they would go away. Not a healthy attitude toward my body, or as the philosophers call it, body image, but in my case it also wasn't particularly destructive.

That is, alas, not true for everyone. The negative thoughts, feelings, and perceptions that people have about their own bodies can have extraordinarily harmful effects, especially—though certainly not only—among women. Some 10 million women struggle with extreme forms of eating disorders, while countless others presumably show symptoms.[5] While men are far less likely to have eating disorders, body image problems are increasingly prevalent among men as well.[6]

Our body image, though, is not formed in the abstract. Just as with architecture, the culture around us establishes a range of "plausible options" for our bodies that we either adopt or reject, and through which we interpret our own bodies. *Maxim, Seventeen, Men's Health, People*—these are the arbiters of what bodies should look like, and the reality is that those of us who look at them can very rarely control the negative twinges of guilt and self-loathing that come in the instantaneous moments when we compare our bodies to the ones on the page.

But we should also be wary of laying *too much* responsibility at the feet of the media. It wasn't, after all, a magazine that informed me that my ears were funny looking—even though the girl might have looked at them from the day she popped out of the womb. Parents (especially fathers), siblings, friends, pastors, teachers—all the people that we interact with, and their sometimes habituated responses to our bodies, reinforce or alter the stories we tell ourselves about our bodies. Inevitably, we see ourselves through the lens of those people with whom we interact.

THE BEAUTIFUL BODY

The images are inescapable—even when we're using the restroom. I am writing at a hipster coffee shop, where the restroom has chalkboard walls so the college students can out-clever each other. Look up, though, and the ceiling is plastered with cutouts of women from fashion and teen magazines. There's no nudity, and most of the cutouts are just faces. But the effect is still numbing, as the sheer volume of images minimizes the impact any one of them might have on their own (which, I suspect, is part of their point).

Young men see more images of beautiful women in a single day than an average man might have seen in a lifetime 200 years ago. Michael Levine, a Hollywood publicist, pointed out in 2001 that most people in agrarian societies would have met and seen images of far fewer people than we do today. Levine argues that the ubiquitous images of beautiful people have had a profound effect on both men and women. He puts the problem this way:

> The strange thing is, being bombarded with visions of beautiful women (or for women, socially powerful men) doesn't make us think our partners are less physically attractive. It doesn't change our perception of our partner. Instead, by some sleight of mind, it distorts our idea of the pool of possibilities.
>
> These images make us think there's a huge field of alternatives. It changes our estimate of the number of people who are available to us as potential mates. In changing our sense of the possibilities, it prods us to believe we could always do better, keeping us continually unsatisfied.[7]

Not only are men's standards of beauty unrealistic, but because that level of beauty is all over the media, we think beauty of that sort is everywhere—except, of course, in our current circle of acquaintances. The normalization of unreasonable standards of beauty undermines men's satisfaction with their spouses while simultaneously makes meeting that standard a full-time job for women.[8]

At the same time, the standard for body image has shifted away from being beautiful toward being "sexy."[9] While thin is still in, the contemporary equivalent of the corset—liposuction—now has to be accompanied by bikini waxes and skin treatments, because simply being thin is not enough. We live in a pornified world, as feminist author Pamela Paul has dubbed it, where showing skin is an inevitable part of being a female star.[10]

The media, though, eventually trickles down and infiltrates the clothing racks—and what normal people like my wife think of as "beautiful" clothing. In a moment of honest self-awareness, my wife realized that she was drawn to more immodest clothes than she would have been in high school, even though her conscious beliefs about modesty have not changed. But living in a world where increasingly revealing clothing is not simply normal, but celebrated, has subtly shaped her desires. Such shifts are rarely perceptible to the people going through them. But if such changes have happened in my wife, who is both authentically beautiful and a saint, not even the Amish are safe.

THE THIN BODY

The Hallelujah Diet. The Weigh Down Diet. The Daniel Plan. Losing Weight Jabez's Way. The Edenic Diet.

Evangelical Christians love dieting because Jesus wants lean bodies (especially ones that are sexually charged). Dieting clearly isn't limited to conservative Christians, but it has taken hold of our community, even beyond the small-group meetings of women who are eager to please their husbands by looking fit. The latest church to get in on the mix is Rick Warren's Saddleback. He announced that he would be doing the Daniel Plan, and 6,000 attendees of his church are doing it with him.

The modern Christian diet movement was actually started by a Presbyterian, Charlie Shedd, who inaugurated it in 1957 with his book *Pray Your Weight Away*. In a few sentences, he manifests all the dangers of identifying fat with sin: "We fatties are the only people on earth who can weigh our sin. . . . Stand on the scale. How much more do you weigh than you should weigh? There it is: one hundred pounds of sin, or fifty, or eleven."[11] While contemporary versions avoid Shedd's overly caustic language, the diet movement perpetuates this identification of cellulite with iniquity.

Consider the story of Neva Coyle. Coyle was an obese person who lost over one hundred pounds before starting Overeaters Victorious and writing several bestsellers on how to lose weight. But after facing a health crisis she regained her weight. In her book *Loved on a Grander Scale,* she writes this prayer; "Forgive me for putting my body size before you. For spending so much time on how I look, how much I weigh, and caring more about pleasing others than I cared about pleasing you."[12] Her confession was mostly ignored by evangelicals, and some women even rejected her for failing at her own efforts.[13]

This focus on our diet is not all bad, of course. To some extent, the movement reminds us that what we do to our bodies matters. It was on those terms that Phyllis Tickle expressed optimism back in 2000. In an article by Lauren Winner, Tickle commented on Weigh Down Diet advocate Gwen Shamblin, saying, "Shamblin is showing us that you diet as a Christian, you choose your food as a Christian, you exercise as a Christian—and that's a fairly new phenomenon. . . . We are beginning to say the world of the body can indeed be approached by a soul who is devout and in service to his or her God and sees the world of the body that way."

Yet holiness is not based on our body type, nor is thinness next to godliness. Health is good, but the dieting movement teeters on the edge of affirming a standard of bodily perfection that owes more to *Maxim* or *Men's Health* than Jesus. R. Marie Griffith says, "Equating thinness with obedience, godly submission, and the thoroughgoing self-abnegation required for salvation, later authors like [*Weigh Down* author Gwen] Shamblin reinforced the sunny picture of paradisiacal slimness with its grim obverse: damnation by fat."[14] Paul's clear distinction between physical training, which is of some value, and godliness has been pushed to the background.[15]

THE iPHONE-SHAPED BODY

I have an iPhone problem. I love my little device. The beautiful screen, the intuitive interface, the limitless possibilities that the app store represents—I am an avowed iPhone fan boy. But I first realized that I had a serious problem when I noticed that my hand was cupped in the way that I usually hold the iPhone, even though the phone wasn't there. It's a natural shape for our hands to make, a bit like carrying a cup or gripping a ball. Except I don't carry cups that often, and it's not the sort of shape that my hand naturally gravitates to when I'm not doing anything else. I had spent eighteen months gripping my iPhone, and now it was gripping me.

Most of us don't notice how our tools shape our bodies. My friend John Dyer, who thinks more clearly about how Christianity intersects with the Christian life than anyone else I know, often uses a shovel to make the point: use it long enough and your hands will have calluses from the wood. He describes the phenomenon this way:

> Over time, as we dig hole after hole, reshaping the world as we see fit, our hands, arms, and backs will be changed as well. Those blisters will turn into calluses, and our once weak arms will grow stronger and more muscular. Our minds too will develop a sense of the land and how best to approach it. When the job is completed, the tool will have transformed both the creator and the creation. Indeed as John Culkin, a student of Marshall McLuhan wrote, "We shape our tools and thereafter our tools shape us."[16]

Contemporary technology is forcing us to rethink what it means to have human bodies. The cyborg, or the Terminator-type fusion of the body and technology, has slowly been making the jump from the screen to reality. Lepht Anonym, a hacker, has inserted magnets and other electronic devices under her own skin—in her kitchen—so she can sense electromagnetic fields.[17] The Internet is littered with "do-it-yourself" guides to become a cyborg. And if you're not interested in the pain of becoming a cyborg, then there's always artificial intelligence, which collapses the categories of human and machine from the other direction. The Steven Spielberg film *A.I., Artificial Intelligence*, which shows a world where machines become (virtually?) human, is a long way off, but it accurately captures the promise and the problems of the movement.

And then there's *Avatar*, the mega-blockbuster that featured Na'vi, humanlike extraterrestrials that humans interact with through bodies that are exact replicas of the Na'vi, but are controlled simply by the human's mind. Pastor Mark Driscoll famously lambasted the weird spiritual forces at work in the story, but those weren't the film's only troubles.[18] The film presumed that humans could not only take on other human bodies, but other *species'* bodies without any loss of personal identity. Ironically, the film's rather overt anti-industrialism and pro-environmentalism ignores the fact that the technological development of the avatars make the spiritual fusion possible. If the advanced technologies of the humans had not been developed, the love story wouldn't even have gotten started. But the technological and spiritual impulses both meet at a single point, namely in minimizing or rejecting the human body's importance to our personal identity.

These movies are fanciful, of course, but they are based on—and reinforce—very real impulses. Hollywood depictions of a world where human bodies are expendable are simply extreme manifestations of trends at work in most of our normal lives. The promise of technological mediation is that we can control how our external lives appear to others. We choose when we want to update our statuses and what we want to say. We are not present online—we present ourselves. But in a mediated world, presentation will constantly threaten to overwhelm our bodily presence, invariably pushing the body to the margins.

When humans gather face-to-face, we take emotional (and sometimes physical) risks. Yet in a mediated world, those risks either go away or are significantly curtailed. Philosopher Roger Scruton made this point in an important essay in *The New Atlantis*. As he puts it:

> To a large extent, life on the screen is risk-free: when we click to enter some new domain, we risk nothing immediate

in the way of physical danger, and our accountability to others and risk of emotional embarrassment is attenuated.[19]

By way of contrast, when we walk into a Starbucks and see the barista, we risk disclosure—by way of our bodily presence, the look on our face, the habitual nonverbal cue—that he or she will see something of our inner life without our realizing it.

Of course, video chat retains some of the risk of our actual presence, but there is still a difference between digital communication and physical presence. In times of sorrow among friends, there simply is no substitute for a long, silent hug. In times of joy, there is no replacing the high fives or the short, ecstatic embrace. There's a reason athletes reach out and touch each other when things are going well or badly on the field or court. In an environment as focused on accomplishing goals as sports, bodily connection among teammates is not only unavoidable, research indicates it may be a key indicator of both the team and individual player's success.[20]

The advantages of the Internet, of course, are incalculable. But a world shaped by iPhones and Facebook is more oriented toward communication than presence. When I communicate something, I intentionally transmit information. The word or thought, in other words, passes through the tools we make to other people who receive the communication. But the body, on the other hand, does not only mediate information about me—it is my presence in the world. Physical presence makes possible a true communion of persons, a communion that requires the sharing of space and time.[21]

Yet for us to be present does require something more than sharing space and time. To be present is to be there in our whole person, both our internal and external dimensions. We are, in a sense, present with and toward others. I may be in the same space as my wife, but if my attention and awareness are directed toward my iPhone, then I am clearly not present with her. Scruton puts this presence in the context of friendship:

What we are witnessing is a change in the *attention* that mediates and gives rise to friendship. In the once normal conditions of human contact, people became friends by being in each other's presence, understanding all the many subtle signals, verbal and bodily, whereby another testifies to his character, emotions, and intentions, and building affection and trust in tandem. Attention was fixed on the other—on his face, words, and gestures. And his nature as an embodied person was the focus of the friendly feelings that he inspired.

Scruton's suggestion is that our bodily presence reveals our character—regardless of whether we choose to disclose our inner life or not. We may be able to communicate through screens, but our presence is the place where our inner life and our visible bodies meet.[22]

In fact, John Dyer has pointed out that the New Testament values physical, face-to-face presence over other forms of interaction. Consider the following passages:

- For I long to see you, that I may impart to you some spiritual gift to strengthen you. (Romans 1:11)
- But since we were torn away from you, brothers, for a short time, in person not in heart, we endeavored the more eagerly and with great desire to see you face to face. (1 Thessalonians 2:17)
- We pray most earnestly night and day that we may see you face to face and supply what is lacking in your faith. (1 Thessalonians 3:10)
- Though I have much to write to you, I would rather not use paper and ink. Instead I hope to come to you and talk face to face, so that our joy may be complete. (2 John 1:12)

John also points out that "Paul and John often connected physical presence with 'joy' and 'completeness.'" Our contemporary emphasis on church communications needs to be tempered by the reminder that it is a secondary good to the embodied, personal, attentive presence that is befitting the ministry of the saints.[23]

JESUS AND THE WORD-SHAPED BODY

"But we have this treasure in jars of clay, to show that the surpassing power belongs to God and not to us. We are afflicted in every way, but not crushed; perplexed, but not driven to despair; persecuted, but not forsaken; struck down, but not destroyed; always carrying in the body the death of Jesus, so that the life of Jesus may also be manifested in our bodies. For we who live are always being given over to death for Jesus' sake, so that the life of Jesus also may be manifested in our mortal flesh. So death is at work in us, but life in you" (2 Corinthians 4:7–12).

The power and the pattern for our bodies are those which we see in Jesus Christ. Rather than sculpting ourselves according to what we see in *Glamour*, our friends, or even our natural families, our bodies are to be conformed to the body of Jesus Christ. We "take up our cross daily," imitating him in grateful response to his salvific work in us, and find our place within the community of those who have heard and responded to the gospel. We need bodies that are shaped by the gospel within gospel-centered communities and trained by gospel-centered practices. While this may take various forms, I highlight three ways here in which the gospel provides an alternative way of living in the body within the world around us.

FREEDOM

The libertarian-minded freedom that we are often presented with in public is simply a cheap imitation of the freedom we have in Christ by virtue of the Holy Spirit. While clothing, health, and communication styles are not intrinsically wrong, a people whose identities are not fundamentally shaped by the love of Jesus will inevitably be prone to identify themselves with the general public. We *are* our Facebook friends, our fitness charts, our caloric intake, and the affirmation of our visible beauty. We have given ourselves to those things in the hope that they would provide something in return. But like all idols, they can only take our offerings—they cannot give.

It is "for freedom Christ has set us free" (Galatians 5:1). But our freedom is not a negation of rules but an opportunity for us "through love" to "serve one another" (v. 13). It is grounded in the reality—not the words—of our life "in Christ," a life that makes us responsible to "walk in a manner worthy of the calling to which [we] have been called" (Ephesians 4:1).[24]

The grace and freedom we have in Christ sets us free from the tyranny of conforming our self-presentation, both online and in our communities, to standards that are extrinsic to love, joy, peace, patience, kindness, goodness, self-control, and the other fruit of the Spirit. When cleanliness and bodily order become required for entrance into our communities, as they clearly are in most evangelical churches, then we have adopted a standard inhospitable to those whose bodies either might intrude at inopportune times (such as infants and the elderly) or who lack the grooming that an affluent society has transformed into a requirement. Crying babies are not a distraction from connecting with God—they are a tangible reminder of our embodied lives (and that Jesus himself once cried as a baby).

What's more, our fitness and our fashion needs to take its cues from the cross and the resurrection. We need an aesthetic that is oriented toward Jesus Christ. It is no accident that the central event of human history, the cross, has spawned some of the world's greatest art and become a symbol many of us wear. As the familiar hymn puts it, "In that old rugged cross, stained with blood so divine, a wondrous beauty I see, for 'twas on that old cross Jesus suffered and died, to pardon and sanctify me."[25]

Embracing an aesthetic of the cross sets us free from the anxieties, the stress, the sense of control that motivate our tireless efforts to conform to the image of beauty that we see in *Cosmo*. It moves our attention away from what we consume and how we clothe our bodies and toward how we live in the world. Most conversations about the proper shape of beauty are focused on what the proper form of the body is. Yet even in our understanding of beauty, this may be the wrong aspect to emphasize. Some scholars contend that physical beauty in the Old Testament is grounded in the body's expressiveness, rather than its form. When the lovers in the Song of Solomon write that "your eyes are like doves," Thomas Staubli and Silvia Schroer argue that the doves "say nothing about the appearance of the eyes, but express the content, the message of the glance."[26] Beauty isn't, in other words, so much about what people look like, but what they do.

That's a helpful corrective, but it probably also overstates the case. The Jewish people seem to have also thought that the form of the body could be beautiful, but they also knew that such beauty was insufficient and could be dangerous. Proverbs 11:22 and 31:30 contain strong warnings against the vanity of physical beauty alone, and Genesis 6:1–4 and 12:11–14 remind us that exceptional beauty could make life difficult.

Against all this, though, stands the person and work of Jesus on the cross. The gospels are silent about whether Jesus was physically attractive or not.[27] They choose instead to focus on his work as the Messiah. But there are hints in Scripture that Jesus would not have been the physical specimen that we might want today in our media-saturated age. Isaiah 53, in particular, underscores the fact that the Messiah would not be good-looking:

> He had no beauty or majesty to attract us to him,
> nothing in his appearance that we should desire him.
> He was despised and rejected by men,
> a man of sorrows, and familiar with suffering.
> Like one from whom men hide their faces
> he was despised, and we esteemed him not. (vv. 2-3 NIV)

The Messiah is the truer and better King David, whose progeny he would eventually be (Matthew 1:6, 16). First Samuel 16:12; 16:18; and 17:42 all make a point to underscore that David is particularly good-looking, a standard for the king that the cross turns on its head.

In one of his most profound moments, Pastor John Piper talked about how we should live in a world whose form is passing away. He writes:

> Christians should deal with the world. This world is here
> to be used. Dealt with. There is no avoiding it. Not to deal

with it is to deal with it *that* way. Not to weed your garden is to cultivate a weedy garden. Not to wear a coat in Minnesota is to freeze—to deal with the cold that way. Not to stop when the light is red is to spend your money on fines or hospital bills and deal with the world that way. We must deal with the world.

But as we deal with it, we don't give it our fullest attention. We don't ascribe to the world the greatest status. There are unseen things that are vastly more precious than the world. We use the world without offering it our whole soul. We may work with all our might when dealing with the world, but the full passions of our heart will be attached to something higher: godward purposes. We use the world, but not as an end in itself. It is a means. We deal with the world in order to make much of Christ.[28]

Piper extended the point to marriage, mourning, and our consumption of goods. We should also extend it to our beauty and our clothing. We are to dress ourselves with a holy indifference to the broken standards of beauty and with the confidence that our identity lies not in our conformity to this world but in the person and work of Jesus Christ.

GRATITUDE

Being grateful for the bodies we have been given might be the most difficult aspect of living in conformity with the gospel in our world. Some people experience debilitating diseases, while others are born with disabilities that seem to unfairly limit their possibilities. Others feel the weight of racism, while others feel self-conscious about their weight or a disfigurement.

But gratitude is, as Karl Barth has put it, "the creaturely counterpart to grace." Regardless of the nature of our physical bodies—and we are all imperfect, longing for the resurrection of the body—we have been invited into the presence of God himself through the work of Jesus Christ and the gift of his Holy Spirit. Our humanity before God is determined not by whether our lives are free from bodily harm or suffering, but whether the love of God himself dwells within and rebuilds the ruins of the temple.

What's more, gratitude is the only response for seeing that the creation that God has given to us is fundamentally and gloriously good. And the expression of our gratitude in worship is the necessary completion of the experience of goodness. C. S. Lewis once said, "I think we delight to praise what we enjoy because the praise not merely expresses but completes the enjoyment; it is its appointed consummation."[29]

Yet gratitude for the pleasures of the world also carries with it an intrinsic modesty and humility before them. God places Adam and Eve in a garden full of delights, but cordons off a single tree to remind them of their creaturely status. We give thanks, in Chesterton's line, "for beer and Burgundy by not drinking too much of them." Or as he said elsewhere, "Keeping to one woman is a small price for so much as seeing one woman."[30] Our recognition of the goodness of the world as a gift from God is at the heart of our proper use and treatment of it.

CARE

Bodies need care, especially in a fallen world. Sickness, disease, hunger, thirst—the more we are aware of the body, the more we recognize just how much care and attentive love people require for their health and well-being.

In fact, seeing suffering human bodies is a far stronger motivator to action than hearing about them—as fund-raisers well know. Many who pursue temporal justice are often motivated primarily by the experiences that they have had. The compassion that motivates people is a visceral response, something that touches them in the deepest parts of their embodied being. As Oliver O'Donovan describes it, compassion is "the virtue of being moved to action by suffering." But such compassion also needs to be tethered to the cross and not simply an emotional response—it is, literally, a *co passion*, a co-suffering, wherein we give ourselves away for the health and well-being of another. We cannot take others' sin away, but the fact that our own sin has been forgiven by Jesus is the grounds for us to "bear one another's burdens."[31]

Yet the church should be more than a place where we "mourn

with those who mourn and rejoice with those who rejoice"—we should also be individuals who demonstrate an appropriate level of care for our own bodies. It might be tempting to read the section above on developing an aesthetic of the cross as a repudiation of our responsibility to care for the body. But no such rejection is allowed. The body in its original and redeemed goodness requires care, and such care is at the heart of embracing our role as creatures before God. Paul writes in Ephesians, "For no one ever hated his own flesh, but nourishes and cherishes it, just as Christ does the church" (Ephesians 5:29).

Discerning what shape our care for bodies should take in our world is one of the intractable difficulties of late-modern life. Yet despite the challenges of discerning *how* we should care for the body, we need to do so without turning it into a task to be accomplished or perfected (as so many diet programs seem to do). For many of us, part of the problem is that our social and work environments do not make us use the body. We drive to work, sit at our desks, drive home; rinse, repeat. I spent a year studying in England, where I was forced to walk everywhere. The need integrated exercise into my life, which made it easier to stay healthy without reducing my health to a task independent of our other good things.

And that is, perhaps, instructive. Caring for the body—whether ours or someone else's—might begin by being attentive to the ways in which we pursue the activities of our daily lives. When I shave in the morning, my goal is to hurry through it so I can move on to the important tasks of reading and writing. Judging by the increasing number of blades incorporated onto razors, I'm not alone. And that's all well and good, most days. But shaving could also become a means of slowing down, of opening myself to restful thought rather than subordinating the time to a list of tasks I feel I must accomplish. We might say the same for the time we spend eating.

In other words, a life lived caring for the body is a life encompassed by what I would call an attentive presence, or a "holy attentiveness." When we care for someone else, we direct our attention to that person—we notice when he walks into the room and we make him the object of our concern. Yet such awareness needs to be cultivated—it is dependent upon a rich inner life out of which we orient ourselves toward others.

It is precisely this inner life that our mediated world has stunted. In the early 1900s, G. K. Chesterton described the coming peril as "the intellectual, educational, psychological and artistic overproduction, which, equally with economic overproduction, threatens the well-being of contemporary civilization. People are inundated, blinded, deafened, and mentally paralyzed by a flood of vulgar and tasteless externals, leaving them no time for leisure, thought, or creation from within themselves."[32]

It's a salient point for the care of the body, as our constant distractions direct us away from attending to the humans who are in our immediate bodily spheres. Our iPhones interrupt our conversations, forcing us to switch our attention away from the person seated across the table from us to the screen we are holding. This diffusion of our focus makes deep connectedness with and awareness of other people difficult at best.

Not surprisingly, the best model for caring for the body is perhaps the Good Samaritan. Unlike the priest and the Levite, he subordinates his plans and his goals for the day (namely, to get to his destination) when he encounters the broken body of the victim by the road. His openness to the surprising and unplanned contingencies of the world around him is joined with a patient, deliberate concern for his neighbor. The Samaritan "bound up [the man's] wounds, pouring on oil and wine," taking him to an inn and paying for the rest of his treatment in advance, with a promise for additional funds if needed. (See Luke 10:25–37.)

The Samaritan's holy attentiveness to the needs and cares of the body are precisely what make him a neighbor to another, and provide a model for us to implement throughout our everyday lives. Some of us might, like the priest or Levite, deliberately reject caring for the bodies of those around us. But the more plausible scenario in our distracted world is that we would walk by without noticing, focused on accomplishing our tasks for the day, attentive only to the music in our ears and the status updates on our cell phones.

CHAPTER SIX

TATTOOS AND
THE MEANING OF OUR BODIES

Body piercing didn't save my life. And it didn't save yours either.

It is a catchy phrase, even if it made for some unsightly T-shirts. Those of us who grew up attending Christian concerts and festivals (and who have spent the past decade repenting both for going and for what happened there) have doubtlessly seen them—Jesus' suffering body hanging on the cross with the oversized spikes through his hands, and the gaudy lettering on the side: "Body piercing saved my life." Not exactly the coolest T-shirt you've ever seen, but the subversive point is clear enough: "Jesus' body was pierced, right? So you know I should be able to get that tattoo, *Mom*."

As a teenager, I rather enjoyed starting arguments in my youth group. That diversion hasn't really gone away, although for the most part I have learned to temper it with a healthy dose of congeniality. But growing up, I would enjoy stirring the pot, watching it come to a boil, and adding as much seasoning to the conversation as I could.

There were few issues that people were more passionately and personally invested in than tattoos. Like the debates over dating vs. courting, we would wrangle over it as though the whole world depended upon it, before happily forgetting those debates as soon as we entered college. Overworked and underdeveloped youth pastors bravely stood in the midst of it all, attempting to placate both parents and students.

But the great tattoo war of the 1990s is finished. And those in favor won.

While the occasional evangelical leader might still raise an objection (as Charles Colson recently did on his radio program), the prevalence of tattoos among younger evangelicals (and their leaders) has drained the energy from the topic.[1] Mostly, we just don't care about the question. We are happily focused on other issues—as we should be.

This shift in focus, though, doesn't minimize the astonishing nature of the tattoo revolution. Nearly 40 percent of people between the ages of eighteen and twenty-eight have tattoos, more than four times the Baby Boomer generation. And we're six times more likely than our parents to have piercings in places other than the earlobe.[2] The practice has become so prevalent within the young evangelical world that when a younger-minded church made a video poking fun at their own worship services, the greeter made sure to reveal his tat to "show he's got a past." And everyone immediately understood. Lauren Sandler, an outside observer, suggested that "Young Evangelicals look so similar to denizens of every other strain of youth culture that, aside from their religious tattoos, the difference between them and the unsaved is invisible."[3]

This suggests that there is room for a post-mortem on the body modification movement. When cultural trends shift below the surface and cease to become points of conscious reflection, we stand at risk of letting ideologies that oppose our Christian witness shape us more than Scripture. Tattoos and body piercings may appear on the body's surface, but they contain a depth of meaning that is worth exploring.

I realize that reopening the question of tattoos might prompt a little eye rolling. I have no pretensions that the topic is as critical as how to feed the poor or how to stop sex trafficking, and that the bulk of our attention and resources should be devoted to those issues and others. But the widespread acceptance of marking our bodies represents a real shift in the evangelical ethos and in our understanding of the meaning of the body. Cultures don't shift capriciously or quickly, and when they shift as much as evangelicalism has on this issue, generally something significant is at work.

My goal in what follows, then, is limited. I want to try to peer beneath the shift to the assumptions about the body. My point is not to examine anyone's motivation or intention for getting a tattoo. You might have had any number of reasons to get that Jesus fish lodged on your ankle, and those reasons may be more or less noble. Instead, I am curious to know why at *this* point in evangelicalism's history, tattoos, piercings, and other forms of body modification have become the preferred option for self-expression. Where other generations might have put the pen to the page or the paintbrush to the canvas, we have turned those tools on ourselves, making our bodies the objects of our own decorative fancies.

THE MAINSTREAMING OF TATTOOS

For the better part of the twentieth century, tattoos were limited to the lower classes and marginalized social groups.[4] Perhaps the most famous example of a tatted star was Popeye, the cartoon sailor created in the early '30s whose popularity endured into the '80s, when Robin Williams played him in a movie. His bulging biceps were marked by two anchors, signs of his status as a sailor and a member of the lower class.

In such a world, tattoos and piercings were—in both senses—a social stigma.[5] They were a sign of deviants and outcasts, like bikers, convicts, and sexual revolutionaries. This was especially true during the emergence of the middle class in the post–World War II era, the so-called *Leave It to Beaver* generation, whose white-bread sensibilities and focus on cleanliness and order extended all the way to markings on the skin. Because of this, the tattoo was an object of resistance against mainstream culture, an act of defiance against standards widely accepted as "normal."[6]

As tattoos have mainstreamed, their content has shifted from themes of war, women, and iconic American imagery toward a more exotic, international flavor. In the late '80s, Japanese characters were introduced and became enormously popular, a surprising and interesting development for a generation once-removed from those who fought in World War II.[7]

The transition toward a more pluralist tattoo world raised the stakes for tattoo artists and aficionados. Tattooing took on a new level of artistry, and the movement developed a self-consciousness and organization. The spontaneous tattoo after a wild night of party-ing was out, and reflective deliberation was in. Rather than a social expression of deviancy or a way of expressing attachment and loy-alty—think the classic tattoo of a girlfriend or wife's name—tattoos became a means of self-expression more akin to playing the piano or painting a picture. As a result, they are rarely purchased with anything but careful deliberation about how we want to express ourselves.

But like all communities, the tattooing world has not escaped the trappings or temptations of consumerism and commodification. Web sites, books, conventions, and other avenues to show people "custom" designs have exploded, which has broadened the appeal of tattoos but has also turned the art form into an industry.[8] What began as a sign of marginalization and resistance to the culturally sterile consumerism of suburban American life has, like so many resistance movements, been co-opted by the very thing it originally rebelled against.[9] When rebellion and breaking boundaries becomes as chic as it has been for the past thirty years, taboos eventually become the norms. And eventually we quit caring.

THE BODY'S MEANING

Tattoos were originally taboo because they challenged popular notions about the body's "proper" shape and the skin's "proper" look. Before angst-filled teenagers got inked to remember their youth group field trips, tattoos had something like a political mean-ing. The sailor might get his tattoo as an indication of his devotion to America, while the prisoner would do it as an act of defiance against his captors, an expression of his own freedom over and against "the man." Gang members would also get the same tattoo as a way of expressing their solidarity as a group—the tattoo provided a sense of identity and self-understanding, as it would set each individual off as a member of a larger community.

In other words, tattoos can have several meanings. Where we might treat them simply as a form of self-expression on the level of painting or poetry, our parents thought of tattoos very differently. It's a point that both young people and parents would do well to keep in mind, if only for the sake of harmony around those dinner tables where it is still an issue.

But for both generations, tattoos are not "empty" symbols. They, along with piercings and other forms of body modification, are important precisely because they are signs that contain deeper meaning. They are not gibberish, like "raerhspdfiajera8ysdfj." Just as the sign of the cross reminds us of our salvation, so tattoos point us to deeper realities about ourselves and our understanding of the world.

In some ancient cultures, tattoos functioned as a sign of ownership, either by the pagan gods or someone else.[10] In more recent times, Nazis tattooed Jews as they entered concentration camps, a dehumanizing equivalent to ranchers branding their cattle. It's common for Christians to mark themselves with Bible verses (cooler in their original language), the cross, or some other religious icon that expresses their faith.

In each of these contexts, tattoos are significant precisely because they draw on a common stock of symbols that point to larger realities. They exist in that fascinating nexus between what we intend by them and what society understands them to be. Yet the fact that there is a social dimension means there are constraints on the nature of our self-expression. To tattoo myself, for instance, with the Seattle Mariners logo surrounded by a heart and then claim that it expresses my undying appreciation for the Texas Rangers is to commit a symbolic party foul. The public nature of symbols must guide how we use them.

In other words, our skin and what we do to it is not self-enclosed. We make personal decisions about how to color our hair and what clothes to wear, but those decisions exist within a complicated web of relationships and symbols, the meaning of which we do not have the license to decide. Because the body is ourselves in our external dimension, how we live in the body—and what we do *to* the body—invariably shapes not only our connection with the world in general but also with the society around us.

The point stands, I think, even for those who choose to cover their tattoos or piercings. The decision to get markings no one else can see only reinforces the public nature of the body. While tattoos and piercings may be hidden from the world, the fact that they must be covered is a constant reminder of the body's social nature. The decision to reveal or conceal our body modifications contains the implicit question, "To whom?"—a question that is unavoidable because the body is unremittingly social.

We all grew up familiar with the line "No man is an island." The same is true of our bodies. The skin stretches beyond its limits into the world around us. It connects us with the world as much as it separates us from the world, and so it is the context where our understanding of what it means to be human plays out. Our bodies exist in communities, and we cannot fail to acknowledge this if we wish to live in them well. What we do *to* our skin matters as much as what we do within the skin.

HOW FAR THE MEANING?

Even though you're just as likely to see a tattoo on the occupant of a pulpit as you are on TV, their widespread acceptance hasn't eliminated fringe and marginalized cultures.

As our technological abilities have improved, our ability to customize and modify our bodies has expanded as well. Tattoos and piercings have mainstreamed—along with nose jobs, breast enhancements, and liposuction—while more fringe forms of body modification continue to break taboos and push boundaries.[11] Whether it is adding spikes or horns on the head or reshaping the tongue or ears, the underlying questions and issues beneath tattoos are simply being repeated, if only in more shocking form.

While such groups and people are on the margins of both society and evangelicalism, it is important to take the questions they are raising seriously. Not all marginalized communities will have the cultural influence the tattooing community earned, but they still push the window of acceptable body types outward, challenging our intuition about what is acceptable for the body's adornment. Regardless of people's individual motivations, the world of body modification poses a challenge to standard understandings of the body's "proper" shape and look.

At the heart of the body modification movement is an aesthetic critique of society and its repressive uniformity. Some people surgically insert implants like stars and other shapes beneath the skin, creating an unsettling effect that highlights the plastic nature of the body. Such modifications don't serve any functional purpose, but are there to break taboos and express a person's individuality and personality.

THE UNSTABLE BODY

Memento is the perfect film for a postmodern world.

Leonard Shelby, the main character, has suffered a head injury and can't create new memories. In order to cope with his forgetfulness, he externalizes his thoughts by tattooing himself with personal notes. But the film doesn't proceed linearly. It has two timelines, one moving chronologically and the other moving in reverse chronological order, and the two are spliced together. The result is—intentionally—disorienting.

Tattoos function in a similar way for many young people as they do for Leonard Shelby (and the viewer). The younger evangelical experience of the world has often been fragmented, unstable, and shallow. The decay of the family, the emptiness of our church experiences, our geographical transience, the inability to find employment—these are the sorts of pressures that have left many young people with a lingering sense of emptiness and instability.

The widespread acceptance of tattoos can be seen as an attempt to navigate and overcome these instabilities, to provide a coherent sense of meaning and unity to our lives. They do this by providing a permanent marker that helps give us a sense of movement and direction. Like the pile of stones that Israel raised when entering the Promised Land to remember God's faithfulness, tattoos remind us of the events that have shaped us, giving us a sense of a stable core.

Yet tattoos don't provide that sense of unity and coherency on their own. Ask any young evangelical about their tattoo and watch their eyes light up as they relate the meaningful event, relationship, or idea that prompted them to choose that particular shape. The "tattoo narrative" is a key part of the tattoo culture and a crucial element in what makes them so significant. We want to live out meaningful stories, and tattoos help us remember and share the key events that give us our sense of identity. This dimension is, perhaps, why tattoos have taken hold so easily in evangelical culture. The "conversion narrative" that has been at the heart of the evangelical experience has been modified—though not necessarily replaced—into one that is broader and less overtly religious, but still meaningful.

I suspect this explains why the central argument parents raise against tattoos is that they are permanent. Even if tattoos were only aesthetic in nature, they mark the body in a more enduring way than either makeup or clothing. And in that sense, they indicate a longing for permanence and stability in a quickly changing world. When everything else fades away, we are at least left with our bodies and the marks we have made on them, just like Leonard Shelby.

TATTOOS, THE ONE, AND THE MANY

The longing for stability and significance isn't unique to younger evangelicals. It is a distinctly human need. We internalize the events that happen to us and incorporate them into our understanding of the world around us, organize them into a coherent pattern, and externalize the meaning through speech, poetry, painting, and other forms of cultural creation. It is how we make sense of ourselves, how we develop our sense of what it means to be a specific person before God.

Yet before the past twenty years, evangelicals would have never thought to express that self-understanding by marking their bodies. With all the possible options for organizing and expressing our self-understanding, my question is simply "Why are tattoos now being embraced?" Something has changed that has made them a plausible option.

At the heart of the tattooing renaissance that brought tattoos from the margins to the mainstream was the shift toward treating tattoos as art and the adoption of "exotic" imagery and characters.[12] As Margo DeMello puts it, "Tattooists are no longer limited by Western imagery, and many have, in fact, completely repudiated it in favor of the more exotic, spiritual, or sophisticated non-Western designs."[13]

This expansion of iconography has fit well with younger evangelicals' desires to have our horizons broadened beyond the suburban lifestyle in which many of us were raised and the Western mentality that many of us have been taught to resist. Through travel, education, and the constant reminders of the limitations of our own culture, we have become entranced by attempting to see the world through other people's eyes. The result is a sort of "cafeteria culture" where we pick and choose from the various (non-Western) cultures we are drawn to.

The expanded options for tattoo iconography were also fuel for the notion that tattoos are an assertion of our individuality over and against a world that inevitably tries to conform us to its standards and ideals. The goal with tattoos is customization and uniqueness, something that expresses the core of the individual's values, personality, or identity. Even while Christians often use an iconography drawn straight from the Christian tradition, the expression is almost always tied to the individual's personal encounter and relationship with God. Susan Benson writes, "What certainly *is* central to a lot of contemporary tattoo and piercing talk is the idea of *individuation*; of the tattoo, as one contributor to the Bodyart Enzine put it, as 'a declaration of me-ness.'"[14]

The cultural logic, then, of tattoos depends upon the body being a canvas for our self-expression, a lump of clay that we style in ways that express the hidden core of who we are. Tattoos are an aesthetic technique—the program of control and domination—melded with a contrarian aesthetic and applied to our own bodies. The practice of tattooing treats the body not as our place of personal presence in the world, but as an object for our self-construction. Once we have organized our own experience, we project it outward not only through the body, but on the body. As literary theorist Terry

Eagleton puts it, "Having moulded the landscape to our own image and likeness, we have now begun to recraft ourselves. Civil engineering has been joined by cosmetic surgery."[15]

Yet the expression of our individuality suffers from what we might call *The Devil Wears Prada* problem. The film—since I haven't read the book—is about a rather plain young woman who takes a job at a fashion magazine. In my favorite scene, she laughs when a fashion designer agonizes over which belt to pair with an outfit, despite their almost identical shades of blue. The editor of the magazine, a fashion legend, dismantles her, pointing out that the color of the sweater she is wearing made it to the Target shelves precisely because it was featured in her magazine two years earlier.

The point is pretty clear: Even though she *thinks* her sweater is a defiant rejection of the demands of high fashion, Madison Avenue decides which colors will be on the clothing racks within the mainstream culture in a given season. While she treats her clothing as an assertion of her individuality, she asserts it in precisely that way in part because of decisions regarding style that have been made by others. She exists, as we all do, within a society that renders certain options for our self-expression more plausible than others. Tattoos have become an acceptable form because the fashion and style taste-makers—Hollywood, New York, and the NBA—have legitimized them. Fashion designers give free clothing to actors and actresses and Nike sponsors give shoes to athletes for one simple reason: it works. Most of us end up adopting the sense of fashion and style we see on TV or in magazines.

So the promise of individuality that tattoos offer may be a false one. In one sense, evangelicals are simply doing what everyone else in the world is doing—consuming the culture around them, which has decided to package its wares under the guise of "individuality" and "freedom." You might get Tweetie bird, while I get Roadrunner. But we're both getting tattoos rather than writing poems, because the world currently ignores poets but counts celebrity tats.

This is the paradox, then, of the cultural ascension of tattoos: While tattoos mark a desire for significance within a destabilized world, they are a live option for most young people precisely because we have not escaped the clutches of the consumerism and the individualism that are so often criticized.

In fact, where ethical reflection about tattoos *does* happen, it almost always starts with the assumption that we have the right to do with our bodies as we please, provided the procedures are medically safe and we are not harming anyone else—the same liberalized notion of the human body that is so often critiqued in other spheres. As I've suggested with other areas, for evangelicals, this notion of freedom and rights often resides beneath our understanding of Christian liberty and the freedom of conscience, and is buttressed by a decidedly inward way of approaching ethics. As long as our heart is "in the right place" and there are no clear prohibitions in Scripture, then even raising the question is a sign of legalism.[16]

In chapter 2, I suggested that where evangelicals have been inattentive to the body and its role in the Christian life, our embodied lives have been shaped more by the society around us than from the revelation of God himself, Jesus Christ. This is a problem that evangelicals—of every age—have not yet escaped. For all our claims to be a postmodern generation, we have tacitly continued one of the central features of modernity—its individualism and our corresponding assertion of our right to do to our bodies what we want. The claim of postmoderns to have rejected modernism leads, in Oliver O'Donovan's phrase, "back to a secret celebration of the features of modernity it claims to have transcended, like a midnight feast on smuggled goodies hidden beneath the bedclothes."[17]

THE COMMUNALLY SHAPED BODY

The prevalence of tattoos among evangelicalism's children is simultaneously a sign of its strengths and an indictment of its weaknesses.

On the one hand, tattoos have found fertile soil among a people who have been trained to see the world through the lens of personal testimonies and conversion stories. Growing up, our evangelistic efforts were almost always tied to our histories with God. The emphasis on conversion, however, is only understandable in light of a God who is living, active, and very much involved in our lives.

Tattoos and their accompanying narratives reinforce that emphasis on authenticity and a sense of personal significance.

But at the same time, tattoos suggest that evangelicalism has not provided a pattern for young people to organize and externalize our experiences through, leaving us to take our cues from the world around us. Our emphasis on our personal relationship with God is the right one to have—but the inner life we have through the indwelling presence of the Holy Spirit takes shape within the community of believers, the church, and the practices through which we respond in gratitude to God. The lack of emphasis on the church and its practices in most evangelical circles has left a void that the consumerist logic undergirding tattoos has inevitably filled.

Yet even though tattoos are an expression of our individuality and a sign of the narrative and meaning that we interpret our lives through, because they are on the body they are necessarily social. Raise the question of tattoos among a group of lifetime evangelicals, and eventually someone will point out that their ink has been a conversation starter with a nonbeliever. Where baptism is a confirmation of our entry into the community of Christians, tattoos inaugurate a community of the searching.

Yet the people of God are not shaped by a narrative of searching, but one that has at its center the unique and unrepeatable sacrifice of Jesus Christ and his glorious resurrection. We have been given the pattern for our identity and life—and it is a pattern of being found in him and conforming our body to his. Our searching has, in a real sense, ended, and our vocation has shifted so that we are "ambassadors of Christ," entrusted with the ministry of reconciliation as a sign that this world has passed away and a new one has come.

As Christians, we are to be a community where the Word of God is active, shaping us and molding us into conformity to the God to whom it bears witness.[18] Even if tattoos are an option because of our consumerism and our individualism, there may be a means of incorporating them in such a way that they align with our witness to the person of Jesus Christ—"to the tattooed I become tattooed." Yet that path needs to be walked carefully, acknowledging that tattoos are neither neutral nor trivial in our society, and our witness to others is not grounded primarily in our cultural identification with them but in Paul's words: "I have made myself a servant to all, that I might win more of them" (1 Corinthians 9:19).

THE BIBLE AND TATTOOS

The fact that I have waited this long to bring up the Bible in this conversation breaks all the youth group rules. That is, of course, quite intentional. It's easy to approach the question of tattoos with a very narrow lens, address only the two or three most obvious texts that deal specifically with the question, and then move on. That limited way of reading Scripture potentially subordinates or ignores passages that might weigh against the conclusions we want to hear, inevitably stunting any conversation by focusing on what will doubtlessly be contested passages.

Let's start, though, with what seems obvious:

There is no straight line that we can draw between the ancient practices of tattooing and its contemporary manifestation. In the ancient Jewish world, tattoos were either used as a punishment or to align people with the local deities.[19] In the Hellenized world of the New Testament, tattoos were primarily punitive. It was less common, though not unheard of, to use them as a way to associate oneself with a local deity. The Bible knows nothing of tattoos for purely aesthetic purposes or of tattoos as simply an external expression of personal significance. They are almost always marks of ownership or punishment, and therefore marks of shame.[20]

While it might be tempting, then, to simply treat the prohibition in Leviticus 19:28 as a proof text against tattoos, the argument is not that simple. While the outright prohibition on marking the body shouldn't be discounted, it raises a host of questions about how Christians should understand and incorporate the Old Testament laws into our practices. There are obvious examples of laws that no one follows, and that no one thinks we should follow. Maybe the clearest example of such a law is the commandment not to mix fibers, a prohibition that if followed would eliminate most of the clothing options available to us (Leviticus 19:19). As has been frequently pointed out, we can't be selective in determining which laws we want to adhere to and which we don't.

Yet the mixing of fibers prohibition simply highlights how complex the Old Testament's position is on such matters. In Exodus and Numbers, the priests are commanded to wear clothing made of— multiple fibers![21] For some reason, the priesthood was commanded to do something no one else was allowed to do. Old Testament scholar Jacob Milgrom has suggested that in the ancient Near-Eastern world, mixtures "characterize the holiness of the sacred sphere and those authorized to enter or serve it." If this is true, then the rejection of mixing fibers wouldn't necessarily always pertain, nor would it simply distinguish Israel from the surrounding nations.[22]

But the prohibition on tattoos has no such tempering parallel, and the dominant Jewish tradition throughout history has continued to apply the prohibition to all forms of the markings. And contrary to piercings, there is no evidence in the Old Testament that the Israelites tattooed themselves for aesthetic reasons.

In fact, the distinction between tattoos and piercings in the Old Testament is interesting. On the one hand, there is lots of evidence that the Israelites pierced themselves for aesthetic reasons, and in ways similar to the surrounding cultures.[23] What's more, rather than tattoo their slaves, the Old Testament commands the Israelites to pierce them—which is in contrast with the surrounding cultures.[24] The difference may point to the relative impermanence of slaves within the culture of Israel, as piercings would leave a hole but unlike tattoos could also be removed. Milgrom, in fact, reads the prohibition of tattooing as aiming at "the abolition of slavery in Israel."[25] If nothing else, it's very clear that the people of God took marking the body seriously.

To fill the point out, consider the imagery of tattoos in the Old Testament. In Deuteronomy, the Israelites are exhorted to know the Shema so well that it is inscribed on their foreheads (6:8). In Isaiah 44, the Lord suggests that some Israelites will one day write on their hands "Belonging to the Lord" (44:5), and later that the Lord has written their names on his hands (49:16). In the former, the marking seems to be tied to the Israelites' perfection as the people of God. Whereas the Old Testament is marked by their infidelity and change, someday they will be so faithful that some will mark the name of the Lord on their bodies. In both cases, tattoos mark a permanent status and an expression of fidelity and ownership.

This is as close as the Old Testament comes to sanctioning tattoos. And the New Testament comes no closer.

The first and perhaps most important passage is Paul's claim that he bears the stigmata of Jesus Christ on his body (Galatians 6:17). *Stigma* is the Greek word for *tattoo,* and Paul's point has sometimes been used to justify voluntary Christian tattooing. But tattoos in both the Greek and Roman cultures were almost exclusively punitive. The Greeks and the Romans treated non-punitive religious tattooing as something the barbaric surrounding cultures did.[26] If anything, Paul is subverting a practice that would have been viewed as dishonorable by associating it with the death of Jesus. But this isn't a point in favor of voluntary aesthetic tattooing; rather, it points to Paul's joyful embrace of his physical suffering as a means of identifying with the person of Jesus Christ.

The other central passages come from Revelation. The famous "mark of the beast" has sometimes been treated as a tattoo, while the people of God get the sign of the Lord sealed on their foreheads (7:3). Like Isaiah, the markings on the body have nothing to do with aesthetics or even self-expression, as they predominately do in our contemporary context; instead, they point to the permanent and unchangeable status of those who bear them. While the Hellenistic culture might not know of tattoos that were for slavery and ownership, the New Testament seems to be transmitting the Old Testament understanding of tattoos faithfully.

More famously, some have suggested that Jesus comes down from heaven with a tattoo on his thigh in Revelation 19:16: "On his robe and on his thigh he has a name written, King of kings and Lord of lords." The verse is a favorite for those who advocate the adoption of tattoos, as it points to a Savior who has the power and the freedom to wear one.

Yet there are problems with this interpretation. For one, the translation leaves the nature of the "tattoo" at best ambiguous. Grant Osborne points out that the sentence is better translated along the lines of "on his robe covering his thigh"—which is to say, "The name is written on that part of his tunic that covered his thigh, the place where his sword would rest and where it would be conspicuous on a mounted warrior."[27] The thigh is the euphemism for the place where covenants were sworn in the Old Testament; and that Jesus has his name written on the clothing that covers it suggests that he is the revelation and fulfillment of God's promise to his people.

Second, it's not clear which way we should interpret the "tattoo." In the Jewish context, tattoos were signs of ownership, yet King of Kings and Lord of Lords is Jesus' title, which would not fit easily in the Jewish understanding. In the Greco-Roman context, tattoos were almost always punitive in nature, but King of Kings and Lord of Lords doesn't fit any better here. While it is possible that John is subverting the stigma (in the way Paul did) by making it a mark of identification, it would represent a remarkable break with the Levitical prohibition on tattoos and introduce a level of discontinuity with the Old Testament that later Christians would ultimately reject.

Finally, people who deploy Revelation as justification for tattoos frequently dip into a surprising bit of literalism that simply doesn't seem to fit the genre. The interpretation seems to rest on the presumption that all markings on the skin have the same meaning, a presumption that simply is not true. Even if Jesus has a tattoo in the Bible, the meaning of tattoos during the time of the writing of Scripture is considerably different than in our own day.

Within church history, the record on tattoos is mixed. On the one hand, where Christian missionaries have gone, the practice of tattooing has largely ceased.[28] Constantine banned the practice of facial tattoos as a punitive measure, a self-imposed limitation on the state's ability to subject and control criminals. And in the fourth century, Basil the Great wrote, "No man shall let his hair grow long or tattoo himself as do the heathen," which is one of the few explicit prohibitions on the practice within the Christian tradition.

That the prohibition had to be uttered suggests that some Christians were open to the practice. Later, soldiers would commemorate the crusades by getting a tattoo. But the most prevalent form of tattoos within the Christian tradition has been as acts of defiance within regimes where Christians are persecuted, as the Coptic Christians currently use them in modern-day Egypt. The small cross on the wrist serves as an act of political opposition and political solidarity around the cross—but it also makes it more difficult for Christian children to be kidnapped and forced to convert to Islam.[29]

In such contexts, tattoos are a form of continuing the tradition of martyrdom and identification with Jesus on the cross. Yet this is an important difference, for they are not primarily aesthetic marks or even a means of identifying with a particular group in order to preach the gospel to them. Rather, they are a subversion of the standards of what it means to be an outcast and to have bodies that are marked as such. They take their meaning not through identifying with predominant social norms, but opposing them. Yet the opposition of the martyr is not an opposition for its own sake, but an opposition that demonstrates a fierce disregard for this world. The martyr turns not to his own body or the markings on it for a sense of stability and permanence, but to the promises of God.

CONCLUSION

What, then, should we make of tattoos? My goal is not to offer an outright dismissal of them as a practice, but simply to raise the question of what tattoos mean in our own culture and whether we are taking our cues from Scripture or from the prevailing winds of fashion.

The fragmentation of American life and the dissolution of identity-shaping institutions like the family, education, and marriage have left young people searching for a coherent and stable sense of identity. Many have turned to tattoos as a means of consolidating and expressing identity. But that decision is a live option for most young people only because the counterculture of the late '50s and '60s has become the mainstream, and the dissolution of cultural norms they sought has occurred. Once rebellion becomes the new normal, though, it inevitably becomes passé.

The line between self-expression and self-construction is hard to find in this culture. Because many of us have not grown up shaped predominately by the church, the selves we are seeking to express are as fragmented as the world around us, which means we are looking for a point that we can organize around. The human body has started to play that role for many of us, as we organize our narratives through our tattoos and fashion.

But our critiques of the consumerism of older evangelicals shouldn't blind our eyes to the role consumerism has played in our reaction against it. After all, it's no accident that tattoos have become a phenomenon within evangelicalism shortly after they became acceptable to the world around us. We are perpetually in danger of making Jesus our brand and the cross our logo.

In that sense, claiming that our tattoos are continuous with Christian tradition or Scripture misses what's unique about tattoos in our late-modern world. Here and now, tattoos function as aesthetic expressions of meaning-making, as we attempt to navigate the hollow emptiness of the world in which we have been raised. The danger with our tattoo preferences is that in a consumerist culture where we are the brands we consume, tattoos can function as a sort of polytheistic expression of devotion to our local deities—as it might have for the poor chap who covered his back with a Twilight tattoo. As Christians, we need to ensure that we do not place Jesus within the pantheon of gods and make him one option among many, but bear witness to his lordship as Christians always have—through sacrificial love, hope in suffering, acts of mercy, and the proclamation of the gospel.

CHAPTER SEVEN

THE BODY AND ITS PLEASURE

If there were a sexual arms race, evangelicals would be winning.

Evangelical Christianity has undergone in the past three decades what is tantamount to its own sexual revolution. Since 1973, when Marabel Morgan's book *The Total Woman* was released, evangelicals have maintained a profound focus on maximizing pleasure between the sheets—or wherever else we happen to be when inspiration strikes. We are living in "the golden age for Christian sex manuals," as writer Mark Oppenheimer has dubbed it.[1]

Like much of our thinking about other areas of life, the evangelical sex manual has an apologetic undercurrent. The implicit—and occasionally explicit—argument is that because God designed sex to be kept within marriage, Christians should be having better and more frequent sex than anyone else.[2] Or as two scholars who analyzed evangelical sex manuals in the early 1980s put it, we are apparently "God's chosen people in matters of sexuality."[3] The increasingly common challenges from evangelical pulpits to have daily sex suggest the calling is irrevocable.[4]

"Rapture," "bliss," "ecstasy," "powerful transcendence"—this is the sales pitch that evangelicals have made for the goodness of sex within marriage, and by all measurable accounts, it's worked. When the University of Chicago did a massive study on sex in America, they found that conservative Protestant women experienced sexual satisfaction far more often than any other religious demographic.[5] A more recent study confirmed the research, finding that evangelical Christian women have sex more frequently and report higher satisfaction levels than other demographics.[6]

This story is rarely told from the pulpit or in the media, both of which seem content to continue to present exaggerated stereotypes of evangelicals as sexual rubes (like the prudish Kenneth on *30 Rock*). Younger evangelicals—particularly those raised within the evangelical subculture—seem to have an acute sense that something has been missing in the evangelical approach to sex. Whether that is expressed through frank talk about sex from the pulpit or calls for connecting sex with God—as Rob Bell did in his book *Sex God*— everyone seems to have the impression that traditional evangelical understandings of sex are deeply messed up.

There is good reason for that, I think. Most young evangelicals were raised within youth groups where discussions of the goodness of sexuality were inevitably drowned out by the understandable attempts to remind everyone to keep their clothes on. Of course, some of that may have been the fault of the youth. When all you can think about is reaching inside the cookie jar, Mom's lectures about the goodness of cookies will be far less memorable than her restriction to wait until after dinner. Young people with raging hormones need little persuasion that sex within marriage is good. Further, presenting healthy sexuality that is enticing enough to make young people want to wait for sex until marriage while at the same time not exacerbating their temptation to engage in sexual fantasies is something of a high art. And evangelicals certainly have not mastered it.

But the disenchantment with evangelical teachings about sex also points to a different, more problematic cause. For all our efforts to recover the goodness of pleasure, our understanding of human sexuality still does not go very deep. The loud arguments within evangelicalism that pleasure is good border on defensively shouting, "Hey, we've got pleasure too!" in a world that cares about little else. Evangelicals can and should win the pleasure war but not on the same terms as the world. And judging by our literature and manner of life, we are closer to treating sexual pleasure as an idol than we have ever been to treating it as a curse.

NAKED AND NOT ASHAMED

God's gift of sexual pleasure started in the garden. But the account of human sexuality seen in the first pages of Genesis is far less clear than we might like. In fact, its ambiguity allowed early Christians to hold differing beliefs about sex, ranging from it being a good, natural part of human creation to it being the inevitable result of the fall and a necessary way to overcome our mortality.

But what is murky in the garden becomes clearer throughout the rest of the Bible.[7] The canon of Scripture interprets itself, commenting on, expanding, and clarifying passages that might otherwise be ambiguous. Theologian Robert Jenson points out, for instance, that the intensely erotic Song of Songs functions within Scripture as "the chief biblical resource for a believing understanding of human sexuality, of the *lived meaning* of 'Male and female he created them.' "[8] The *Song of Songs* depends for its poetry and allusions on a rich affirmation of the goodness of the created world (see 2:16–17; 4:12–15ff.). As something of an elaboration on the first pages of Genesis, it affirms that sexual desire can still be as it once was—"very good."

This affirmation of the goodness of the original creation is also prominent in some of the key texts in the New Testament. When asked about divorce in Matthew 19:5, Jesus responds by affirming that in marriage male and female "are no longer two but one flesh." He underscores twice in the passage that it was this way "from the beginning," reinforcing that the original pattern for human sexuality can be found in Genesis. Paul makes the same move in rebuking the Corinthians' understanding of sexuality in 1 Corinthians 6.

Ephesians 5, though, goes one step further, making the primary referent for marital love Christ and the church. Paul adopts the language of Genesis, but then points to its deepest, clearest manifestation: " 'Therefore a man shall leave his father and mother and hold fast to his wife, and the two shall become one flesh.' This mystery is profound, and I am saying that it refers to Christ and the church."[9] Paul adopts this marriage imagery from various places in the Old Testament.[10] As Christ and the church are the primary referents for the marital relationship, it is Christ who is the pattern for our sexuality rather than our sexuality providing the pattern for our understanding of Jesus.

The narrative of Adam and Eve in the first pages of Genesis, then, is the heartbeat of Christian sexuality, but the dynamic of their love together is not clarified until the cross, which reopens the possibility of healthy and intimate sexual pleasure for us as humans. Whatever we make of the historical content of Genesis—a phrase not meant to minimize the importance of the question—Jesus and Paul both treat the original innocence and goodness of human sexuality as our history, as revealing a pattern that was broken by sin and that was reestablished and restored through the redemptive love of Christ.

What follows in the rest of this chapter, then, is not a comprehensive treatment of human sexuality, but my attempt to outline what I think is distinctive about Christian sexuality in a world that worships sex. My goal is to say what I think Scripture thinks sex *is* rather than focusing primarily on what sex *is not*. Naturally, I draw on the account of the body I have sketched in earlier chapters to make my case. But I should also note that much of what follows is heavily influenced by—though not a direct translation of—John Paul II's *Theology of the Body*.

SEX AS SELF-GIVING

"It is not good for the man to be alone." And with that, Genesis highlights the essentially social nature of the human person. At each step of creation, God saw that his work was good. Yet the goodness of humanity is not fulfilled in our solitude, but in our connection and relationship with others who stand before God in the same way that we do.

This is, I think, the basic thrust of Adam's recognition of Eve: "This at last is bone of my bone and flesh of my flesh."[11] He goes on to highlight one way they are different, but his first impulse is that they are of the same kind, unique in the order of creation and uniquely related to God. The first creation account puts it, "So God created man in his own image, in the image of God he created him; male and female he created them." The third clause expands the first—male and female are made in the image of God together, which means that our relationship toward God as bearers of his image is the grounds for a healthy and Christian sexuality.

Moving on to the last phrase of chapter 2, we see that the sexuality of Adam and Eve is inextricable from the totality of their lives together. "And the man and his wife were both naked and were not ashamed." There is no dimension of the other that is preserved or held back. Yet to call their nakedness a "self-revelation" is almost misleading: their fundamental lack of conscious awareness of their own bodies meant that there was no gap between their bodily visibility and their personal presence. Their self was manifested in and through the body, and vice versa. Or as John Paul II puts it, there is no "interior rupture and opposition between what is spiritual and what is sensible."[12] There was no gap, in other words, between their bodies and their personal presence in the world.

Yet the communion between Adam and Eve is not static. The personal presence of man in the world is active and externally minded—it is a presence where we give ourselves to others for their benefit and receive their gift to us in gratitude. Human sexuality, as seen in the fact that Adam and Eve were naked in the body without shame, is constituted by this mutual self-giving. In the act of sex itself, the man gives himself to the woman and the woman (by way of freely opening herself) gives herself to the man.[13]

In that sense, Christian sexuality is not simply an expression of an abstract or vague inner desire—it is a dynamic encounter between a man and a woman in the fullness of their humanity before God, which is constituted by their mutual self-giving to the other for the other's good.

Here again, what is murky in the early chapters of the Bible is clearly revealed on the cross: It is love that marks a Christian sexuality, but our model for love is the sacrificial self-giving on the cross by the person of Jesus Christ. As John says in 1 John 3:16: "By this we know love, that he laid down his life for us." God gives himself to man, for man, and in doing so reveals the nature of the love that has bound husbands and wives together from the very beginning. This Christ-centered sexuality is precisely what Paul is talking about in Ephesians 5, when he affirms the goodness of Christian marriage by pointing to the relationship between Christ and the church.

This Christ-shaped love stands in contrast to contemporary notions about sex in one important way: it subordinates or delays the pursuit of one's own sexual pleasure to the good and well-being of the other. Pursuing an orgasm may seem like a "healthy sexual selfishness," as Douglas Rosenau puts it in *A Celebration of Sex*.[14] But our joy as Christians is not fundamentally driven by our experience of physical pleasure, but by the self-giving love that unites us together in the bond of peace. And that may mean delaying or forestalling sexual satisfaction in pursuit of the other's good. "Count others," Paul reminds the Philippians (2:3) in a passage that is pervaded by Christ, "more significant than yourselves."

SEX AS SELF-GIVING IN FREEDOM

Adam's embrace of Eve as companion and lover is his response to an awareness of his solitude in the world. God acknowledges that it is not good for Adam to be alone, then immediately gives him the responsibility to name the animals. This demonstrates Adam's authority in the world, but also serves a role in his search for a mate. He is the first frustrated single: "But for Adam there was not found a helper fit for him" (2:20). This search provides Adam with a sense of his own uniqueness within the created order. When Eve is created, he celebrates her entrance on the scene with the poetic joy of someone whose longing has been fulfilled: "This *at last* is bone of my bones and flesh of my flesh" (emphasis added).

The body is ourselves in our external dimension. But Adam's experience in naming the animals must have made him even more aware of the uniqueness of his body and his position before the Creator. This deepened attentiveness to how we are different from the world is at the heart of our inner life—which is why as children grow up they become more and more aware of their own and others' internal states. This holy attentiveness prepared Adam to recognize and receive Eve's uniqueness as a gift and give himself to her without shame or recrimination.

But gifts are given out of freedom, not necessity. Authentic human sexuality is something more than a physical act done for the purpose of bodily stimulation or pleasure. It is the mutual self-giving of two persons in their external dimensions, inaugurating a union that encompasses the totality of their lives. It is an overflow of love that starts in the heart and shows itself in the very members of our flesh.

As we said before, this love becomes clear in the person and work of Jesus Christ, who gives himself for us not out of compulsion or necessity but in the joyful freedom of love (John 10:17–18). God's own freedom is never impinged in his self-giving—he never ceases to be anything less than God himself. Likewise, our freedom to give ourselves away in love and affection conforms to God's freedom when the Holy Spirit is poured into our inner lives and manifests himself in our bodies.

Giving ourselves away freely, though, inherently requires self-control—a fruit of the Spirit that is essential to love (Galatians 5:22). As Paul writes to the Thessalonians, "For this is the will of God, your sanctification: that you abstain from sexual immorality; that each one of you knows how to control his own body in holiness and honor, not in the passion of lust like the Gentiles who do not know God" (1 Thessalonians 4:3–4). Paul's suggestion that we control our bodies in "holiness and honor" isn't grounded in the negation of sex or sexual pleasure, but in the idea that gifts are given freely rather than out of instinct or uncontrollable urges. The contemporary reduction of sexual desire to the level of an animalistic drive is nothing less than a sub-personal account of human sexuality that devalues the intrinsic goodness of God's created order.

SEX AS UNION

There is an enormous amount of confusion within Christian teaching regarding the nature of the "one flesh" union. We have a deep tendency within evangelicalism to speak of sex as something like a fusion of souls. Even conservative ethicist Daniel Heimbach, whose work on sexual ethics is otherwise excellent, suggests: "Sex is truly spiritual and unites soul with soul. That much is true."[15]

In fact, that much is probably *not* true—depending on what Heimbach means by the "soul." Our bodies are the place of our personal presence, which means that our union in sex is very real. Intercourse establishes a union of persons in this visible dimension. Inasmuch as husband and wife live, move, and act toward others—including their children—they do so as one.

But from within the relationship, husband and wife remain two. The joy of sexual delight is that the union preserves rather than destroys all the differences that make love possible in the first place. Our inner lives—our souls—are still distinct from the other, providing the necessary backdrop for our interaction and our self-giving in love that constitutes the marriage. In this sense, the "one flesh" union is strictly that—a union of our bodied, visible lives in the world.

When we compare this to Christ and the church, we see that in the church's relationship to the world around us there is no division between the people of God and their Savior. We are the "body of Christ," and those around us make no differentiation between who we are as Christians and the God we serve. Yet from within the church, the gap is infinite. There is only one Savior, one Lord Jesus Christ, and the church is not him, but is formed in response to his death and resurrection. The church is constituted in its inner life by the worship of God and in its external dimension by the ministry of reconciliation, through which God is drawing all people to himself. But the church and her Savior remain distinct from each other.

It's worth pointing out two other dimensions of the visible union that sex ratifies. First, because we are temporal creatures, the union of our bodies in sex involves our personal histories. Our lives are inextricable from time—and when we have sex, we enter into it in ways shaped by our past and that will reshape our future. It is for this reason that Scripture says the man will "hold fast" to his wife. The visible union ratified by sex is stretched out through time, just like our bodies are; the sexual act cannot be separated from the covenant that the marriage vows express. And because we live in a fallen world, we need to be attentive to the ways in which our histories and biographies are shaping the nature of our union—for good and for bad.[16]

Second, because the union of our external dimensions is real, it gives the other authority over us. Paul's argument that we should not join ourselves to a prostitute because we become "one body" with her (1 Corinthians 6:16) rests on this logic. Sexual immorality goes against the order God established for sexuality, and the authority the Spirit should have over our bodies does not fit with the authority a prostitute gains over us through sexual union.[17] First Corinthians 7 develops Paul's insight: "The husband should give to his wife her conjugal rights, and likewise the wife to her husband. For the wife does not have authority over her own body, but the husband does. Likewise the husband does not have authority over his own body, but the wife does" (vv. 3–4).

Yet it's important to point out that nowhere does Paul say that it is beneficial for people to claim their authority to have sex with their spouse. His point is that husband and wife should "give" their conjugal rights to the other. His focus is on the self-giving that constitutes Christlike sexuality, which he reinforces in his next breath by rejecting sexual manipulation: "Do not deprive one another" (v. 5). As in all things, it is a courtesy to ask for sex as much as it is a courtesy to give it. And relationships shaped by the love of God are constituted by asking and receiving, rather than demanding or domineering.

In fact, there is a hint that Paul would think claiming our "sexual rights" over the other person's body might contradict our witness to Christ's love. In 1 Corinthians 9:1–18, Paul points out that while he has the right to receive money from the Corinthians, he refuses to claim it so he might be free to proclaim the gospel. In 1 Corinthians 6:1–8, Paul argues it is better for believers to "be defrauded" than to pursue their rights against other believers in court.

The assertion of sexual rights within marriage, then, represents the failure of love and undermines the true meaning of sexuality. Paul's focus is always on cultivating hearts that freely respond in gratitude, rather than legislating Christian behavior.

SEX AND HOLY ATTENTIVENESS

Because sex is a mutual self-giving in freedom and love, it requires the sort of holy attentiveness that is in short supply in our world. When Paul reminds the Ephesians: "No one ever hated his own flesh, but nourishes it and cherishes it" (Ephesians 5:29), he points to the delicate care and concern for the other's bodied life that should mark a marriage. The words *nourish* and *cherish* literally mean "to feed and clothe the wife," but also carry connotations of "bringing someone to maturity"—a lengthy process that can be very time-consuming.

Being attentive to the rhythms and movements of the other person's body—both within the marriage more broadly, and in the sexual union itself—helps us to pursue that one's own good more deeply. But our attentiveness is not simply to help the other gain sexual pleasure. Rather, it is fundamentally a lavish affirmation of the other's beauty and goodness. For in marriage, we are to nourish and cherish each other—"as Christ loved the church" (Ephesians 5:25–27), who sanctifies her "so that he might present the church to himself in splendor, without spot or wrinkle or any such thing, so that she might be holy and without blemish."

Cultivating a holy attentiveness toward the other in marriage is an important part of learning to love her as Christ loves her, to delight in her and proclaim that she is a "crown of beauty in the hand of the Lord" and in ours (Isaiah 62:3). If our attentiveness to the other is holy, then it will fundamentally see the other's humanness as oriented toward God himself. It attends to the totality of the other, respecting the freedom of the other's inner life and freeing her to offer herself as a gift in mutual love. It is, in other words, ordered toward experiencing the "communion of persons" that is an intrinsic part of our human flourishing.[18]

SINGLENESS AND CHRISTIAN SEXUALITY

Jesus couldn't get hired as an evangelical pastor, and neither could Paul.

Most evangelical churches are wary of single male pastors (especially young ones). The belief is that single men are incapable either of controlling themselves sexually, or of counseling married couples on the dynamics of human sexuality. This basic inhospitality toward single people in church leadership suggests, I suspect, a tacit commitment to standards of sexuality that are taken less from Scripture and more from the world around us.[19]

Celibacy has a crucial role in Christian sexuality. When the Sadducees posed a puzzle to Jesus about which husband a particularly unfortunate wife (who had lost seven of them) would be married to in heaven, Jesus responded that "in the resurrection they neither marry nor are given in marriage, but are like the angels in heaven."[20] Then in Matthew 19, after affirming the goodness of created sexuality, Jesus tells us that "there are eunuchs who have made themselves eunuchs for the sake of the kingdom of heaven."[21]

This idea of a vocation—or a calling—to lifelong celibacy for the kingdom of God does not minimize the importance of marriage. Each calling bears witness to different aspects of our world. Oliver O'Donovan puts it this way: "[The New Testament church] conceived of marriage and singleness as alternative vocations, each a worthy form of life, the two together comprising the whole Christian witness to the nature of affectionate community. The one declared that God had vindicated the order of creation, the other pointed beyond it to its eschatological transformation."[22] In other words, marriage points to Genesis, singleness to Revelation.

The "communion of persons" that marriage exemplifies is, in this sense, a temporary reality. Paul tells the Corinthians in the same passage where he commends singleness, "For the present form of this world is passing away" (1 Corinthians 7:31). The New Testament's basic contention is that our human flourishing is not found in marriages or the natural families that they inaugurate, but in bearing each others' burdens in love within the church.[23] The only alternative is to minimize the humanity of Jesus by treating his celibacy as an aberration rather than a possibility for our lives.

The possibility of finding full human flourishing without sex stands in stark contrast to one of the most prevalent notions of sexuality both inside and outside the church: Thanks in part to Sigmund Freud and Abraham Maslow, sex has been transformed from an expression of our humanity to a physiological or psychological need that is essential to our human flourishing.

Probably the most famous infusion of the language of "needs" into evangelical sexuality has been through Willard Harley's enormously popular *His Needs, Her Needs* (of which we received multiple copies when we got married). Harley suggests that one of the main ways to prevent an affair (an instantly troubling way to frame marital advice) is for the wife to meet the husband's "sexual need." Nearly every Christian sex manual carries the torch, including Douglas Rosenau's *A Celebration of Sex* and Ed Wheat's *Intended for Pleasure*. Rosenau encapsulates most of our attitudes toward sex when he writes, "If we are always other-focused and if we always repress or ignore our own needs, we forfeit complete sexual fulfillment."[24]

Theological ethicist Daniel Heimbach calls this mindset "therapeutic sexual morality," in which "people fulfill or actualize themselves through sex, and everyone must have sex in order to be whole. No sexual behavior is right or wrong in itself because what matters is a person's inner sense of satisfaction."[25] Humanity clearly needs to procreate—at least until Jesus returns—but that does not mean our flourishing depends upon our fulfilling our sexual "needs."

The teaching that our wholeness depends upon sexual fulfillment lies behind many of the problems in evangelical teaching about sex. We implicitly convey to young people that sex is a need by marginalizing those who are single or cordoning them off in singles groups so that they hopefully will get married. Then we expect them to live some of the most sexually charged years of their lives without yielding to temptation. No wonder young people struggle to stay sexually pure: either sex is essential to their flourishing as humans or it isn't. And if everyone who is married thinks it is, then young people will too—regardless of whatever else we tell them.[26]

I realize there are deep difficulties here, not the least of which are discerning the call of singleness and establishing structures and systems of support within the church for those called to it. But the absence of visible, lifetime singleness within our communities suggests that our affirmation of marriage and the goodness of sexual pleasure have overstepped their boundaries. We cannot affirm the goodness of the created order as Christians without also seeing how it has been caught up and renewed in Christ—which those who are called to celibacy bear witness to by their lives and their love. A church without singles has lost one of its main ways of warning against a sexual idolatry that has driven the whole world mad.

THE PROBLEM OF PORNOGRAPHY

We now know that every male in his twenties looks at pornography.

Researchers at the University of Montreal had been planning to conduct a study on the effects of pornography by comparing young men who watched porn regularly to those who had never seen it. But in December 2009, they announced that the research failed before it began: they couldn't find anyone who didn't watch pornography. Researcher Simon Louis Lajeunesse told the university's School of Social Work: "Guys who do not watch pornography do not exist."[27]

That's an overstatement, but the fact that researchers at a major Western university came up empty for their study certainly isn't good news. While things may be somewhat better within evangelical circles, the problem is still rampant among most young men—and a growing problem for young women as well.[28]

At the heart of the pornography problem is the commodification of sexuality, which turns other people—and the images of them—into objects for our own sexual pleasure. The pornography culture has taken our sexuality and industrialized, packaged, and sold it. This objectification of women in a pornified world reduces them to instruments or tools for self-gratification—which means that even if they *did* choose to enter the pornography world voluntarily (and many do not), it would still be fundamentally wrong to treat them as sub-personal creatures.

Yet the objectification of women—or men—in pornography depends upon a prior objectification of our *own* bodies. When we turn people into sexual objects so we can have an artificial sense of connection with them, we treat our bodies as machines meant to maximize our experience of pleasure. It is fundamentally depersonalizing for *everyone* involved—for the viewer and the viewed. Wendell Berry writes, "Our 'sexual revolution' is mostly an industrial phenomenon, in which the body is used as an idea of pleasure or a pleasure machine with the aim of 'freeing' natural pleasure from natural consequence."[29]

This is the fundamental problem of lust, one form of what the ancients would have called concupiscence. Disordered desires undermine our own personal integrity—that is, our own proper functioning as children made to love God and those around us. When Jesus said that anyone who looked on the opposite sex with lustful intent had already committed adultery in their hearts, he wasn't suggesting that the consequences (in this life) would be the same as if we actually committed adultery. Rather, he was pointing to the basic corruption that happens when we give ourselves over to desires that do not conform to the reality of God's love and his good creation.

When Jesus told us to love our neighbor as ourselves, he not only gave us a commandment, he also described a basic feature of human existence. One way or another, we will ultimately treat others the way we treat ourselves, which is why lust and sexual promiscuity are so often entangled with self-loathing. The more we see ourselves in light of the gospel—"You have died, and your life is hidden in Christ with God"—the more we will be set free from treating our bodies as objects, instead seeing them as the place of our personal presence and the indwelling presence of God himself. The Lord has come to his temple!

The reality that lust destroys the viewer as much as the viewed must be kept at the forefront of our evangelical teaching on sexuality. One of the more successful recent arguments against pornography is its link to sex trafficking—a horribly dehumanizing practice that depends on pornography for its existence. Pornography fosters a climate that encourages sex trafficking and child prostitution because men (primarily) are shaping their hearts and their minds to treat human bodies as objects.

But the sex-trafficking link won't be a compelling argument forever. Evangelicals need to be prepared for the day when pornography can be entirely computer generated. The scenario isn't an idle possibility. What will be created is a type of pornography that does not require actual women, taking away one of the most forceful arguments against the practice, a practice that destroys the lives and families of those who engage in it as well as those who create it.[30]

It is important, perhaps, to also say something about masturbation. While I remain skeptical that masturbation as a regular practice can be separated from looking at pornography or creating mental fantasies based on real women or men (the equivalent of lusting), the practice treats the body as an instrument for personal pleasure and gratification. Human sexuality is inherently social, and masturbation is not. In that sense, it represents a failure to fulfill the nature of Christian sexuality as God designed it.

CONCLUSION

"With my body I thee worship."

It's what I wrote to my wife in dedicating this book to her, and it's a bit of an inside joke. We were married according to an old form of the Book of Common Prayer, and that line was part of the vows. My wife, worried that people would misunderstand it, wanted to take it out. I love the line and thought we should keep it in and add an explanatory footnote in the wedding folder. She won.

Worship doesn't mean that I've turned my wife into an idol. Though she is practically a saint in every way, not even she is worthy of what is owed to God alone. But it does mean that I give her all the reverence, honor, and adoration due her because of her beauty and loveliness. And I do this with my body, giving myself up for her and seeking as much as possible, by the grace of God, to place her interests above my own.

Our confusion, though, over God and creation is at the heart of our sexual dysfunctions and brokenness. C. S. Lewis wrote in his famous passage:

> We are half-hearted creatures, fooling about with drink and sex and ambition when infinite joy is offered us, like an ignorant child who wants to go on making mud pies in a slum because he cannot imagine what is meant by the offer of a holiday at the sea. We are far too easily pleased.[31]

We have broken sexual lives. We have objectified our own bodies and the bodies of others. We have turned sex into a technique wherein we seek to maximize our own pleasure at the other person's expense, rather than seeing them as the temple of the Holy Spirit, the place where God himself dwells.

Yet the God who died for us, who revealed the pattern for our true humanity in Jesus Christ, has forgiven our sins and washed away our iniquities. And the Holy Spirit, his empowering presence, lives in the very sinews and bones of our mortal bodies, reshaping them and reforming our members into instruments of righteousness.

It is through this—the good news of the gospel—that we are set free from the shame of rejection and pain and empowered to respond in love to the one who gave himself for us—and then in turn to give ourselves to others. The gospel sets us free from the frustration of impotence and the fears caused by abuse, allowing us to enter into a journey of discovery filled with joy and freedom. It gives us the hope of a fulfilled, joyous, and abundantly flourishing life, even if we never taste the goods of marriage at all.

"We do not yet know what we shall be!" It is joy that awaits us in the kingdom of heaven, joy and pleasures forevermore. When we are raised up on the last day, we will not escape our physical bodies, but they will be marked by such a glorious beauty and splendor that we will barely recognize one another, and the transient moments of ecstasy will become the permanent features of our lives. Our bodies cannot hold such joys now—for all their splendors, they are too weak for the pleasures that await us, when we are transformed from "glory into glory." As Lewis once put it:

> It is a serious thing to live in a society of possible gods and goddesses, to remember that the dullest and most uninteresting person you talk to may one day be a creature which, if you saw it now, you would be strongly tempted to worship, or else a horror and a corruption such as you now meet, if at all, only in a nightmare. All day long we are, in some degree, helping each other to one or other of these destinations. It is in the light of these overwhelming possibilities, it is with the

awe and the circumspection proper to them, that we should conduct all our dealings with one another, all friendships, all loves, all play, all politics. There are no ordinary people. You have never talked to a mere mortal.[32]

CHAPTER EIGHT

HOMOSEXUALITY AND THE CHRISTIAN BODY

It was an awkward conversation when it started, but I wasn't prepared for the turn it took.

A new friend and I were sitting on the patio of the cafeteria at our conservative evangelical university, enjoying our lunch and debriefing our philosophy class. We eventually found ourselves talking about what the conversation often turns to among college men: women. We discussed past relationships and future prospects, but the conversation proceeded in fits and starts. It was clear my new friend wasn't very interested, and I wasn't about to pry.

I was ready to move on when the conversation took a more serious turn toward the nature of sexuality. It wasn't that surprising, given that we were both philosophy students. The conversation progressed and my friend slowly opened up, but I wasn't prepared for what came next. He was attracted to the same sex.

I grew up in small-town America where I had very little interaction with people who identified as gays or lesbians. I didn't join the party scene as a high school student, and generally kept to myself, so I have no idea if my friends were curious or experimenting back then. The only significant contact I had with the issue was when Ellen Degeneres came out as a lesbian and the discussion about its significance made its way into the classroom. And there were the snide insinuations by classmates that I was gay because I was happily celibate (well, happy most of the time).

So when my friend in college told me he had struggled with same-sex attraction, I was at something of a loss. I had access to the platitudes about homosexuality I had picked up through the years, but they suddenly struck me as counterproductive to any sort of decent or interesting conversation. So I listened. He talked of the confusion that he felt and his feelings of alienation and isolation. He spoke of anger toward God and of a bitter frustration with how he had been treated by others. Though we have lost contact, I have always appreciated his willingness to be forthright with me.

If there is an issue that separates the generations of evangelicals, it is the question of homosexuality. I suspect my experience is typical of many of the younger crowd: we grew up in a world where the way we thought about the question was primarily shaped by politics and the media. But as we have grown older, we have met and known people who identify as gay, lesbian, bisexual, or transgender (GLBT). The proximity of the issue to our personal lives and friendships has prompted us to seek ways to reframe Christianity's public witness on this issue so that it is, if nothing else, more hospitable and charitable toward those with whom we disagree.[1]

Inasmuch as this shift represents an attempt to ground the conversation within the context of personal friendships, it's a welcome development. The fundamental humanity of GLBT people is obscured when celebrities or the media are setting the terms of the discussion, as it inevitably reduces what should be thoughtful dialogue to sloganeering. When we get to know those who identify as gay or lesbian, our need to be constantly reminded of their fundamental human dignity and our equality as children of God recedes into the background.

But these newfound relationships and the increasing awareness of homosexuality within the church have made many younger evangelicals aware of our inability to respond to the questions the issue raises with confidence, clarity, and love. Even those who want to hold on to conservative positions on the question are often uncertain as to how to voice them in ways that won't contribute to the already negative perception of evangelicals among the gay and lesbian community.

Here, perhaps more than any other issue, evangelical inattention to the body has left us woefully underprepared to understand and respond to this question with grace. And as a result, evangelicals are in danger of allowing secular categories to dominate our discussion, undermining our witness to the good news of Jesus Christ. While our individual witness should be placed within the context of our personal relationships with gays and lesbians, we also need to ensure that our speech corresponds to the Word of God, which bears witness to the one who is "full of grace and truth."

One note: There are few books I would recommend more highly to you than Wesley Hill's *Washed and Waiting*. I realize my own limitations on this issue, as I am not someone who struggles with same-sex attraction. Hill, however, is, and his book is a profound and thoughtful meditation on why he has chosen celibacy and how his struggles have played out in the church.

HOMOSEXUALITY AND CHRISTIAN ETHICS

In the past three decades, mainline Protestants have watched— and talked—while the question of homosexuality has ripped their denominations apart, leaving a string of divisions and lawsuits in its wake. Hostility and animus aren't vices that restrict themselves to one side of the issue or the other; there has been plenty all around.

While evangelical churches have been mostly immune to these challenges, the dispute is now racing toward us. When Jennifer Knapp came out as a lesbian in the pages of *Christianity Today*, she was met with widespread acceptance by younger evangelicals, even while LifeWay (the Southern Baptist chain of bookstores) dropped her music.[2] Soul Force, an organization dedicated to equal rights, has been making bus trips to evangelical college campuses to raise awareness since 2004. Andrew Marin, the most prominent younger evangelical thinker on the question, has drawn international attention by reaching out to the gay community in Chicago. His book

Love Is an Orientation is an important and impassioned plea for more civil conversation with the gay and lesbian community. Additionally, the past decade has seen a full-court press to legalize same-sex marriage, a movement that younger evangelicals have met with either indifference or a warm embrace.

In her book *The Great Emergence*, Phyllis Tickle suggests that the coming conflict will be a "battle to the death" over the understanding of Scripture that Protestants have affirmed since the Reformation. As she puts it, "When it is all resolved—and it most surely will be—the Reformation's understanding of Scripture as the base of authority will be dead. That is not to say that Scripture as the base of authority is dead. Rather it is to say that what the Protestant tradition has taught about the nature of that authority will be either dead or in mortal need of reconfiguration."[3]

While I don't think the Protestant doctrine of *sola Scriptura* is in as much jeopardy as Tickle does, her decision to frame the debate over homosexuality within the church in terms of authority is precisely right. Near the heart of the question is whether or not there is an authority that should govern our experiences, and how that authority wants us to shape our lives and desires.

For much of the past thirty years, the tendency within the burgeoning subfield of theology known as "body theology" was to treat our experiences—in either the narrow sense of what we feel and desire or in the broad sense of what psychology and sociology reveal—as authoritative alongside Scripture. This was the strategy of James Nelson, a liberal Lutheran theologian who was one of the most prominent advocates for body theology. In a line that was written thirty years before Brian McLaren would sound a similar note in *A New Kind of Christianity*, Nelson boldly proclaimed, "There are times when we must challenge specific moral traditions of our heritage in the light of new empirical knowledge, new experience, and God's ongoing revelation."[4]

Though at this point I have no way of proving it, my suspicion is that mainstream evangelicalism will prove fertile soil for letting experiences be the authority in our moral discussions. One of the standard critiques of evangelical theology has been its purported Biblicism, or worship of the Bible. But evangelical piety is still often shaped by experience, even among those who are most wary of the charismatic movement. The emerging church's success in moving practices more toward the center of many people's theological reflection provides some evidence that this shift is already underway.

That said, the insistence by liberal critics that Christian churches have been inhospitable to those who identify as gays and lesbians strikes me as fundamentally correct. When professional number-cruncher Bradley R. E. Wright questioned whether Christians have "warm, charitable attitudes toward gay people" in *Christians Are Hate-Filled Hypocrites,* his answer was a blunt no.[5] And Wright is the guy with the most generous and sensitive reading of the state of evangelical Christianity.

The gospel does reach across barriers, but evangelicals haven't shared that very well with the gay and lesbian communities. When Jesus was lifted up on the cross, he stretched his arms in an open embrace that drew all people to himself.[6] As Brian McLaren points out in *A New Kind of Christianity,* Philip welcomes a eunuch into the kingdom of God by proclaiming the good news of the salvation of Jesus to him before baptizing him (Acts 8).[7] The eunuch probably castrated himself for religious or political purposes, and would have been revered among pagans, but rejected in Jerusalem, where he was returning from. McLaren's point that the good news of Jesus touches the sexually marginalized is fundamentally right.

But the gospel also leaves no one alone—including the eunuch. It transforms each of us into the image of Jesus, a transformation that reaches down and reworks every aspect of our humanity, including our sexual lives and practices. The question of Christian ethics is not what we were but what we are to become once we have heard and responded to the gospel call.

Appeals to the authority of experience are insufficient for our ethics to bear witness to the love Jesus demonstrated on the cross. The Bible is the authorized witness to the reality of God's revelation in Jesus Christ, and it stands as merciful judge over our experiences,[8] helping us discern the shape in which God wishes to mold our bodies and our lives. When our ethics are faithful to the gospel of Jesus Christ, they challenge the patterns and habits of our hearts and our world.[9]

Yet while ethics cannot be subordinated to our experience, they do need to be attentive to experience. We need to listen to the voices of those who wrestle with same-sex attraction in our midst, if only because moving from Scripture to our lives requires a sensitive and careful understanding of the world in which we are called to live. The more we understand both the nature of same-sex attraction and the shape of Christian theology, the more welcoming we can be without compromising Scripture.[10]

One word of caution: Locating our experience under the authority of Scripture cuts both ways, as it means we cannot make the heterosexual experience of the world normative on psychological or social scientific grounds either—at least not within the church, whose proper objective is to bear witness to the gospel and the life that it inaugurates.

In other words, we are all under sin. As many have pointed out, as heterosexuals our first duty is to pluck the log out of our own eye. Scripture speaks to us as much as anyone else, calling us to reform our disordered desires and to confess our sins. Whatever else we make of Romans 1, in Romans 2 Paul spares no one: "Therefore you have no excuse, O man, every one of you who judges. For in passing judgment on another you condemn yourself, because you, the judge, practice the very same things." It is what theologian Richard Hays calls a "homiletical sting operation." As he puts it, "The radical move that Paul makes is to proclaim that all people, Jews and Gentiles alike, stand equally condemned under the just judgment of a righteous God."[11] And, we might add, heterosexuals, gays, lesbians, and everyone in between are included.

At the heart of human sexuality is the question of authority. Whose body is it? And what is its proper shape? The experience of same-sex attraction within our late-modern world poses that question to us all. It is not only a question for those who are friends with people who struggle with same-sex attraction; it is a question about the church's public witness in the world.

A CONVERSATION THAT CAN'T GO FORWARD

Part of the difficulty of discussions on this topic is that while they operate under a veneer of neutrality, the presuppositions and expectations of the participants establish tacit criteria for what is and is not permissible speech and conduct.[12] Many of the lay-level conversations about the relationship between homosexuality and Christianity are based on assumptions that not only undermine the possibility of a straightforward, civil dialogue but also do not fit with Scripture's teaching about the nature of sexuality.

The gospel proclaims that because of the atoning sacrifice of Jesus Christ, Christians have died and their life is hidden in Christ with God.[13] Galatians 3:28 indicates that those aspects of our identity that we treat as core have been pushed to the margins by the encompassing love of Jesus Christ: "There is neither Jew nor Greek, there is neither slave nor free, there is no male and female, for you are all one in Christ Jesus." The basic equality of humanity that existed in our original innocence is reestablished by the person and work of Jesus Christ. Paul's logic identifies us with our Savior. He writes in Galatians 2:20, "I have been crucified with Christ. It is no longer I who live, but Christ who lives in me."

The good news is that our relationship with God himself determines our fundamental identity as humans—not our sexual desires or actions. And as Christians, locating our identity in the person of Jesus Christ undermines all other attempts to claim the center of our being. In doing so, the gospel establishes the possibility of civil dialogue on sexual ethics. In *Homosexuality and the Christian*, Mark Yarhouse points out the fact that discussions about homosexuality often conflate three different categories: same-sex attraction, homosexual orientation, and gay identity. In the first category, people experience attractions to the same sex, but they are not nurtured. In the second, those attractions are frequent enough and sustained enough that the persons are oriented toward the same sex. In the final category, people have incorporated their sexual orientation into their identity, making it a feature of who they are in such a way that "being gay means not only that you are attracted to the same sex, but you are personally fulfilled through engagement in same-sex behavior."[14]

In other words, labeling oneself gay or lesbian treats sexual orientation as a core part of one's identity as human persons. Unfortunately, this narrative of sexual identity stops any dialogue about the morality of same-sex desires and practices before it can even begin; any disagreement goes against the core of the other person's identity. Andrew Marin writes:

> Since the GLBT person's mindset attests that same-sex sexual behavior is the dominating characteristic that sets them apart from everyone else, their sexual behavior is who they are . . . their same-sex sexual behavior is their identity. As a result, when gay and lesbian sexual behavior is challenged or questioned, they perceive their entire being as a person—their whole identity—as being under attack.[15]

This means that as long as those with same-sex orientations treat the fulfillment of their sexual desires as a necessary part of their identity, the most sensitive traditional responses to same-sex attraction and acts will inevitably be reduced to bigotry. The possibility of real conversation is over before it begins.

But what of the log in our own eye? The language of "sexual identity" (rather than attraction or desire) glorifies sexual expression by establishing it as necessary to our humanity. And as I suggested in the previous chapter, it is heterosexuals who first took this step and made sexual expression a "need" on which human flourishing depends. With some modifications—like taking over the language of the civil rights movement, for instance—the gay and lesbian communities have simply followed our lead, using the language of sexual fulfillment and identity that heterosexuals have been using since at least Freud.

Evangelical attitudes about our *own* sexuality, then, are part of the inability of the church to speak firmly on this issue without being heard as spiteful and to speak charitably without ceasing to be clear. And unfortunately, the stalemate undermines Christianity's public witness, which does not depend only upon *what* conclusions we come to about homosexuality but *how* we come to those conclusions. For if we speak with the tongues of truth and exegesis but have not love, we are little more than a noisy gong or a clanging cymbal.

None of this yet approaches the question of whether same-sex acts can be practiced in faithful conformity to the gospel. But the prefatory material is more than throat-clearing. My suggestion is that discerning the proper expression for our sexual desires can only happen in response to the good news that God has given us a new name in Christ, and that the primary reality about who we are in the world is that our lives are hidden in God with him.

THE POSSIBILITY OF ORIGINAL SIN

Where does homosexuality come from? Until recently, evangelicals found themselves embroiled in a debate over whether gay and lesbian tendencies are chosen or inherent. Yet as *gay* has slowly ceased to designate a lifestyle and instead marked out a sexual orientation that may be expressed in a variety of lifestyles, this debate has receded into the background. For Christians of any position on this issue, the question of how our orientation is formed should be irrelevant to the question of what order it should be conformed to.[16] The focus on whether sexual orientation is a choice or not distracts us from the deeper, more fundamental questions about the proper shape of human desire, and it unnecessarily alienates us from those non-Christians who have accepted their same-sex attraction as their identity.

What's more, the psychological, environmental, or social factors behind a tendency are always imperceptible to us, as St. Augustine understood. In a famous episode in his writings, he spends a good bit of time reflecting about why he stole a pear. He examines most of the plausible options, such as peer pressure or hunger. But at the end of the analysis he is no clearer than when he began—suggesting that desires, sinful or otherwise, are the sorts of things that are particularly resistant to unraveling.[17]

In chapter 5, I argued that we shape the world and then the world shapes us. Our desires and embodied experiences are

147

inevitably formed by the environment in which we place ourselves.[18] We cannot simply force ourselves to desire something through a superhuman exertion of our will without placing ourselves in the proper context and engaging in the sorts of practices that cultivate those desires.[19] The reason advertisers carefully choose colors, sounds, and other sensory stimuli is because they work. Stare at enough Victoria's Secret catalogs, and that will be your vision of the ideal of female beauty—regardless of what you affirm when asked.

This account is an oversimplification, of course. While the raw material for our interior lives is shaped by our presence in the world, we also have the freedom not only to "take every thought captive," but to place ourselves in environments that may be more conducive to our formation in the kingdom of God—such as worship in the church, which should be a regular part of the Christian life for this very purpose.[20] If we denied this, we would be ignoring our individual freedom before God and transferring the responsibility for our formation over to the environments that produced us.[21]

But even if environmental factors were completely responsible for causing heterosexual or gay desires, that would have no bearing on whether such desires are proper or not.[22] We are all formed by the same fallen world and all have disordered desires as a result. To quote Oliver O'Donovan:

> Desire is, however, one aspect of what Christian doctrine used to speak of as "concupiscence," a brokenness of the world reflected in a confusion of desire that our human society itself instills in us. A recovery of the length, breadth and depth of the doctrine of original sin would rid us of a lot of misunderstanding at this point. The gay Christian who complains that the good news is difficult to hear because his position is treated as compromised from the outset could learn that it is not his position, but the position of the human race, that is compromised from the outset.[23]

O'Donovan's suggestion here is subtle. Rather than simply locate concupiscence—or disordered desires—in the individual, he suggests that they "reflect" the "brokenness of the world." Under this account, homosexuality is—as Wesley Hill writes—"a tragic sign that human nature and relationships are fractured by sin."[24] That fracture, though, extends beyond our sexuality into our relationships with food, money, and every other sphere of human life. From this standpoint, desires of any sort cannot tell us whether they are properly formed or not. That can only come from outside us, from the counsel of the Scriptures.

The basic irrelevance of the biological dimension to the question of our formation should also be noted.[25] In fact, the push to find a "gay gene" represents the moral schizophrenia of the scientific establishment. On the one hand, the slim evidence for a genetic basis for same-sex attraction is put forward as evidence that it is normal. On the other hand, the slim evidence for the genetic basis for alcoholism is put forward to find therapies to change it.[26]

The question of how same-sex attraction is formed is important for discerning the pastoral response to same-sex desires and acts. But it has no bearing on whether gay and lesbian activities are a faithful expression of the life we have in Christ, or whether those desires are themselves properly ordered toward the gospel. The more important questions are whether same-sex attraction can be incorporated into Christian ethics without alteration, how those Christians with same-sex desires can bear faithful witness to the gospel, and how the church can incorporate those with same-sex attraction into its midst in a way that faithfully submits to the authority of Scripture.

HOW DOES THE BODY MATTER?

In a provocative and profoundly meditative article, Archbishop of Canterbury Rowan Williams writes:

> Same-sex love annoyingly poses the question of what the meaning of desire is in itself, not considered as instrumental to some other process, such as the peopling of the world. We are brought up against the possibility not only of pain and humiliation without any clear payoff, but, just as worryingly, of nonfunctional joy—of joy, to put it less starkly,

whose material "production" is an embodied person aware of grace. The question is the same as the one raised for some kinds of moralists by the existence of the clitoris in women: something whose function is joy. If the Creator were quite so instrumentalist in "his" attitude to sexuality, these hints of prodigality and redundancy in the way the whole thing works might cause us to worry about whether "he" was, after all, in full rational control of it. But if God made us for joy . . . [27]

Williams' suggestion is an interesting one, but his case also rests upon the supposition that sexual pleasure in heterosexual acts is "instrumental" to procreation. Yet that simply isn't the case. The pleasure of sex serves no other purpose than to enhance the delight and the joy that the husband and wife take in each other.

Nor is pleasure itself a sufficient justification for a desire or action. To use an extreme example, the pleasure that someone takes in sadomasochism seems irrelevant to the morality of the action. In fact, the pleasure that people take in sadomasochistic acts is itself wrong. Pleasure may not be instrumental, but it's not neutral either. It reinforces the desires and behaviors that it accompanies and so contributes to their moral status.[28]

What's more, the separation of sexual pleasure from the sexual complementarity—"male and female he created them"—that is revealed in Genesis 1–3 is grounded in an impulse that borders on minimizing the importance of the body.[29] As Williams says later in the same essay, "In a church that accepts the legitimacy of contraception, the absolute condemnation of same-sex relations of intimacy must rely either on an abstract fundamentalist deployment of a number of very ambiguous biblical texts, or on a problematic and non-scriptural theory about natural complementarity applied narrowly and crudely to physical differentiation without regard to psychological structures."[30] Or as Gerard Loughlin, another progressive Christian writes, "Indeed it may be suggested that only when theology begins to think of sexual difference starting from the homosexual couple as its paradigm of sexual difference will it be possible to think of the difference not in crudely biologistic terms . . . but in more properly theological ones."[31]

The contrast between the "crudely biological" and the theological highlights the difficulty with which theology understands the body's role in relationships of love. The tendency within liberal sexual theologies to ignore the sexual complementarity evident in humanity's original creation rests upon an ethic that minimizes the differences in male and female bodies—and between Christ and the church, which is the pattern for marriage.[32]

Gilbert Meilaender offers a helpful corrective:

> The body is the place of our personal presence. And moral significance must therefore be found not only in the spirit that characterizes our relationships with others, not only in mutuality and communion, but also in the bodily relationship itself. To suppose that mutual love is all that is needed to make a relationship right is to ignore the moral significance of the body. It is, in fact, a kind of dualism that separates our true self from the body. If we want to know how rightly to use the body, therefore, if we want to distinguish between fulfilling and corrupting sexual relationships, we cannot talk only of love, consent, and mutuality. However much my neighbor's wife and I are drawn to each other, our bodies are already promised to others. However deep and intense may be a father's affection for his adult daughter, to give himself sexually to her is a perversion of love, not a fulfillment.[33]

In other words, for Christian morality, the types of bodies we have and who our bodies belong to matter. Even while we evangelical Protestants emphasize the covenantal nature of marriage, we must not overshadow the other dimensions of marriage, namely the physical union that ratifies the covenant and the procreative aspect that depends upon sexual complementarity. Marriage bears witness to the original creation, and the first commandment is to "be fruitful and multiply." Marriage is a covenant between two persons, but it is a covenant that is sealed in a physical union of the kind that produces children.

It is for this reason that Jesus joins together the two creation narratives in Matthew 19: "Have you not read that he who created them from the beginning made them male and female, and said, 'Therefore a man shall leave his father and his mother and hold fast to his wife, and the two shall become one flesh'?" The affirmation of the union of marriage flows immediately upon the affirmation of the original creation as male and female. The suggestion that scripturally, sexual complementarity is insignificant to the morality of Christian marriage simply does not hold up to scrutiny.[34]

At the extreme end of the tragic undermining of the "moral significance of the body," as Meilaender puts it, are transsexualism and gender dysphoria, or "gender identity disorder." GID is a psychological condition wherein people believe they have a body that is the "wrong" sex. This sometimes leads those who suffer from it to pursue hormonal treatments or sex-change operations to conform their body to their psychological state.

The pastoral questions raised by transsexualism are extraordinarily complex, and as Christians we need an extraordinary measure of grace and discernment in knowing how to respond to them. The central issue, though, seems to be whether the body establishes limits on how our sexuality takes shape in the world. Can we receive our bodies as created gifts that are loved by God rather than reshaping them according to our psychological state? It's very true that such a position may make some people feel as though their bodies are "damaged goods" upon delivery. But it is the Lord's pleasure to make damaged goods his temple, a temple that he himself destroyed, only to raise it again.

THE BODY FOR THE LORD

Does Scripture sanction, then, same-sex sexual acts or desires as appropriate expressions of the life to which we have been called in Jesus Christ? I realize that addressing the question head on inevitably runs the risk of overinflating the problem. After all, our sexual desires are only one way in which the sinfulness of our hearts plays out in our world. And as Richard Hays suggests, "The Bible hardly ever discusses homosexual behavior."[35]

Yet as even liberal theologian Walter Wink acknowledges, "Where the Bible mentions homosexual behavior at all, it clearly condemns it."[36] The explicit rejections of gay and lesbian practices are not "clobber verses," but rather the tip of an iceberg sticking above the surface: they reveal a much larger and deeper understanding of human sexuality and its relationship to our lives before God.

The center of the debate is the relationship between creation and new creation, between the revelation of marriage in Genesis 1–3 and the affirmation of celibacy in Jesus. In other words, does the New Testament give a different answer than the Old Testament? I have argued that marriage reveals the original goodness of the created order, a created order that presupposes "male and female he created them."

Yet the "created order" is a theological revelation, not a scientific or empirical reality.[37] And the gap between what is and what should be is the tragedy of living in a fallen world, a world where the disorder introduced by sin goes all the way into the very bones and chemicals of the bodies we are born with. The pastoral question of how this gap is bridged is a matter of prudential judgment that has been shaped by Scripture—but it must be bridged in ways that do not undermine our Christian witness to the truth of the Christian life.

The first chapter of Romans, which is probably the central and most controversial passage about homosexuality, reinforces this point. Paul argues that we are all guilty before God, but as Richard Hays argues, the sins he lists are not the *reason* for God's wrath but the *result*. Paul is "presenting an empirical survey of rampant human lawlessness as evidence that God's wrath and judgment are already at work in the world."[38]

Although Paul lists same-sex sexual practices among the sins that Jesus' death paid for, that is no sanction. Instead, Paul's point is that it is grounded in humanity's rejection of God as Creator. In verse 25, it is precisely because they "worshiped and served the creature rather than the Creator" that God gives them up to dishonorable passions. This is clearly a reminder of Genesis 1, where God establishes Adam and Eve in the garden as male and female. As Richard Hays puts it (arguing against Rowan Williams above):

> Thus the complementarity of male and female is given a
> theological grounding in God's creative activity. By way of sharp

contrast, in Romans 1 Paul portrays homosexual behavior as a "sacrament" (so to speak) of the antireligion of human beings who refuse to honor God as Creator. When human beings engage in homosexual activity, they enact an outward and visible sign of an inward and spiritual reality: the rejection of the Creator's design.[39]

There is an enormous debate, though, over what sort of same-sex practices Paul is referring to in Romans 1. The scholarship of Robin Scroggs has perpetuated the notion that Paul is not referring to long-term, committed monogamous relationships but is challenging the practice of pederasty.[40] Unfortunately, the claim has all the advantages of a good story without the benefits of being true. As Mark Smith argues in his devastating analysis of bisexuality in the ancient Near East, the evidence suggests that same-sex relationships then and now had more in common than we usually hear. Paul's mention of lesbian relations in Romans 1:26 suggests he knew of non-pederastic same-sex relationships that would have shared the level of commitment that contemporary lesbian relationships share. As Smith writes, "When it comes to sexual behavior, there are only a limited number of options, and the evidence demonstrates that the Greeks and Romans were busily engaging in almost every form of expression known to us, with perhaps some variation in emphasis." And Paul would have certainly known this.[41]

Additionally, when Paul writes that women exchanged their natural function for that which is "against nature," he is not taking his cues from the animal world or the environment we see around us. Instead, he is suggesting that bad theology is inextricable from sinful sexuality. Our worship of God himself is inextricable from the form our sexuality takes. When we align our sexual desires to God's revealed order in Genesis 1–3, we confess our belief that God is indeed "maker of heaven and earth." Paul writes in Romans 1 that God gives those who reject him up to their sinful passions "because they exchanged the truth about God for a lie and worshiped and served the creature rather than the Creator, who is blessed forever!"[42]

Yet things get trickier at this point, if that's possible. Eugene

Rogers, who is one of the more sensitive theologians attempting to defend the idea that same-sex orientations are compatible with Scripture, points out that Paul describes the engrafting of the Gentiles into the covenant people of God as being "contrary to nature" in Romans 11:24.[43] The very Gentiles whose idolatry had led them into gay and lesbian relationships have been engrafted—by God!—into the people of God. As he puts it, "The community of the baptized must be open to the possibility that the Holy Spirit is able to pour out holiness also on gay and lesbian couples, without erasing the distinction between gay and straight, as the Holy Spirit rendered the Gentiles holy without circumcision and keeping the Torah."[44]

Yet God's acceptance of those who act contrary to nature does not necessarily mean that such desires and actions would still be approved or normative within the community. After all, if same-sex sexual acts are a manifestation of a society's idolatry in Romans 1, then the community of those who worship the Creator rather than the creature would view same-sex acts as wrong (in the same way that it would view adultery or divorce as wrong).[45]

And that is precisely the sort of logic we see Paul use elsewhere. In 1 Corinthians 5:7–9, Paul argues that we should separate ourselves from those who claim to be Christians but sin sexually and are unrepentant. Paul's logic depends upon an "in-group" and an "out-group" distinguished by an aggressive promotion of sexual purity. As Alistair May writes, "Christian social identity is, for Paul, symbolized in assumptions about moral difference. 'We' differ from 'them' in regard to ethics, and particularly sexual ethics. Believers are ['holy']: unbelievers are [sexually immoral ('pornoi')]." Unrepentant sexual immorality reveals that someone is an unbeliever.[46]

Sexual purity is a communal concern within the church because what each person does with their body affects everyone else. As the place of our personal presence in the world, our bodies and what we do with them are inextricably bound up with the lives of those around us—a fact that is true especially among those who are "members one of another" through the Spirit's indwelling presence (Ephesians 4:25). Stanley Hauerwas writes, "How we order and form our lives sexually cannot be separated from the necessity of the church to chart an alternative to our culture's dominant assumptions."[47]

Yet for Paul, sexual immorality also has a unique effect on our sense of the Holy Spirit's presence within us. In 1 Corinthians 6:13–20, he writes:

> The body is not meant for sexual immorality, but for the Lord, and the Lord for the body. And God raised the Lord and will also raise us up by his power. Do you not know that your bodies are members of Christ? Shall I then take the members of Christ and make them members of a prostitute? Never! Or do you not know that he who is joined to a prostitute becomes one body with her? For, as it is written, "The two will become one flesh." But he who is joined to the Lord becomes one spirit with him. Flee from sexual immorality. Every other sin a person commits is outside the body, but the sexually immoral person sins against his own body. Or do you not know that your body is a temple of the Holy Spirit within you, whom you have from God? You are not your own, for you were bought with a price. So glorify God in your body.

While Paul's immediate target is the issue of sex with prostitutes, his logic is rooted in Genesis and the nature of the union of persons we see there (3:16). Paul's basic belief is that sexual union gives the other authority over our body (see 1 Corinthians 7:3 as well). Because of that, sexual union outside the covenant of marriage represents a conflict between God's authority over our body and those with whom we have been joined.[48]

Yet the indwelling presence of the Holy Spirit means that our bodies are not our own to do with as we please. The body is "for the Lord" and so we do not have the authority to live in it according to our own desires. Our bodies—both the physical substance and our lived experience—are to be conformed to the person of Jesus ("take up your cross!") and submitted to the authority of the Father. The submission, as I have pointed out before, is grounded in our response to the gracious presence of God himself in us. The body is a temple, the place where God dwells. And the one who dwells in the temple shall act for its welfare: "the Lord is for the body."

Paul's implicit understanding that how we unite our body with another in sex—a point fundamentally motivated by his affirmation of Genesis and the "one flesh" union there—means that sexual sins uniquely affect our sense of the Spirit's indwelling presence. "Every other sin a person commits is outside the body, but the sexually immoral person sins against his own body" (1 Corinthians 6:18). Every sin is subject to the judgment of grace at the cross. But because "the body is for the Lord" and the "temple of the Holy Spirit," unrepentingly uniting with others in ways he has not authorized in Scripture are uniquely corrosive to our sense of his presence.[49]

Does the New Testament, then, sanction same-sex attraction? In two of the major texts on Christian sexuality, Paul's argument depends upon the sexual complementarity in the original creation. What's more, in 1 Corinthians 6, he simultaneously affirms a Christological understanding of the body—that it is a "member of the Lord" by virtue of the Holy Spirit's indwelling presence—and appeals to Genesis to make his case. The resurrection of Jesus does not destroy the normative of male-female sexual complementarity; rather, it establishes it in its fundamental goodness. As Oliver O'Donovan puts it, "New creation is creation renewed, a restoration and enhancement, not an abolition. . . . God has announced his kingdom in a Second Adam, and *Adam* means *human*."[50]

SAME-SEX ATTRACTION WITHIN THE CHURCH

"You were washed, you were sanctified, you were justified in the name of the Lord Jesus Christ and by the Spirit of our God" (1 Corinthians 6:11).

Whatever our sexual sins or our sexual past, as the redeemed people of God we have been washed clean and have entered into the love, freedom, and joy of the Holy Spirit. The causes of our sinful desires may be ambiguous to us ("Who can discern his errors? Declare me innocent from hidden faults").[51] But the clarity of grace transforms all those whose lives are hidden in Christ alone. The same Spirit that raised Jesus from the dead dwells within his temple, patiently and lovingly preserving and sanctifying it until our long-awaited adoption as sons and daughters, "the redemption of our bodies."

The gospel is good news for those with same-sex desires, just as it is good news for those who are addicted to masturbation or who have committed adultery or who have in any way put their own interests above those of their spouse. But as the wisest among us know best, the gospel does not always work its way into the marrow and bones of our lives quickly. Sometimes progress seems easy—other times it is nonexistent. And occasionally, it feels as though we are going in reverse, as the Lord shines his light on the hidden, unknown reaches of the human heart and calls us to confess and repent. The fruit of the Spirit is patience, and often the Lord uses our own sanctification to remind us just how much we need it.

Our identity in Christ takes shape within the church, the community that is formed in response to the gospel and whose practices reform our own desires. And it is precisely the church's obligation to discern how the gap between our lives now—sexual or otherwise—and the life to which we are called can be lessened. The need for prudential judgment shaped by grace among our pastors and leaders has never been more pressing.

But the path to closing that gap may not always seem straight, especially as same-sex relationships become more embedded in the structures of American life. For instance, what would happen ten or twenty years from now if an atheist lesbian couple and their eight-year-old adopted daughter became Christians and affirmed traditional sexual morality? Should the home be broken up so the child can have a father? Should the couple live together as celibates so the child's stability is preserved? And do the answers change if the child is six—or sixteen? The questions are but variations on a theme: How does the gospel pervade cultural institutions that are inhospitable to its presence? Does Paul's suggestion in 1 Corinthians 7 that each person should "remain in the condition in which they were called" provide a template for a sensitive pastoral response, one akin to that which some missionaries have taken in polygamous cultures?

These are hard questions, and my point is not to legitimize

same-sex relationships. But as these relationships are normalized, navigating changing social conditions that will accompany them requires an incredible amount of pastoral prudence and wisdom.

I am convinced that voluntary celibacy and heterosexual marriage are the two patterns of sexual expression that Scripture reveals. But in saying this, I want to suggest that we should be wary of reducing celibacy to a corrective to same-sex attraction. Christian celibacy, as I argued in the previous chapter, is a life uniquely oriented toward our eschatological transformation, a life that bears witness to the kingdom of heaven in a unique way. And it needs to precede same-sex attraction in our order of proclamation if we wish to authentically present the good news of the gospel.

Our hospitality as evangelicals toward those with same-sex attraction depends upon recovering this idea of celibacy as a vocation if we are going to support and sustain them beyond their initial introduction into the community. One of the benefits of monastic orders is their visibility; they serve as a reminder both to the church and the world that "the present form of this world is passing away" (1 Corinthians 7:31). Whatever form it takes within our local churches, we need to provide systems and structures of care for those who wish to lead celibate lives, regardless of whether they struggle with same-sex desires.

Sanctification is a community concern, for it is a matter of retelling the story of the gospel to each other and reminding one another of the holiness and purity to which we are called in grace. It is a matter of bearing one another's burdens, of fulfilling the law of love, and giving ourselves away to others for the glory of God and the good of the world. We "rejoice with those who rejoice, and weep with those who weep," for the gospel calls us to carry the burden of a joy we did not earn and a grace we did not deserve, a burden too heavy for us to carry alone. It is an invitation open to all.

CHAPTER NINE

THE MORTAL BODY

Even though most of us could probably quote it, it's not really a question we often ask.

The opening to Shakespeare's most famous soliloquy from the most famous of his plays—*Hamlet*—captures the fundamental rupture of the universe that death represents: "To be, or not to be: that is the question." The Dane has suffered from what amounts to literary overexposure, but the poetry is still among my favorite bits.

Though Hamlet only presents us with two options—being or not being—he somehow manages to linger between them, suspended between the recognition of life's toils and sorrows and the "dread of something after death, the undiscover'd country from whose bourn no traveler returns." It is this terror of judgment, the fear of God, which keeps him mucking about on earth, pursuing his father's business. His is not a glorious affirmation of the goodness of life so much as the ambivalent acceptance that for all the sufferings of this world, it is better than the possibility of having to face his own conscience.

Some 1,500 years before Shakespeare was scribbling out Hamlet's lines, the apostle Paul was sitting in a Roman prison facing that very decision—though he approached it from a very different set of presuppositions and came to a very different conclusion. Staring at the end of his life and ministry, Paul poured his heart into his pen, sending a letter to the Philippians that is itself a beautiful and tragic commemoration of the love he had for the church. This is not the Paul who is the brilliant thinker of Romans or the sarcastic combatant of Galatians. This is Paul at his most vulnerable, entreating the church at Philippi to be unified, passionately pleading with its people to fix their eyes on Jesus, and rejoicing in the joyful bonds of love and peace.

"To live is Christ, and to die is gain" (Philippians 1:21).

The first time I remember this line striking me was in a high school English class. We were discussing a Nathaniel Hawthorne short story, I believe, about death or aging. I remember putting forth some (mind-numbing, I'm sure) attempt at an insight about the horrendous evil that death is, only to have my English teacher toss this passage at me. I have never quite recovered.

Paul wasn't endorsing suicide. No Christian ever has, that I can find. As Chesterton put the case against it:

> Not only is suicide a sin, it is the sin. It is the ultimate and absolute evil, the refusal to take an interest in existence; the refusal to take the oath of loyalty to life. The man who kills a man, kills a man. The man who kills himself, kills all men; as far as he is concerned he wipes out the world.[1]

In fact, Paul's earnest desire "to depart and be with Christ" (v. 23) is the grounds for his sticking around. It is precisely because he is so entranced by the beauty and glory of Jesus Christ that he will "remain and continue" (v. 25) with the Philippians so that they will glory in Jesus Christ when they are reunited with Paul. Paul isn't backing out of the earth—he's doubling down, making plans to see them again even though he's in chains and has every reason to believe he's not going to make it out alive (v. 26).

The glorious paradox of Paul's line is that it fundamentally rejects Hamlet's categories. Though Paul is facing death, he refuses to choose between "being" and "nonbeing." His choice is between life in the Spirit and the perfection of that life "with Christ." It is between seeing as in a mirror dimly, but then face-to-face. It is between knowing in part and knowing fully (1 Corinthians 13:12). It is between earthly joy and a joy so powerful that the sufferings of this world fade to oblivion. It is between glory and glory, between a lowly body subject to the pains, aches, and hurts of corruptibility and a glorious body that has been transformed by the power that rules the universe (Philippians 3:21).

Death shook the universe when it put Jesus into the grave, but was reduced to nothing when he came out. "O death, where is thy sting? O grave, where is thy victory?" (1 Corinthians 15:55 kjv). The resurrection makes death impotent, vanquishing its only tool of breeding and preying upon our fears of dissolution, destruction, and the unknown.

DEATH AND LIFE IN AMERICAN CULTURE

The way we interact with death reveals how we think about life.

One hundred fifty years ago, Americans kept the bodies of the dead in their homes while mourning, and then took them to the churchyard or to the homestead where they would be buried. Now we send the bodies to funeral homes, wheel them into inter-faith chapels, and bury them in our nonsectarian cemeteries—if we bury them at all. Nearly one-third of Americans who die will be cremated.[2] What was once a ritual shaped by communities of family and faith has become a consumer experience managed by professionals whose practices are shaped by profit and sanitation.

A few of the more artistic and free-spirited folks among us reject this industrialization of death, and for good reason. Yet their alternative is similarly uninspiring. Wade Funeral Home in St. Louis promises "services as unique as your loved one," and sells caskets custom themed to fit the personality of the departed. The over-amplified individualism has sometimes been combined with a murky New Age spirituality that traffics in "feel-goodisms."[3] Thankfully, the trend, known as "designer funerals" has never quite cracked the mainstream.[4] But its replacement might. Green burials, where people either go straight into the ground or are placed in an eco-friendly box, are on the rise.[5]

People will obviously think about death when it thrusts itself upon them. But for many of us, death remains at the margins of our lives and consciousness. And that's a feature, not a bug, of our American social fabric. In rural America, graveyards were most often attached to churchyards or on family plots of land. People would walk by Uncle Charlie on their way to meet with the Almighty. But in the mid-1800s, cemeteries—cities for the dead—emerged and began undermining the tie between churches and their dead.[6] Many major American cities actually banned cemeteries within their city limits.[7] San Francisco, St. Louis, Chicago—each banished the dead not just to the suburbs, but to what was then the rural country.[8] When Bellefontaine Cemetery in St. Louis opened in the mid-1800s, it was five miles out of town—a considerable distance before the Model T. And the speaker who dedicated the cemetery pronounced that it would be "the shadow, the counterpart" of St. Louis.[9]

The American city has no room for death—and neither do most of its churches. We have no catacombs, and most of the church graveyards are long gone. Our cities have been built on this denial of death, and it has worked its way through the rest of our culture. Aging has become a "disease" that we are bent on eradicating just as we have polio—and we nip and tuck ourselves to hide its marks until we succeed. Conquering space quit being cool once the USSR fell, so the new technological visionaries have turned to immortality. We do not need the resurrection from the dead if we can recreate it ourselves—or at least build a close approximation.[10]

In his provocative little book *Death and Life: An American Theology*, Arthur McGill examined the various aspects of the American ethos and concluded that Americans are fundamentally characterized by our efforts to "appear to be full of life." We worship success and punish failure, and exclude from the fabric of our lives "any evidence of decay or death and helplessness." Fundamentally, the ethic of avoiding death is characterized by the worship and adoration of youth. As he puts it, "Youth is the time that is full of life, when all the negatives are only minor and accidental. Youth is the actualization, then, of the American ethic. It is to be expected that the American people, so far as they want to create a living world that seems to have no place for death, will idolize youth as the best and truest time of life, and will teach individuals to value anyone who can maintain the style and appearance of youth."[11]

McGill is after an ethos, a certain temperament. But his description of our fundamental worship of youth is undoubtedly correct. The fundamental aversion to wrinkles, gray hair, and loose skin drives a $189 billion cosmetic industry that is roughly twenty times the size of Hollywood.[12] The constant glorification of college and high school as "the best days of your life" and the steady consumption of adulthood by adolescence—these are the marks of a culture that has forgotten that *sic transit gloria mundi*—thus passes the glory of the world.

How different from the early church we are, a church that was constantly teetering on the edge of being a little too eager about martyrdom.[13] The early church was formed in a world where the average life expectancy was under twenty-five, and only 4 percent of men—and even fewer women—lived to be over fifty. The presence of death was everywhere, and Christians made no attempt to avoid it. In the second century, the physician Galen spoke of Christians' "contempt" for death.[14] By the fourth century, Christians were founding hospitals in Constantinople. And they kissed the dying and diseased to demonstrate not only their compassion but also their belligerent rejection of death's power.

We cannot speak of the body without speaking of its mortality, for the God who became flesh did so in order that he might die. For Jesus, death was the precursor to the resurrection. For us, it is the power of Christ's resurrection that allows us to stare death in the face. Easter Sunday and the life we have in Christ shape our understanding of the Friday on which humanity died and the grounds by which we call it "good." When we experience the power of the resurrection through the indwelling Holy Spirit, we will age as though not aging, be in pain as though not in pain, and die as though not dying.

DEATH AS JUDGMENT AND DISSOLUTION

Justin Key was one of those exceptional young men whom you suspected might not have been affected by the fall. Always pleasant and exceptionally earnest, he built organizations and ministries aimed at converting and discipling the world. He could woo women with ease—especially with his electric salsa moves.

Justin was also an explorer's explorer, a fellow who found himself frequently enjoying front-row seats at the theater of God's glory—the created world. We all expected that he would die fighting lions in Africa, sky-surfing in California, or succumbing to dysentery in some remote jungle. He was practically indestructible. Yet he died at the age of twenty-six, alone in his house in Virginia, a victim of a blood clot in his lung.

The sense of tragic loss we feel when loved ones die is very real and appropriate. My grandfather had been in declining health for many years before he passed on. His ongoing problems were a constant reminder to us that he would not always be with us. But though his death was not completely unexpected, as Justin's was, the sense of loss and emptiness were still irrepressibly present. For death is a radical irruption in the goodness of the created order, a brokenness of the world that suggests that things are not the way they are supposed to be.

Within the creation narrative, death stands as a possibility over Adam if he is disobedient to the God who made him. When God establishes the limits on Adam's life, limits that remind him of his fundamental creaturely status and his dependence upon God for his sustenance and existence, he points out that "in the day that you eat of it [the forbidden tree] you shall surely die." Christians have often discerned a double meaning in the warning, and for good reason. Our bodies live by the pleasure and goodness of God, and our fundamental separation from him in sin would inevitably contribute to their degeneration. "You are dust," God tells Adam after their sin, "and to dust you shall return."

Death, then, is inextricable from the judgment of God for the rebellion of humanity against him. But there is no one-to-one correspondence between any specific sins that we commit and how we die. Even in the creation narrative, Adam continues his life by the grace of God despite the pronouncement of God's judgment. Death may take some of us quickly, but it eventually takes us all. And while the sense of tragedy may be more acute in natural disasters or accidents, such heartrending disruptions point to the fundamental importance of death's presence to our lives.

In other words, death is not only the event when our bodies cease to have life. It is also a power at work in the world and in us, a condition of our brokenness and our separation from God himself. Our bodies do not just happen to die—they are mortal, incapable of avoiding the reality of decay and degeneration. As theologian Arthur McGill describes it, "Death is the losing of life, that wearing away which goes on all the time."[15]

Death's power over us manifests itself through the body's corruption. As a sixteen-year-old living in western Washington, I often found the gravitational pull of the massive pools of water that rainstorms would leave too difficult to resist. I seized every opportunity to drive through puddles five or six inches deep. But though my station wagon was probably large enough to be one, cars aren't boats and water in their engines has an unavoidably corrosive effect.

Though the body isn't a machine, it is an organic system that has interdependent parts. And like any such system, the decay of one part slowly corrodes the whole system. As any mechanic will point out, having a bad air filter doesn't simply reduce your fuel mileage—it makes your engine work harder and shortens its lifespan. Everything is connected, and as anyone with an old car knows, once decay takes hold it can be hard to reverse it.

At the heart of Adam's sin was a rejection of his status as creature—as an embodied person living in dependence upon God and thereby subject to the law of God. The isolation from God as a result of his sin undermines the integrity and harmony of his own body. Death did not simply mean an event wherein Adam would quit breathing, but the corresponding decay and degeneration of his own body.

At the heart of the relationship between death and resurrection, then, is a conflict between the impermanent and transitory nature of a life under sin and the permanent, incorruptibility of the physical resurrection from the dead. Paul writes, "For the trumpet will sound, and the dead will be raised imperishable, and we shall be changed. For this perishable body must put on the imperishable, and this mortal body must put on immortality."[16] As C. S. Lewis put it, "If flesh and blood cannot inherit the Kingdom, that is not because they are too solid, too gross, too distinct, too 'illustrious with being.' They are too flimsy, too transitory, too phantasmal." The solidity and permanence of the bodily resurrection is too strong for the frailties and contingencies of our current bodies.[17]

PURSUING PERMANENCE

The movies and media have been good to vampires.

Vampire legends have been around a long time. The publication of Bram Stoker's book *Dracula* in 1897 revived the genre, but only with help from its many cinematic adaptations. The book was a minor success, but when Bela Lugosi's thick Hungarian accent droned "I vant to suck your blooood" for the film-going public, America's torrid love affair with the undead was on. Now over seventy years later, vampires are inescapable. Hollywood continues to turn out film variations, and Buffy and Angel brought them back to TV by reducing the myths into the angst-filled teenage dramas that were popular in the late '90s.

The most recent iteration, *Twilight,* continues the "vampire rehabilitation" trajectory that was first mainstreamed by Angel. The plot is functionally *Romeo and Juliet* on steroids. Edward Cullen— a nice vampire who never sleeps, has superhuman abilities, and practically glitters because he's so good looking—falls in love with a teenage girl, Bella. Or he wants to suck her blood. It's never quite clear. But that drives the erotic tension to the max—if they get too frisky, he really may consume her.

We are a nation of people who want to be vampires like Edward Cullen. Driven by a nearly unrestrainable desire that denies human limitations, we pour our resources into cultivating the beauty and immortality that mimics the resurrection from the dead. While the fascination with Cullen may in some way point to our longing for the resurrection of the body, his pseudo-body depends upon the consumption of other creatures. While he may point to our longing for transcendence and immortality, he can only do so within the imaginative paradigm of a broken creation.

Culturally, we have reversed Paul's maxim that while our "outer self is wasting away, our inner self is being renewed day by day" (2 Corinthians 4:16) in our attempt to live like Edward Cullen. We invest our energies in maintaining the illusion of having life, devoting ourselves to the skin and superficialities in order to fill the deadness within. We have become what psychologist Phillip Cushman dubbed "empty selves," which he suggested seek "the experience of being continually filled up by consuming goods, calories, experiences, politicians, romantic partners, and empathic therapists."[18]

We want, in other words, all the benefits of the resurrection without acknowledging our dependence upon God as mortal creatures. The attempt at having the appearance of resurrected bodies without the power of resurrected bodies—the Holy Spirit—necessarily denies that we are dependent upon God for our lives. While there are numerous forms such a denial can take, allow me to mention two.

First, *we refuse to observe the Sabbath in our pursuit of self-aggrandizement through our own work*. Like death, the notion that we are to rest one day out of seven establishes a limit on our human existence. Unlike death, however, it is not an intrusion into the created order but an expression of the created order's perfection and completion. When God created the world, he rested on the seventh day and enshrined that day as holy. In Exodus, the Sabbath regulations are repeated twice, and the episode in between is the construction of the golden calf, the apostasy of the people of Israel. In Hebrews, the Sabbath is swept up into the new creation; creation restored, perfected, and redeemed.

Keeping that day holy—or as Chesterton calls it, "that holiday"—bears witness to the frailty of our existence and our dependency upon God. The recreation we enjoy on the Sabbath is more than entertainment—it is a time for us to be *re-created* through our worship of the one who made us.

Inasmuch as it is an act of worship and rest, the Sabbath also affirms that the permanence of our cultural labors cannot be brought about by our own efforts. Psalm 90, a psalm that starts by contrasting God's faithful permanence with our transience, exhorts us to "number our days" so that we can be wise in how we spend them. While the notion of our transience and mortality might undermine our work, the psalmist goes in the other direction, asking God to "establish the work of our hands." The Lord builds the house—and any other artifacts of our current world—with human hands. But unless he is present, "those who build it labor in vain" (Psalm 127).

Second, we deny our mortality and creaturely status when we refuse to sleep. Psalm 127 points out: "It is in vain that you rise up early and go late to rest, eating the bread of anxious toil." Our attempt to stay awake—when driven by anxious thoughts about work, consumption of entertainment, or the perversions of pornography—is a denial of the limits on our embodied lives.

In that sense, sleep approximates death. As John Paul II writes regarding Adam's sleep in the garden of Eden:

> Considering the specific language, first it must be recognized that in the Genesis account, that sleep in which man is immersed—thanks to God-Yahweh—in preparation for the new creative act, gives us food for thought. . . . Perhaps, therefore, the analogy of sleep indicates here not so much a passing from consciousness to subconciousness as a specific return to nonbeing (sleep contains an element of annihilation of man's conscious existence).[19]

Our sleep is a foreshadowing of death, a way in which we relinquish control of our bodies and our lives to God himself. Compared to our contemporary reticence about death, it is remarkable that children once grew up praying, "Now I lay me down to sleep, I pray the Lord my soul to keep. If I should die before I wake, I pray the Lord my soul to take." The prayer perfectly captures our dependency on God for life, a dependency that is hidden from view most of the day but is crystallized when we release ourselves to the unknowns of our dreams.

As Christians, sleep manifests our dependence on the power of God who calls being out of nonbeing. It is not simply an act we do for health benefits or to accomplish more, but is an affirmation of the providence of God, whose kindness and mercy govern our lives.

DEATH AND FORMATION OF THE COMMUNITY

In C. S. Lewis's prophetic novel *That Hideous Strength*, the physiology professor Filostrato asks, "What are the things that most offend the dignity of man?" The answer? "Birth, and breeding, and death."[20] Lewis isn't endorsing the view—quite the opposite, in fact. His basic critique is that these events offend precisely because the role of the body in our existence is never clearer than in them.

It is not surprising, then, given the fact that the body is ourself in our external, social dimension, that all three events are at the foundation of human communities. When a person dies, the community of those whose lives were intertwined is inherently changed, just as it is reconfigured when a new social unit is formed in marriage or a new member enters through birth. But there is also a historical dimension that marks the events as sacred moments. Babies make us look forward, death backward, and weddings in both directions.

As evangelicals, the rituals at the heart of our human communities have been deeply formed by our evangelistic sense. While the motivation is sound, the danger is that funerals and weddings are reduced to appeals to non-Christians to enter the community of faith rather than richly textured, uniquely human and gospel-centered responses to the sacred moments that bind communities together. We need to keep that evangelistic sense around, but our direct appeals to others should be the by-product of the ways in which we bear witness to the hope within us in our mourning and our celebration.

The funeral, in particular, is an opportunity to engage in communal remembering and storytelling. When we remember, we locate ourselves in a particular place in a story, which gives us perspective on our own situation and context. The "inside jokes" that mark the fellowship of friends do not depend on a snobbish desire to exclude, but on the fact that any group is formed by its memory of shared experiences, and the retelling of those experiences reinforces the group's identity and character.

But the process of mourning and remembering is also important to the community's life going forward. The body that loses an arm, a foot, or a fingernail has to adjust to a new reality by exploring the different possibilities and prospects in front of it. It cannot do this well without remembering where it came from and the way the arm or foot shaped its presence in the world. The body's sense of what is missing deeply affects its awareness of its new possibilities, or lack thereof.

This remembering is neither an act of tragic nihilism nor an attempt to create meaning where it does not exist. It is, instead, a sober act of faith, and therefore must also be a forward-looking act. When the gospel is at the heart of our communities, our memorializing takes its character not simply from our having lost the person, but from the deeper and more powerful fact that we will someday meet again. Our remembering is bound up in our anticipation and our trust. The thematic pair of Psalms 105 and 106 remind us of God's faithfulness and Israel's failure, and end with the cry of anticipation that God will save his people. Christ has died, Christ is risen, and Christ will come again. This is the lodestar for our Christian experience and the way our remembrance of the dead shapes our Christian community.

Christianity declares that the tragic intrusion of death on the goodness of creation is not the end of the story. The silence of death is but a pause in the symphony of our lives. We must "play the rests," as my piano teacher repeatedly reminded me. Within the dynamic power of the resurrection, death is not the end of the melody, but is swept up in a glorious concluding theme that begins with a trumpet call.

What's more, because we are historical creatures that are born, live, and die, our lives are shaped by those who go before us. The life of any local church is not only made up of those who happen to be walking around at the moment. That would entail, as G. K. Chesterton put it, the "tyranny of the living." Such a tyranny is rooted in a falsehood, for the space the people of God inhabit was built by those members who are no longer alive. The truism that our forgetfulness of the past dooms us to repeat it misses the deeper truth that we cannot understand ourselves without knowing where we came from.

This, of course, is a point in favor of listening to the traditions that shaped our communities, of giving ear to what Chesterton

The Mortal Body

famously dubbed "the democracy of the dead." Yet as Plato understood, any democracy can devolve into a tyranny, leaving behind an empty traditionalism that hands the pattern down without the reason for it. We need tradition without traditionalism, a memory of the past that appreciates what we have at hand while still reaching for the resources of the Christian experience throughout the centuries. Those who have gone before us have shaped the character of our world, as well as our Christian community. Ours is a unique period in human history, if only because every period of history is unique. But remembering the ways the gospel went forward throughout history can provide insight into the shape our lives should take now.

As evangelicals, then, it should trouble us if our only remembrance of the dead happens on Memorial Day, the secular holiday set aside to remember those who died while defending our country. While I wholeheartedly endorse the practice, it is not enough if we want to ensure that our communities are firmly rooted not only in Scripture, but in continuity with the church throughout history.

If we wish to deepen our sense of identity as the people of God, there are resources in the broader Christian tradition to draw from: the church calendar used by the Anglican church, for instance, memorializes certain saints throughout the year, providing opportunities for the church to tell the stories of the faithful departed and to reinterpret its own identity in the context of their lives and deaths. But we also have other resources in our own tradition. The times of sharing evidences of God's grace that I grew up with reinforced the perception that God was at work within our community. Broadening those stories to include the lives of those who have departed would reinforce the perception that God has been at work in our community, giving people a sense of his faithfulness in the past that deepens our hope for the future.

Most important, the central memorial service is the communion meal, where we are confronted by the death and resurrection of Jesus Christ, the good news of the gospel. This is the center of our identity as the church, for we are formed in response to Jesus' work. Whatever I have said above does not take precedence over this singular reality. But neither does understanding ourselves

173

primarily in light of the cross preclude remembering the dead. The stories of those who died are one way to imitate those who imitate Christ, who walk according to the pattern that we have in Paul, Epaphroditus, and Timothy.[21] It is a way of honoring those men and women whose lives have reflected the glory of Jesus Christ and of orienting our own lives and community around the cross because of their witness.[22] We are "surrounded by so great a cloud of witnesses," and the more we know their stories, the more we will look to Jesus, "the founder and perfecter of our faith."[23]

DEATH AND THE POST-DEATH BODY

The notion of "proper care" for the dead raises a host of questions about the possibility of Christian ethics having something to say about the matter. While Christian ethics is primarily a matter of how we treat living bodies, beneath our practices of caring for the dead stand presuppositions about the nature of the body, the bodily resurrection, and the body's relationship to the church.

As in other practices, we need to carefully deliberate about our rituals of caring for the dead, lest we adopt secular practices or simply affirm tradition without understanding the reasons behind it. Since the 1960s, cremation has exploded in America and no church tradition has been able to resist it. In 2010, nearly one-third of those who died were cremated, and within twenty years sociologists expect that number to reach 60 percent.[24] When surveyed, evangelical leaders were predominantly opposed to cremation, but even the president of the National Association of Evangelicals said, "Almost all those who responded to the survey indicated this is their preference and not a mandate. My guess is that cremation will increase in popularity and frequency among evangelicals along with the rest of American's population."[25]

Nearly everyone grants that Scripture does not directly address the question, but David Jones concludes, "While Scripture is silent on the specifics of how to treat the deceased, both the example of biblical characters and the general trajectory of related passages seem to be in a pro-burial direction."[26] That's a very judicious conclusion on the question. But while Jones mentions that Jesus' burial is ordained by God in Isaiah 53:9, he does not make much of it. It's worth suggesting that if our ethics is to be Christological—if we are to take the pattern for our embodied lives from the person and work of Jesus, specifically—then we should give more weight to the fact that Jesus was buried in trying to discern what the proper shape for the care of the dead is.

There may be certain situations where Christians might cremate their dead. But the notion that the body is the temple of the Holy Spirit makes it difficult to see why cremation should become commonplace within the biblical community. I am not Catholic, but their pastoral position on cremation seems right. The Catholic Church began permitting cremation in 1963, even though it "earnestly recommends" burial and suggests that cremation "does not enjoy the same value as burial of the body."[27]

Even if cremation is permissible, there are arguments for the practice that Christians should *not* make, as they rely on intuitions that are sub-Christian. For instance, the pragmatic argument that cremation saves money could be made against a host of church practices that are oriented toward shaping the community around the beauty of God. This pragmatism is often allied with the idea that it is the family (and their more limited resources) that is responsible for burying the dead, which undermines the reality that it is primarily as members of the church that we live and die.

The church and its practices do not exist in a vacuum. Our ceremonies and rituals are public acts and have meanings that we cannot ignore—and it is difficult to separate the meaning of cremation in America from its pragmatic and individualistic roots.[28] Cremation was initially introduced in ways that directly undermined traditional Christian orthodoxy, but in the 1960s it finally took hold by appealing to pragmatism and personal creativity. The customization (and commercialization) of urns undermined the rituals and practices that had shaped Americans' responses to death. Specialized urns are far more cost-effective than caskets, and with the emphasis on personal expression and individuality in the 1960s, the church lost her authority over funeral practices. The recent rise of green burials may be one way of preserving both the form and the meaning for

Christian burial, as it could potentially reduce the cost and preserve the theological significance of the act.

Because Christians believe the body is intrinsically good, we have historically been wary of cremation. The public act of burying our own communicates that the body's return to dust is the result of the inevitable decay that comes from living in a fallen world rather than from a technologically driven attempt to find a more sanitary way of disposing of the dead. While we don't entirely understand how bodies will be resurrected on the last day, that gap in our knowledge indicates that Christian burial is an act of faith. It cuts against our senses of pragmatism and individualism by affirming that our bodies—living or dead—are not our own to do with as we'd like, but rather are God's and are subject to the counsel of the church.

Perhaps more important, we need to keep in mind that our bodies are who we are in our external dimension, in our relationship to one another and to the world around us. Against this, cremation seems to say that the body is only a tool we use to communicate with others. If our bodies are who we are, then they deserve honor and care, for they will be raised up on the last day. It is hard to see how destroying the body through cremation honors it, as by doing so we intentionally contribute to its destruction.

There are certainly many issues more central to Christian ethics than cremation. Yet issues on the fringes of our thought are helpful for exposing the intuitions and assumptions that shape our everyday lives. Everyone knows that as Christians we need to get our approach to euthanasia and abortion right. But our philosophical attitudes on these issues are connected to those on cremation and burial, and an uncritical adoption of the world's response toward the body after death may signal that we are less consistent in our thinking than we should be. How we treat the dead reveals how we think about the living.

In that sense, evangelical ethics need to proceed beyond the explicit prohibitions and sanctions of Scripture to discern how the practices within Scripture and the person of Jesus Christ should shape our witness to the world. We should be wary of critiquing those who have escapist theologies that indicate that the world is going to burn while we drive Grandma down to the crematorium. Our practices need to conform to our theological anthropology, and if they do not, then we undermine the church's witness to the fullness of our faith.

DEATH AND PHYSICAL SUFFERING

My wife's uncle John has lived in almost unremitting physical pain for nearly seven years. He was bitten by an incredibly rare spider, Ctenus hibernalis, which destroyed his nerve endings and caused his muscles to seize up, making the normal activities of life impossible. John has become a testing ground for painkiller cocktails, most of which work for only a short time before his body develops immunity to them.

I think about John a lot. I first met him when my wife and I were dating and was astonished by his overwhelming cheerfulness, which has remained throughout his trials. He and I had similar aspirations and goals: He worked for Campus Crusade for Christ, reaching out to faculty members at secular universities and equipping them to do their work in a Christian manner. One of the first times we talked, he told me how fervently he and his wife had prayed for my wife when she was a child. He is one of those rare souls who can confess such a thing without a hint of pride, and without your ever doubting that he's telling the truth. He is truly an Alabaman in whom there is no guile (except, perhaps, his fervent love for Auburn).

John Myers has suffered unlike anyone I have ever met. In a world that prides itself on its ability to avoid physical pain, John has had no escape short of suicide or euthanasia—a suggestion that repels me even as I write it. Yet for people in John's situation, those are the options our culture has grown to accept. In our anesthetized world, where feeling good both physically and emotionally is what constitutes human flourishing, enduring unrelenting physical suffering like John's is incomprehensible. As John wrote to me:

> Dread of coming, or continual, pain will drive one to contemplate death as an escape. I contend that most people, if

they were honest, don't dread death nearly as much as they dread pain. We know what pain feels like; we don't know what death feels like, although we may have closely observed it. So we would choose death over horrific pain, the unknown over the known. Dread will drive us to contemplate ideas we never thought we would.[29]

I have never known the sort of pain John has lived with for seven years, but I think his suggestion that we think of death as an escape from pain is exactly right. That feeling of dread is sanctified by our Lord, who saw the agonies of the cross ahead and sweat tears of blood in anticipation: "Father, let this cup pass from me" (Matthew 26:39).

Yet Jesus did not succumb to dread, but willingly accepted the pain before him, placing our interests ahead of his own. His death and our identification with it is the treasure we have "in earthen vessels, that the excellence of the power may be of God and not of us" (2 Corinthians 4:7 NKJV). In the next breath, Paul catalogues the torments he has experienced—he has been "hard pressed on every side, yet not crushed . . . perplexed, but not in despair; persecuted, but not forsaken; struck down, but not destroyed." He and those with him were "carrying about in the body the dying of the Lord Jesus, that the life of Jesus also may be manifested in our body" (vv. 8–10).

For Paul, Jesus, and John Myers, the experience of physical pain did not prevent them from pursuing the welfare and interests of those around them. But it very well might have, as physical pain inherently focuses our attention on ourselves. Stub your toe on a door and your whole body might writhe, but your conscious awareness will inevitably be drawn to a very small but suddenly influential part of your body—and directed away from anyone else.

Yet the turn inward that accompanies pain isn't necessary. In the midst of excruciating suffering, Jesus turned his attention outward, directing it toward the Father and his neighbor. He did not ignore his own comfort or needs, acknowledging his thirst. But at the same time, his needs did not overwhelm him or cause him to ignore those around him.

When Christians suffer like Jesus, we resist the temptation to let the self-consciousness of pain consume us, and instead orient ourselves backward toward the cross, outward toward the needs of our neighbors, and forward toward the resurrection from the dead. We can only do this when empowered by the Holy Spirit, who conforms us to the pattern of Jesus' life, death, and resurrection . . . with one important difference. Whereas Jesus' suffering and death preceded his resurrection and opened the way for us to have the Holy Spirit, the Spirit's empowering presence in us precedes and enables our ability to "share [in] his sufferings" (Philippians 3:10). In other words, the order is reversed. We can carry our cross because we have the Spirit, suffering with the hope and joy of the resurrection only in the power of the one who made the way for us.

Physical pain isn't senseless, even though it may seem like it sometimes. Instead, it points to the brokenness of the world and to the goodness of a God whose power is revealed in our weakness. The agonizing suffering of people like John Myers is an unspeakable horror that is only understood in light of a more powerful grace. John would take physical healing if the Lord wanted it for him. And sometimes it's hard to see why the Lord hasn't given it to him. But John's life is a living indicator that the goodness of God is greater than all our immense sufferings. It is not our physical comfort that marks us as the people of God, but our union with the one who died on a cross and rose again the third day. When we see our Savior face-to-face, the sufferings and pains of this world—even those as heartrending as John's—will seem but a trivial and momentary sorrow in the face of an incomprehensible joy.

DRINKING DEATH LIKE WINE

At Justin Key's funeral, the same quote from G. K. Chesterton was read several times—and fittingly so. It was a favorite of Justin's, and it both encapsulated his life and gave us comfort and encouragement in his death:

> Courage is almost a contradiction in terms. It means a
> strong desire to live taking the form of a readiness to die. "He

that will lose his life, the same shall save it," is not a piece of mysticism for saints and heroes. It is a piece of everyday advice for sailors or mountaineers. It might be printed in an Alpine guide—or a drill-book. . . . He can only get away from death by continually stepping within an inch of it. A soldier, surrounded by enemies, if he is to cut his way out needs to combine a strong desire for living with a strange carelessness about dying. He must not merely cling to life, for then he will be a coward and will not escape. He must not merely wait for death, for then he will be a suicide and will not escape. He must seek his life in a spirit of furious indifference to it; he must desire life like water and yet drink death like wine. No philosopher, I fancy, has ever expressed this romantic riddle with adequate lucidity, and I certainly have not done so. But Christianity has done more: it has marked the limits of it in the awful graves of the suicide and the hero, showing the distance between him who dies for the sake of living and him who dies for the sake of dying.[30]

Though we live in the valley of the shadow of death, we shall fear no evil. Our warfare is not through anesthetizing every pain or technologically triumphing over our oldest, darkest foe. Rather, our victory is won for us in the person of Jesus Christ: "O death, where is your victory? O death, where is your sting?" (1 Corinthians 15:55). To die is gain, precisely because we will dwell with God himself until the end of all things, when the world and our bodies shall be restored to us.

As Christians, we have nothing to fear. The disintegration, the corruption, the instability that death works and that culminates in our departure from this world is not the deepest reality of the Christian life, even though the suffering and pain are extraordinarily difficult to live with. As a pastor once told me, all healing begins with pain. Even the needle to anesthetize the patient begins with a prick. Or as John put it, "Unless a grain of wheat falls into the earth and dies, it remains alone; but if it dies, it bears much fruit" (12:24). We can stare death squarely in the face without quavering, for the God whom we serve has defeated it in the person of Jesus Christ.

CHAPTER TEN

SPIRITUAL DISCIPLINES: THE BODY SHAPED BY GRACE AND GRATITUDE

When you look at her, she's dancing, even though she's made of stone.

My friend Abraham is a sculptor. But unlike many modern practitioners of his craft, he approaches his work old school, Michelangelo-style. Massive pieces of rock, hammers, chisels—all of it. My favorite piece is a flamenco dancer that he carved from a block of orange-colored marble. I'm no art critic, but the sense of movement in the stone is remarkable.

I was fortunate to be there before Abraham began carving the piece. We spent some time at his studio and I noticed the rock, which was tall and narrow. When I asked about his plans for it, he didn't hesitate: "It's a flamenco dancer." Just like Michelangelo, Abraham thinks of his work as chipping away what *isn't* there to let the form within the stone emerge.[1]

Sculpting is a long, laborious process. Between the stone's original shape and its final gracefulness as a flamenco dancer, Abraham spent hours knocking away bits of marble that a less artful eye would not have noticed. The subtle changes are hard to measure day-by-day, but set photos of the original stone next to the completed work, and the differences are remarkable.

Abraham doesn't use explosions or fireworks, and he's not shooting up balloons full of paint. His work is much more mundane in the most literal sense possible. *Mundane* is not "boring" or "trivial," but that which has to do with this world—*mundus* in Latin. He spends hours looking at a rock, and even more hours chinking away at it by hand.

Evangelical spirituality, which is shaped in response to the good news that our salvation has been purchased for us, is inescapably mundane. It takes our position in the world seriously, and the body as our connection with it. The body is both the place of our personal presence and the temple of the living God—it is the place we meet with him and he lives in and through us. Yet evangelical spirituality is also mundane in the more familiar sense—our transformation by the sculptor's hand is slow and frequently imperceptible to us on a day-to-day basis. The restoration of our "earthen vessels" tends to go much more slowly than we would like.

It's important to underscore that our transformation is not a technique. We do not sculpt ourselves into the image of Christ. The good news of the gospel sets us free from turning our sanctification into one more body project, like attaining tight abs, clear skin, or perfect SAT scores. It is not a task that we complete. The work of sanctification is not ours, but God's. He is the one who gives himself to us, and as we open ourselves to his presence the impurities that we mistakenly treat as essential to our humanity will fall away without our effort. "You were washed, you were sanctified, you were justified in the name of the Lord Jesus Christ and by the Spirit of our God" (1 Corinthians 6:11).

Our sanctification, our transformation into the image of Jesus Christ, is a response of gratitude to the good news that we have been forgiven. As Karl Barth said, "Gratitude is the creaturely counterpart to grace." Our gratitude, our worship, our adoration is precisely what marks us as people who are conscious of their dependency on the extraordinary mercy of God.

Our worship, our grateful response to the presence of God, doesn't only transform our relationship with God. It makes us agents of reconciliation and restoration within the world. As members of the body of Christ and members of each other, it is impossible to experience transformation within the body without a corresponding transformation of our social lives. The dignity of redeemed humanity is that God himself, the Holy Spirit, dwells within us and remakes us and our world according to his plan and purposes.

PRESENTING THE MEMBERS

In their journey from captivity in Egypt to the Promised Land, the people of God built the tabernacle, the place of worship where God would dwell among his people. The level of detail the author of Exodus conveys is extraordinary. It spans some fifteen chapters of Exodus and surrounds Israel's rejection of God in favor of the golden calf—an instance where the people of God clearly exchanged the Creator for the creation (Exodus 25–40). If nothing else, the author of Exodus's point is manifestly clear: God cares not only that his people worship him but how and where they worship him.

The New Testament stands within that tradition, adopting it and modifying it. On the one hand, Paul co-opts it for the church, suggesting that the Spirit indwells the church's social life and is the sinews, if you will, for the body of Christ.[2] On the other hand, he contends that the individual physical body is also the dwelling place for God—the sense in which I have predominately used it.[3] In this chapter, I will focus on the individual aspect, while saving the corporate dimension for the next chapter.

God's presence cannot be in us in any way that destroys the uniqueness of our personhood. Though he is certainly inside of us, the Holy Spirit is also *with* us, testifying with our spirit about our adoption into the life of God (Romans 8:16). We are not machines that he controls. Instead, the indwelling of the Spirit opens the possibility of a life that is patterned after Jesus' life. Ingolf Dalferth writes, "God's presence is not a contingent fact in [a believer's] life but . . . the absolute presupposition of their life." God's presence allows new possibilities, changing not just one aspect of our existence, but remolding every fiber and sinew of our being. Dalferth further says, "The sense of the presence of God . . . displaces or dislocates persons from their given ways of life and relates them in a new way to reality."[4]

In the previous chapter, I suggested that death is not only an event that happens at the end of our lives, but is a constant possibility that shapes our decisions and way of life. In the same way, the Holy Spirit's presence allows the power of the resurrection, which enables the possibility of new life, to establish a different form of life in us. We are to, in Wendell Berry's phrase, "practice resurrection." Eugene Peterson writes in his beautiful book by the same name, "The resurrection of Jesus establishes the conditions in which we live and mature in the Christian life and carry on this conversation: Jesus is alive and present."[5]

Practicing resurrection, though, means not only confessing sin and being reminded of our forgiveness, but cultivating the life we have in the Holy Spirit. The body's habits and dispositions, which have been trained by fallen people in a fallen world, need to be reformed according to the reality of our redemption in Christ. This, I think, is what Paul is getting at in Romans 6:8–14:

> Now if we have died with Christ, we believe that we will also live with him. We know that Christ, being raised from the dead, will never die again; death no longer has dominion over him. For the death he died he died to sin, once for all, but the life he lives he lives to God. *So you also must consider yourselves dead to sin and alive to God in Christ Jesus.* (emphasis added)

Paul goes on:

> Let not sin therefore reign in your mortal body, to make you obey its passions. Do not present your members to sin as instruments for unrighteousness, but present yourselves to God as those who have been brought from death to life, and your members to God as instruments for righteousness. For sin will have no dominion over you, since you are not under law but under grace.

The reality of our new life in Christ is already ours. Paul's exhortation is for us to practice the reality that the Spirit made present to us in salvation.

Paul suggests a twofold strategy for living in the power of the resurrection: On the one hand, we are to consider ourselves dead to sin, and on the other, alive to God. Our minds and hearts are to be reoriented toward our new identity. This means that the beliefs and attitudes that make up our body image need to be brought into conformity with the resurrection, as the pattern of self-loathing fueled by our inability to conform to the false standards of perfection in the world is replaced by the pattern of love that takes shape at the cross.

At the same time, Paul suggests that we are to present ourselves to God and the members—or parts—of our bodies to God as instruments of righteousness. The body's habits, its unreflective responses to the world, need to be reformed according to the gospel of grace. And our presentation of our body to God is essential to that reformation.

What does it mean to present our members to God? When I am conscious of my fingers, I become aware of the way the keyboard feels under them, the stiffness with which my joints move, and even how my ring feels on my finger. (Go ahead. Look at your hand, move your fingers.) When we present our members to God, we direct our awareness toward the parts of our body—our hands, our arms, our shoulders, our eyes—but in a particular way.

This awareness isn't simply to notice them, but to offer them before God. Part of what this means is telling ourselves (and being told by others) the gospel regarding the members of our physical body. Some of us may struggle with body image issues, and we do so regarding specific members. Part of our sanctification means presenting those parts to God and grounding our attitudes toward them in the forgiveness and power of the gospel.

This process of cultivating a holy attentiveness inevitably fragments our sense of the body into parts. Try directing all your awareness, for instance, to your hands while simultaneously keeping it on your toes.[6] It's almost impossible to do. Yet that fragmentation is precisely what has to happen if we wish to retrain the body's habits. The expert pianist can be wholly focused on the music and its performance. He doesn't need to attend to how his fingers are curved (though he might). But the beginner has to concentrate intensely on his fingers as he plays the scales. That process gives him a heightened awareness of his fingers, his relationship to them, and the possibilities and limitations they currently have.[7]

Presenting our members to God is at the heart of what it means to practice resurrection. To put it in practical terms, when Job says he "made a covenant with [his] eyes," he is expressing the very heart of what it means to present our members to God.[8] To make a covenant with your eyes is to cultivate a holy attentiveness in them—to bring them into the presence of God, to relinquish control of them, and to retrain them to look in ways that are shaped by purity of heart. In a practical sense that may mean no longer looking up every time a girl walks by or into a room—the subtle glance of the eyes that most fellows don't even realize they are doing. Our lips, our tongues, our hearts, our brains—these muscles and organs have been trained to be "slaves of sin," but have been set free by God and can become "slaves of righteousness."

One personal example: In recent months I've realized that my forehead, of all places, is a place where I am clinging to my own righteousness as I worry about the thoughts and ideas that are going into this book. I have literally had to relax my eyebrows and allow the blood to flow there as a way of relinquishing control and giving my head back to God. I have done this while praying and reading Scripture, and have asked God to make me aware of his presence in my life. The book is by no means perfect, but I have grown in the freedom of knowing that if I fail miserably, "my life is hidden in Christ with God."

This is not technique. It is not a task that we perform. Rather, it is opening our bodies and their members to the empowering presence of the Holy Spirit, the Lord and giver of life. Cultivating a holy attentiveness is an act of worship, an ordered response in gratitude for the grace of God in Jesus Christ. Paul writes in Romans 12:1, "I appeal to you therefore, brothers, by the mercies of God, to *present your bodies* as a living sacrifice, holy and acceptable to God, which is your spiritual worship" (emphasis added).

YOGA AND THE LIMITS OF PRACTICES

In chapter 3, I described the contemporary shift of attention away from doctrine toward practices. Part of what has led to the movement is a reaction against what many see as an overly cognitive and cerebral understanding of *belief* that is fundamentally a capitulation to modernism and individualism. In good theological hands, like those of James Smith in his book *Desiring the Kingdom,* the emphasis on church practices doesn't eliminate doctrinal claims, even while it attempts to position them within the church and her practices.

There's a real critique here that we should listen to. Getting the doctrinal propositions right is absolutely essential, I think, for faithfully expounding the contents of Scripture. Yet the word *belief* in Romans, for instance, is reliance on the power of God in Christ Jesus, which reforms human bodies and conforms them to his will and desires. It is a change in the mode of our whole lives, not just one aspect of them. When we have faith in the redemptive power of God in Jesus Christ, we are transferred by his grace from the kingdom of darkness to the kingdom of light. Right belief is not *less* than assenting to the propositions in Scripture as expressed in the creeds, but the faith that Paul talks about is something *more* than that assent. It is an affirmation that involves the entire person, body and soul. For the "righteous man lives"—which is to say, has *life*—"by faith."

The real question of practices is the criterion by which we determine their appropriate form. Do we use Scripture alone? Church tradition? Personal experience? Few things make me feel as alive as taking walks through the country on blustery days and feeling the wind blow through my hair. It fills me with gratitude for God's creation. But to equate my pleasure with the presence of the Holy Spirit potentially minimizes the uniquely transformative nature of God's salvific presence. My pleasure isn't wrong—it's the proper response to the goodness of God's creation. But it also doesn't necessarily mean I'm seeing Jesus or sensing his nearness at that moment.[9]

Few practices crystallize the difficulty of understanding precisely what orthopraxy should look like as yoga, which has become increasingly popular within Christianity in America. In his book *Church Re-Imagined,* emerging church leader Doug Pagitt describes the yoga sessions that his church, Solomon's Porch, hosts. He quotes one of their leaders about these yoga sessions: "This state of being is holy. It is at this time that we become closer to God, aware of our bodies, of the divine."[10]

On the other hand, Southern Baptist Albert Mohler has hard words for those who think practicing yoga is acceptable for Christians. In an article that made national news, Mohler writes:

> When Christians practice yoga, they must either deny the reality of what yoga represents or fail to see the contradictions between their Christian commitments and their embrace of yoga. The contradictions are not few, nor are they peripheral. The bare fact is that yoga is a spiritual discipline by which the adherent is trained to use the body as a vehicle for achieving consciousness of the divine. Christians are called to look to Christ for all that we need and to obey Christ through obeying his Word. We are not called to escape the consciousness of this world by achieving an elevated state of consciousness, but to follow Christ in the way of faithfulness.

Mohler suggests that the physical positions themselves are "not the main issue," but that they are "teaching postures with a spiritual purpose." They cannot be done, he claims, without "intense meditation."[11]

Like Mohler, I'm wary of the increasing acceptance of yoga (or, for that matter, massages, long walks in the park, sniffing flowers in the springtime, or whatever else happens to give us pseudo-religious experiences of pleasure) as a regular practice that we use to connect our bodies to God. The reality is that a sense of "the divine" is very different than a confrontation with God through his Holy Spirit. The possibility that someone might do yoga and feel the Holy Spirit's presence does not itself sanctify yoga as a means of grace.

At the same time, a lot hinges on Mohler's claim that the physical postures (which he grants are "not the main issue") cannot be separated from the New Age spirituality of yoga. While Mohler's original post claimed that the positions of yoga require "intense meditation," the more appropriate descriptor for many Christians might be "mental concentration"—the same sort of concentration that might be necessary for someone to train their fingers to play the *Moonlight Sonata*. In a follow-up post to his original essay, Mohler grants this and suggests that those who practice "yoga" in this way no longer call it yoga. As he writes:

> I have heard from a myriad of Christians who insist that their practice of yoga involves absolutely no meditation, no spiritual direction, no inward concentration, and no thought element. Well, if so, you are simply not practicing yoga. You may be twisting yourselves into pretzels or grasshoppers, but if there is no meditation or direction of consciousness, you are not practicing yoga; you are simply performing a physical exercise. Don't call it yoga.[12]

The question, it seems, is to what end the practices of yoga are being done. As manners of stretching the body for the sake of health, it's hard to see why they would be "unchristian"—any more than lifting weights would be "unchristian."[13]

There is, I think, some solid biblical justification for distinguishing those embodied practices that are oriented toward our physical health from those that are oriented toward "presenting our members to God as instruments of righteousness." Paul writes to Timothy: "Train yourself for godliness; for while bodily training is of some value, godliness is of value in every way, as it holds promise for the present life and also for the life to come."[14] Bodily health is not sufficient to reverse the power of death, and hence its value is inherently temporal. It is an unqualified good—but it is a good that is subordinate to pursuing the life that we will have in the next. Our pursuit of physical fitness needs to be kept in the context of the rest of our Christian life, with our primary focus being on the formation of our character (building discipline, diligence, self-control) rather than on the pursuit of physical health per se.[15]

Yoga also highlights one of the central problems I mentioned in chapter 3 regarding practices: There is an inherent ambiguity about what *practices* means. Two people can perform the same yoga pose, but to very different ends—and potentially with very different effects on their lives. One might empty himself and his mind and connect with the divine, while another might direct his consciousness toward stretching muscles he may not have felt in years. It's for this reason that orthopraxy requires orthodoxy. It is not simply the form of the practice that shapes Christian character—it is the understanding of it and the manner in which the form is practiced.[16]

The impulse to have a mundane spirituality is the right one. Like Brother Lawrence washing pots and pans to the glory of God, our sense of the presence of God is something we can cultivate throughout the rhythms of our normal lives. But the shape of the presence is specifically Christological—it means presenting our bodies to God as instruments of his righteousness. Any "incarnational spirituality" needs to remain tethered to the incarnation of Jesus Christ. But as Karl Barth pointed out, the New Testament rarely presents Jesus exercising, walking through the forest for fun, or doing most of the things we do in our daily lives. He writes:

> But the four Evangelists were not concerned about anything that this man may have been and done apart from His office as the Christ.... Even when they say of Him that He was hungry and thirsty, that he ate and drank, that He was tired and rested and slept, that He loved and sorrowed, was angry and even wept, they touch upon accompanying circumstances in which we cannot detect a personality with its characteristic concerns and inclinations and affections independently of its work.[17]

Barth's point is a helpful caution to ensure that we do not too quickly separate God's presence from the uniqueness of his work in drawing people to himself.

The fact that we don't see Jesus going to a yoga class doesn't mean it's wrong. But I think it does mean that we should be wary of doing it for the purposes of connecting with God. The cultivation of a holy attentiveness is a different sort of thing, I think, than what happens when people practice yoga for the sake of their health—a purpose that Paul says has "some value" but needs to be structured around the practices that train our bodies in righteousness. Treating yoga as a substitute to or supplement for those embodied spiritual practices we see in Scripture potentially undermines the uniqueness of Christian spirituality, which is oriented around the cross.

It's worth pointing out that awareness of the body is good, but it can easily lead to a sense of self-indulgence, wherein our happiness depends upon the particular feelings of our bodies, or a hyperactive desire to sculpt the body. Or it can become a means of manipulating others, as we become attuned to how our bodies affect the world. A holy attentiveness wherein we present the body as a "living sacrifice" and the members as "instruments of righteousness" has a defined shape—namely, a cross, wherein we give ourselves to others.[18] In that sense, when determining the shape of our spiritual practices—those done to become attentive to the presence of God—we should be wary of engaging in practices that we do not see in Scripture.

The calling of our lives as Christians is to discern the way the cross intersects with the fabric of our daily lives—and how it does not. A mundane spirituality is not oriented around the feelings of bodily health that we gain—though those are good—but around a life of self-giving to others, a life wherein our bodies become signs of the love of God in the world. God gives the pattern of worship in the temple, instructing the Israelites how to respond to him in gratitude for his merciful grace. In a similar way, we are called to "deny [our self] and take up [our] cross," to "share his sufferings, becoming like him in his death," in order that we too might attain to the resurrection from the dead.[19]

SCRIPTURE, FASTING, PRAYER, SILENCE, AND SOLITUDE

The spiritual disciplines are not techniques wherein we dominate our bodies with our wills. They are not tasks that we accomplish as a means of self-perfection or to maximize our experience of God. Rather, they are the God-ordained patterns of response to his presence in our lives, and are means of opening ourselves to his transformative power, which empowers us to live authentically Christian lives.

The body is a social reality, which means there is no such thing as a spiritual discipline that does not transform our relationships. When we present our bodies to God, we begin to discern the ways in which we have trained them to damage others. The more I attend to my facial muscles, the more I can see the ways my eyes, my lips, my forehead communicate stress, anger, judgment, or pride and how those expressions can distance others from me. In presenting ourselves to God, we allow his presence to empower the transformation of our habits, freeing us to express love to others as he loved us.

In what follows, I will examine several disciplines that (I think) are central to the pattern Jesus set for us and that will help us cultivate a holy attentiveness. My focus is not on the proper mechanics of these disciplines, but to establish how they are ways of "presenting the body" and our members to God. The following is by no means comprehensive, and I happily commend the work of Dallas Willard, Donald Whitney, and J.P. Moreland to you for more on the subject.

CONSUMING SCRIPTURE

It may seem odd to think of consuming Scripture as a practice in which we offer our bodies to God, but that is precisely what it is. The Word of God not only reorients our minds, it establishes new possibilities for our bodies to live in by drawing attention to those points where our embodied lives and the love of Jesus are not harmonized.

The life of the Holy Spirit is inextricable from the words of God. When Jesus is tempted by Satan to turn stones into bread, Jesus reminds him that "Man shall not live by bread alone, but by every word that comes from the mouth of God" (Matthew 4:4). Food is absolutely necessary for our continued bodily existence on the earth, but it is not all we need. If we do not consume the Word of God as Ezekiel consumed the scroll, then we will not know the power of the resurrection, which reverses the decay of death. The Word of God does not abolish biology, but reestablishes it on its proper foundation—our union with God himself. Deuteronomy 32:47 tells us the law of the Lord is "your very life, and by this word you shall live long in the land."

There are, of course, various ways of consuming the Word of God. For the earliest Christians, the Scriptures would have almost certainly been heard in community; there were few manuscripts, and some believers couldn't read, so the few copies of Scripture they had would have been read aloud. As manuscripts proliferated, more individuals had access to the Bible—but would still read it either aloud or mumbling the words to themselves. When Augustine visited Jerome, he was stunned to see him reading the Bible visually, moving only his eyes from word to word.

There's no reason to choose between these ways of reading Scripture. In fact, practicing all of them is a good way to hear Scripture anew. Each manner of consuming Scripture changes our bodily presence. For example, our ears have no built-in way of blocking sound. While we can avoid environments where the Word of God is proclaimed (e.g., by not attending church), when we are there, we cannot control how the words of Scripture enter us. We can only control whether or not we pay attention. In reading or speaking, though, we move muscles to take in the Scriptures' content. This different activity takes a different sort of discipline, requiring not only mental attention, but something physical as well.

The habits of our body enable—or hurt—our ability to consume Scripture. After spending large quantities of time on the Internet for the past five years, I find my eyes skimming over Scripture the way I would a blog post. They dart up and down the page, refusing to settle in and move slowly over the words. While I am able to get the broad movements of the text quickly, I find it harder to attend to the nuances of the words. While I think my heart is in the right place, the habits of my eyes are working against me.

As we cultivate a holy attentiveness to the Word and allow its language to work its way into the deep structures of our minds and hearts, we give the Holy Spirit resources to draw on to make our attentiveness holy, to reveal to us how our faces, our arms, our eyes, and the rest of our members are affecting others. Proverbs 20:27 says, "The spirit of man is the *lamp of the Lord*, searching all his innermost parts."[20] Scripture isn't simply one word among many—it is the fuel on which the fire of the Holy Spirit depends. It gives us the pattern of love and grace into which the Holy Spirit molds us.

FASTING

Abusus non tollit usum.

This phrase is one of those handy lines that every Christian should have in their readiness tool kit. Not only does it carry a decisive gravitas because it's Latin, it is also a helpful response to many of the most prevalent and popular criticisms of Christianity: the abuse does not invalidate the proper use. Because someone might hit another with a hammer isn't an argument against hammers, but an argument for their proper use. The wrong use of sex (or food, or money, etc.) doesn't mean that sex is bad, but that any good thing can be distorted.

Probably no discipline has been more abused throughout church history than fasting. This has led some people to be wary of asceticism—i.e., spiritual practices of self-denial—altogether. Even Paul levied his own caution against it:

> If with Christ you died to the elemental spirits of the world, why, as if you were still alive in the world, do you submit to regulations—"Do not handle, Do not taste, Do not touch" (referring to things that all perish as they are used)—according to human precepts and teachings? These have indeed an appearance of wisdom in promoting self-made religion and asceticism and severity to the body, but they are of no value in stopping the indulgence of the flesh.[21]

Paul's caution is against "self-made religion," an asceticism that puts on a good show of piety, even while it fails to accomplish what it sets out to do: "stopping the indulgence of the flesh." It is a technique, a way of fashioning the body and its desires through the brute exertion of the will rather than seeking to respond in gratitude to the gift of grace. It is the asceticism of Angelo from Shakespeare's *Measure for Measure.* He had destroyed all his sexual desires, which gave him the appearance of virtue—an appearance that manifested itself by his imposing a law punishing sexual infidelities with death. Yet when he is confronted by beauty, he finds his desires awakened and himself unable to restrain them.

Where asceticism has been turned into a technique for self-improvement, it has inevitably led to abuses. But *abusus non tollit usum*. Ascetical practices—chief among which is fasting—are ordered responses to God's movement in our world. In fasting, we turn our bodies toward God in response to his presence—a turning John Piper suggests deepens our "hunger for God."[22] In Scot McKnight's excellent book on fasting, he suggests that fasting is a "response to a grievous sacred moment" rather than something we do to "get something."[23]

Fasting is inseparable from our desire for God's presence, which means that one of its core dimensions is our awareness of his absence. In Matthew 19, Jesus indicates that when he departs, his disciples will fast—but as long as the bridegroom is around, the party is on. Most of the sacred moments McKnight points to—death, sin, fear, threats, needs, sickness—are manifestations of the brokenness of this world, brokenness that can only be finally healed when Christ himself returns.

Fasting orients us toward our eschatalogical life and brings it into our human bodies. In 1 Corinthians 6, Paul differentiates between the body's status in the resurrection and the stomach's. The body is for the Lord and the Lord for the body—and God will raise it up on the last day. But " 'Food is meant for the stomach and the stomach for food'—and God will destroy both." We are headed toward the "wedding feast of the Lamb," a metaphor that indicates that there will be food in heaven. But the body's dependency on the world's resources for its endurance and life will be severed, as the indwelling Holy Spirit will permanently animate us.[24]

The cultivation of our longing for God through fasting doesn't devalue food—rather, it properly places it within the structure of the kingdom of God. "Seek first the kingdom," Jesus tells us. But we need to be careful not to minimize what follows: "and all these things shall be added unto you" (Matthew 6:33 KJV). In fasting, we acknowledge that our fundamental relationship to creation is not one of dependency, but rather that creation is a gift from God himself that we have broken and depend upon him to restore.

Fasting, then, is an essential practice for the mature Christian—or for those who want to grow to maturity. In Matthew 9:15, Jesus says his disciples *will* eventually—not might, or should—fast. John Piper writes, "Fasting is a periodic—and sometimes decisive—declaration that we would rather feast at God's table in the kingdom of heaven than feed on the finest delicacies of this world."[25] It is the nonverbal expression of the psalmist's cry, "How long, O Lord, how long?" "Even so, come quickly Lord Jesus!"

Our fasting, then, is not a negation. It is not a denial of the world and its goodness, but an affirmation of our dependency upon God himself. As such, it is impossible to fast properly without prayer and reading of the Word. Fasting is feeding of a different sort—it is a radical commitment to the belief that God can reshape the material world according to his power. Not only does he keep us alive biologically for a season without food, but he gives us new life, the life of the resurrection.

Our feeding for a season on the Word of God and prayer is our presentation of the stomach as an "instrument of righteousness." When we do so, we realize how it has become an "instrument of unrighteousness." When I first fasted, I became irritable at the slightest inconvenience or disturbance. What I quickly realized was that I had buried my desire to control the world around me through my dependency on food. My love, joy, peace, patience, kindness, goodness, self-control—the fruit of the Spirit—were thwarted in me without access to three solid meals a day!

By reshaping our bodies, fasting reshapes our world. Most human community happens in the presence of food, and the decision to alter or forgo meals introduces new limitations and possibilities for relationships. In fact, because fasting establishes relationships on a different plane, Jesus warns us to do our fasting in secret. In the Sermon on the Mount, he says:

> And when you fast, do not look gloomy like the hypo-
> crites, for they disfigure their faces that their fasting may be
> seen by others. Truly, I say to you, they have received their

reward. But when you fast, anoint your head and wash your face, that your fasting may not be seen by others but by your Father who is in secret. And your Father who sees in secret will reward you.[26]

While it's easy to jump straight to the caution against hypocrisy here, I think understanding the nature of the stomach itself is crucial to appreciating Jesus' warning. Hunger has a tremendous power over us. We don't know whether most of our organs are functioning until something goes wrong. But the stomach is different. In order to fulfill its proper function, it needs our conscious attention. Unlike breathing, which generally happens (at least most of the time) without our being aware of our lungs, the grumbling of our stomach intrudes itself into our lives and demands our attention. For most of us, our stomach has mastered us—rather than the other way around. We meet the stomach's demands as soon as we can because for most of us our feelings of happiness depend upon whether our appetite has been sated.

Because we are so used to having full bellies, the loss of energy from fasting makes our faces difficult to control. When I fast, physiologically I have a more difficult time smiling and making my eyes bright—at least initially. When that happens, I am tempted to go about looking downcast. After all, my body has less energy than normal. But giving in to that temptation undermines the point of fasting—which is to orient ourselves around God. When we fast, we confess that it is God who is our salvation and not our food. In Psalm 42:5, David writes:

> Why are you cast down, O my soul,
> and why are you in turmoil within me?
> Hope in God; for I shall again praise him,
> my salvation and my God.

"My salvation" in this verse is literally "the salvation of my face." This is why the New American Standard Bible translates it "Hope in God, for I shall yet praise Him, The help of my countenance and my God." Fasting brings the salvation of God to our faces through the Holy Spirit's empowering presence. The temptation to disfigure them is a temptation to have the appearance of holiness, but not the substance—God himself.

Finally, fasting dethrones food from our lives as an idol. Paul writes to the Philippians:

> For many, of whom I have often told you and now tell you even with tears, walk as enemies of the cross of Christ. Their end is destruction, *their god is their belly*, and they glory in their shame, with minds set on earthly things. But our citizenship is in heaven, and from it we await a Savior, the Lord Jesus Christ, *who will transform our lowly body to be like his glorious body*, by the power that enables him even to subject all things to himself. (3:18–21, emphasis added)

The transformation of our bellies is at the heart of the transformation of our bodies, and when we submit our stomachs to God, we live by the same power that raised Jesus from the dead.

Two practical points: First, what I've written here is not a comprehensive "how to" guide to fasting. That's not my goal. And before you start, you should definitely check with a doctor, pastor, and spiritual mentor (and if the latter two have never fasted, you may want to find new ones). Second, fasting can actually be addictive. While it is a divinely ordered response to our sense of our dependence upon God's grace, there is an ever-present danger that our fasting might be reduced to a technique. For that reason, in my own life I have learned to structure my fasting around the church calendar. As evangelical Protestants, I realize talking about Lent, Advent, and other seasons makes some folks nervous. Yet they are there not to turn fasting into a law but to order and structure our corporate response to God's grace by conforming the pattern of our feasting and fasting to the life of Jesus. Our embodied experience of the Spirit needs direction, and the church calendar provides that.

The church calendar is also deeply countercultural. Our world has a neurotic relationship with food—we either binge and purge or maniacally count calories. The cycle of the church calendar undermines both tendencies, ordering our lives instead around the life of Jesus. We lay down some foods in penitential seasons and party like crazy during the feasting seasons. In patterning the seasons of our lives on the life of our Savior, we are constantly reminded of the brokenness of our world and the power of his redemption.

PRAYER

Prayer is not only an activity, it is a way of life.

Within evangelicalism, prayer is largely treated as a practice that happens in the morning or evening (or not at all) that is distinct from all other practices of the Christian life. While most evangelicals reject the formalized prayers of traditional denominations in favor of more (purportedly) spontaneous conversations, we inevitably find our own ways to structure our prayer times. Growing up, I was taught to model my prayers according to the rubric ACTS: adoration, confession, thanksgiving, supplication.

Ordered times of prayer are crucial practices for cultivating a holy attentiveness. Yet if prayer is what Christians think it is—namely, being brought into the presence of the Maker of the universe—then it is a practice that spills beyond our quiet times into the rest of our lives. Prayer is a posture of our whole person. Paul writes to the Thessalonians: "Rejoice always, pray without ceasing, give thanks in all circumstances; for this is the will of God in Christ Jesus for you."[27] Prayer is simply holy attentiveness, for in prayer we open ourselves to God to invade our space and our activity.

This is no argument against the concentrated, intentional practice of conversational prayer with which most of us are familiar. My goal instead is to narrow the gap between praying and doing. When we serve others, we make the love of Jesus on the cross visible. But if it is to be the love of Jesus that is made visible, then it needs to be shaped by the inner life we have with Christ—an inner life constituted by our holy attentiveness toward the world.

At the same time, the routine of a daily quiet time of prayer is like playing scales when learning to play piano. It is a concentrated time of practice that makes us more attuned to the dynamics of God's presence throughout the whole of our lives and worlds. The analogy breaks down, of course. Our prayers in our concentrated times are just as effective in the world as our "doing." In fact, the more we do the more we will find ourselves having times of prayer—and vice versa. We confront our need for God when we serve others, which can drive us to our knees. And our time there turns our hearts outward, shaping us into agents of reconciliation.

Because of the constant interchange between our concentrated times of prayer and our service in the world, our bodies need to play a central role in both. Consider Jesus' confrontation with the cross in the garden of Gethsemane. His time of prayer was a time of preparation, where he intentionally set aside his (perceived) well-being and opened himself to the will of the Father. And then throughout his trial and crucifixion, Jesus practiced what his time of prayer had prepared him for.

Jesus' submission in the garden was only possible because of his connection with the Holy Spirit, which enabled him to stay awake. When Peter, James, and John fall asleep, despite Jesus' requests that they stay awake, Jesus chastises them: "Watch and pray that you may not enter into temptation. The spirit indeed is willing, but the flesh is weak." His discipline over his body in his concentrated prayer time is a manifestation of the Spirit's power in his life, which enabled him to walk in the calling that had been prepared for him.

Our concentrated times of prayer will be enhanced if we practice praying with everything we have—body and soul. While there is a certain sort of intimacy to praying as we fall asleep in bed (akin to the apostle John's lying on Jesus' breast), if that becomes our practice, we will miss out cultivating the attentiveness essential for dwelling in the presence of God in every part of our lives. Lying facedown to pray penitently, standing with our arms raised high in worship, holding our hands open in a posture of acceptance—these are the postures we see in Scripture that help us open ourselves to God. In my own life, I have taken to kneeling as I pray in order to practice the posture to which Paul says every creature will eventually conform: "Therefore God has highly exalted [Jesus] and has bestowed on him the name that is above every name, so that at the name of Jesus every knee should bow, in heaven and on earth and under the earth."[28]

While times of attentive prayer, then, reshape the whole body, bringing our requests to God is also a function of presenting our tongues and lips to God. In one of the most challenging sections of Scripture, James writes:

> So also the tongue is a small member, yet it boasts of great things. How great a forest is set ablaze by such a small fire! And the tongue is a fire, a world of unrighteousness. The tongue is set among our members, staining the whole body, setting on fire the entire course of life, and set on fire by hell. For every kind of beast and bird, reptile and sea creature, can be tamed and has been tamed by mankind, but no human being can tame the tongue. It is a restless evil, full of deadly poison. With it we bless our Lord and Father, and with it we curse people who are made in the likeness of God.[29]

James' point is obvious: Even though the tongue is a smaller member (or part) of the physical body, its size belies its influence and stature. As Proverbs puts it, "Death and life are in the power of the tongue" (18:21). Presenting the tongue to God as an instrument of righteousness means conforming our speech to the speech of God, and this begins with a life of prayer.

This isn't simply a point about our vocabulary before God. Rather, our speech is a manifestation of our attentiveness—or lack thereof—to God and to the world around us. In a phrase that should make us all attentive to our habits and patterns of speech, Jesus promises: "On the day of judgment people will give account for every careless word they speak, for by your words you will be justified, and by your words you will be condemned."[30] It is the habitual, pre-reflective remarks we make that say more about our inner lives than those that are well planned. By becoming attentive to the tongue in and through prayer, we close the gap between the saving presence of God in our lives in the Holy Spirit and our practice and presence in the world.

There are many ways, of course, to become more attentive to our words when we pray. One of the most helpful in my life has been to quiet and compose myself before speaking to God. Even when praying before meals, I will often take a moment to pause and remind myself of God's nearness and the gravity of speaking with him.

Allow me to make one slightly contentious point: One of the cultural differences within the young evangelical world is that we are far more comfortable with profanity than our parents' generation. While it's easy to write this shift off as insignificant, Jesus' challenge regarding our speech makes it impossible. Without descending into the vagaries of word-level translations, we should step back and examine what exactly makes profanity *profane*. To *profane* something is to take what is properly a mystery and to place it in public for anyone to view. As a rule of thumb, you can measure what we culturally think of as sacred by charting what counts as profane.[31] And the death of profanity in our culture suggests that we have no more mysteries left—except within evangelicalism, where profanity is still treated with a wary eye. Christians who habitually use profanities should realize that even profane words lose their power if used too frequently (we would not be debating the meaning of *skubala* if Paul deployed it in every sentence). More important, profanity might represent conformity to patterns of speech that do not fit comfortably with the gospel. Language is inherently social—we pick up our accents and our vocabulary from the people around us. And the more we pray, the more our patterns of speech will both affirm what is good in the world while undermining ways of speaking that are not in line with Scripture.

Two practical points, then, about prayer: First, as prayer is a matter of retraining our lips, we need to learn how to pray in the ways God has set out for us. We are told not only that we should pray in Scripture—we are given the pattern as to how we should pray. The Lord's Prayer is a prayer that I think we would do well to say daily. But the textbook for prayer is the Psalms. Reading the Psalms as a regular part of our prayer life gives us language to use before God, retraining our lips according to the patterns of speech we have in them.

Second, God has the freedom to break forth into our lives in new and spontaneous ways through our prayers. And that's a good thing. But our openness to the power of God doesn't mean we should never repeat prayers that are in Scripture or that others have written. Just before teaching his disciples to pray the Lord's Prayer in Matthew 6, Jesus says, "And when you pray, do not heap up empty phrases as the Gentiles do, for they think that they will be heard for their many words. Do not be like them, for the Father knows what you need before you ask him." Yet the possibility of "empty phrases"—or as the King James puts it, "vain repetitions"—presupposes that there could be phrases and repetitions that are *not* empty. Many of our prayers—extemporaneous or otherwise—are grounded in an anxiety that we are not being heard, which manifests itself through repeating the same thing over and over.[32] Yet when we pray in faith that God is present, we can repeat phrases not out of a manipulative heart, but out of our gratitude to him and a desire to see him work in our lives.

One closing point about prayer: The evangelical tradition has emphasized prayer as a means of connecting us with the triune life of God, which is the right thing to emphasize.[33] Yet inasmuch as we are drawn into the inner life of God through prayer, we will also participate in his work to renew the cosmos. Our prayer doesn't just change us as individuals; it is at the heart of the advancement of the kingdom into the world around us. At the very heart of the book of Romans, Paul writes:

> For we know that the whole creation *has been groaning together in the pains of childbirth until now.* And not only the creation, but we ourselves, who have the firstfruits of the Spirit, *groan inwardly as we wait eagerly for adoption as sons,* the redemption of our bodies. For in this hope we were saved. Now hope that is seen is not hope. For who hopes for what he sees? But if we hope for what we do not see, we wait for it with patience.
>
> Likewise the Spirit helps us in our weakness. For we do not know what to pray for as we ought, but the Spirit himself intercedes *for us with groanings too deep for words.* And he who searches hearts knows what is the mind of the Spirit, because the Spirit intercedes for the saints according to the will of God. (8:22–27, emphasis mine)

Paul's understanding of creation locates humans at the center, just as Jesus does and Genesis does. It is we who have the firstfruits of the Spirit because of the resurrection of Jesus from the dead. Yet the groaning of the created order is a groaning—a deep yearning and longing—that we share *and that the Spirit shares with us.* When faced with the devastation that comes from living in a fallen world, the Spirit moves in us at a level that words cannot reach. Paul says in 2 Corinthians 5, "For while we are still in this tent, we groan, being burdened—not that we would be unclothed, but that we would be further clothed, so that what is mortal may be swallowed up by life. He who has prepared us for this very thing is God, who has given us the Spirit as a guarantee" (vv. 4–5).

When we enter into the presence of the Spirit in prayer, we reform not only our lips but the subterranean parts of our bodies. In short, we are moved to *com-passion,* a visceral, guttural response to the brokenness of the world that is joined together with an intense longing for "our adoption as sons, the redemption of our bodies." God will someday renew the whole creation, restoring peace and reestablishing harmony on the earth. But until he does, the first and primary work of the Christian is to participate with the creation's groaning in and through the holy attentiveness that is constituted by prayer.

SILENCE AND SOLITUDE

We live in a world where the possibility of an inner life has been undermined by the constant presence of cell phone rings, TV, the Internet, and the myriad electrical noises that make up our lives. For many of us, the possibility of becoming creators rather than strictly consumers has been undermined by our addiction to the inescapable noise—both visual and auditory—of our late-modern world.

Particular disciplines will take on a unique level of importance depending on the context in which the church lives. I have become convinced that in our culture silence and solitude—which are sometimes treated as separate disciplines—are essential for making visible the life of the Holy Spirit. There is an enormous cost to living in a world dominated by amusements. As a people, we are "distracted from distraction by distraction," in T. S. Eliot's words. But distractions are not only *mental* realities, but *physical* realities. A noise enters our heads by way of our ears, forcing us to choose whether to attend to it or not. A world of externals distracts us from the empty hollowness of our inner lives, warding off boredom at every turn.

Long before the Internet, the philosopher, mathematician, and theologian Blaise Pascal wrote, "I have often said that man's unhappiness springs from one thing alone, his incapacity to stay quietly in one room." He argues that the royalty of his day sought amusement and entertainment in order to be free from the burden of thinking about their mortality, their responsibilities, and the potential loss of their authority through rebellion. This is why, he says, "Imprisonment is such a horrific punishment. That is why the pleasure of being alone is incomprehensible."[34] For Pascal, there is a restlessness of the passions that is largely motivated by our ethic of avoiding loss and death. As he says later on, "It is easier to put up with death without thinking about it, than with the idea of death when there is no danger of it." Superficiality and shallowness are the result of leading lives where we never know silence or solitude.

Being alone forces us to recognize our own limitations and needs. When we are alone and still, we have no recourse but to confront the hollowness and emptiness of our inner lives. "It is not good that the man should be alone"—but it is good for the man *to know* that it is "not good for the man to be alone." For Adam, that knowledge came by way of his frustrated search for a mate among the animals. While it might seem like Adam's solitude was individualistic, it was actually *anti*-individualistic, for it made him conscious of the limitations of his creaturely status and his need to give himself to another in love. The irony of modern individualism is that its promise of independence has made us all incapable of being alone, for when we are alone we can't help but recognize how empty our lives are.

Solitude and silence establish community on its appropriate basis—as Jesus not only demonstrated in his life but also in his death. Teaching about solitude often points us to the times when Jesus isolated himself to pray, as in Luke 6:12. But we often neglect that in the movement from Good Friday to Easter, it is the silence of Saturday

205

that we call holy. There are no cries from the cross, nor is there the triumph of the resurrection. There is only waiting in hope, confusion, and—for us, though not for the original disciples—the anticipation that the Christ who lives will reshape our lives and our world.

Embracing solitude and silence is not a pietistic withdrawal from the world for the sake of our own personal feelings of well-being. Rather, it is detaching ourselves from the structures and systems that shape our daily lives so that we can reenter the world and participate in human community out of the transformative love of God. Dallas Willard writes, "The normal course of day-to-day human interactions locks us into patterns of feeling, thought, and action that are geared to a world set against God. Nothing but solitude can allow the development of a freedom from the ingrained behaviors that hinder our integration into God's order."[35] Our silence and solitude is one way in which we imitate the death of our Savior, fellowshipping with him in the silence and isolation of the grave so that we too can burst forth in glorious light, with abundant springs of joy and love flowing from the depths of our inner lives out into the world.

CONCLUSION

You are not your own. This is the good news of the gospel applied to human bodies. It is the source of our freedom and our power, for our transformation into the people of God is the work of God. "You were washed, you were sanctified, you were justified."[36] He is the one who sculpts us—it is only given to us to open ourselves to his life and his presence.

We live in a relationship of mutual self-giving with the Maker of the universe. He gave himself to and for us, and we give ourselves back to him. But the deep paradox of our lives and our sanctification is that our honor and glory consist in giving to God what is already his. We may ask God to take our lives—but the good news is that he already has in redeeming us on the cross. "You were bought with a price. So glorify God in your body."[37]

CHAPTER ELEVEN

THE BODY AND THE CHURCH

They had everything but the pyrotechnics—and they probably would have had those too, had not cooler heads prevailed.

I was visiting a high school group at a standard evangelical mega-church in Southern California. The students were pleasant and the leaders sincere, and having led worship for much of my life, I have no problem with energetic music and an aggressive bass. But I was stunned when they turned on the fog machine and the strobe lights to supplement worship. Outside of the words, the experience was virtually indistinguishable from a standard '90s rock concert.

In the past several years, the "worship wars" have become a permanent feature in the life of the church. The elder generation wants its hymns, while the younger generation wants its rock music. Or so it seems. The sides aren't always so clear cut. My wife and I visited one dying church shortly after moving to St. Louis that was totally convinced the way to reach kids was to turn up the volume and repeat the chorus one more time. But many younger evangelicals (and some mainstream Protestant youth as well) have reservations about entertainment-driven worship and are returning to the depth of hymns—even if we prefer them with a modern edge.[1]

I have no interest in reviving the worship wars, as I have always suspected that they rest on the sort of false dichotomies that make discussions heated and unproductive. But by this point, it should surprise no one that I am troubled by the lack of attention evangelical churches have given to the way the body shapes our corporate gatherings as the people of God. When young people leave the evangelical movement for Eastern Orthodoxy, Roman Catholicism, or high-church Anglicanism, they often emphasize the richly embodied nature of the worship.

Giving a full account of the church and its mission in the world is beyond both my skill set and the goal of this chapter. Instead, I want to focus on what happens when the church gathers corporately as the body of Christ to respond to the Word of God, and how the fact that our bodies are our personal presence in the world plays out in a corporate context.

The central challenge when it comes to Christian worship is that one man's *syncretism* is another man's *baptism*. What appears to one person as giving Christianity over to false ideologies may appear to someone else as the contextualization of Christianity to the culture around it. But before we get to that argument, it's important to unpack the ways a biblical anthropology might help pastors and theologians make their worship practices more faithful to Scripture. That may mean bad news for light shows, but so be it. Christians will never win the entertainment war anyway, so no church should pour the resources into crafting a "worship experience" that U2 puts into crafting their concerts. After all, we're not charging $95 a ticket.

EVANGELICAL FREEDOM AND STRUCTURED WORSHIP

Discussions about proper worship invariably are influenced by our wariness of legalism—and with good reason. God has harsh words for those who perform the visible actions of the faith without the interior life that comes from the empowering presence of God himself (Matthew 12:34–35). Paul writes to Timothy, "I desire then that in every place the men should pray, lifting holy hands without anger or quarreling." It's not simply the visible action God wants—it is the lifting of hands that are *sanctified*, presented to God as instruments of righteousness in grateful response to his mercy and forgiveness.[2]

The inner nature of the Christian life is made visible in and through the practices of the church. In other words, the good news of our salvation sets us free, but our freedom as Christians cannot be separated from our presence within the community of believers, the body of Christ of which we are members and which the Spirit knits together with "the bond of peace" (Ephesians 4:1–6). Our freedom as Christians is not for eating and drinking—or rock music or hymns—but righteousness, peace, and joy in the Holy Spirit.

The question of our communal response to God, then, is how we can preserve a form of Christian worship that is grounded in Scripture without falling into the life-denying, legalistic formalism that undermines our witness in the world. The only way to do that is to repeatedly reinforce in the form itself that our worship is a response to the gospel rather than a means of our salvation. It is because we have been washed, we have been sanctified, and we have been justified by Jesus Christ that we can respond to him in freedom in the ways God has established in Scripture, such as kneeling or lifting up our hands in praise.

Most evangelicals will happily affirm this. Yet many of us also add the corollary that the bodied response to God in corporate worship is fine as long as it happens spontaneously, as an overflow of a sense of the Spirit's presence in our midst. Kneeling or lifting our hands is great, provided we do not make them regular features of our Christian worship, lest we devolve into empty and inauthentic formalism.

Here's the problem: The danger of turning worship of the living God into theater isn't limited to any denomination. The evangelical liturgy—welcome, worship, announcements, worship, prayer, giving, reading, sermon, worship—has just as much room for becoming theater as the "highest" liturgical church. Mega-church corporate gatherings are always in danger of being reduced to professionalized productions, complete with stage directors, worship coordinators, and crying rooms so the babies don't mess things up. "Excellence" is reduced to a technique, as we carefully craft and control the "production" (which, alas, worship ends up being called). We are always in danger of industrializing the way we respond to the presence and power of God. In some ways, the multi-service structure of many churches (liturgical or otherwise) undermines *any* possibility of spontaneous movement by the Holy Spirit, especially when we have to end on schedule so the parking lots are opened up for the next round of attendees.

That's an overly cheeky way of putting a rather mild point: It isn't the form of worship that prevents formalism—it's the Spirit's presence in the people of God, and the Spirit's presence alone, that prevents a Christian form of worship from devolving into emptiness and vanity. The Holy Spirit animates the body of Christ and unites us with our Head. He opens our ears to hear the gospel and our hearts to receive it joyfully, and then moves our bodies as we respond in faithful obedience to him.

At the same time, as argued earlier, we make the world and then the world makes us. Our visible life doesn't simply express our inner life in ways that are random or arbitrary. Rather, our inner life takes shape within a context that establishes the plausible parameters for self-expression, and that directs our awareness without our realizing it. For American Presbyterians, dancing with joy isn't a plausible expression of their faith, regardless of their internal dispositions, while it may be par for the course in a charismatic church in Africa. But the nature of those formal expressions, which may be corporately determined, also provides grist for our interior lives with God. Kneeling in church and folding our hands on the rails provides an opportunity to be more attentive to God with our bodies than simply sitting and standing might, if only because we so rarely kneel throughout the week.

The forms that we enter into with our bodies, then, actually present the possibility of shaping the inner attitudes and dispositions that constitute our hearts. It is common within evangelicalism to affirm that the Holy Spirit changes people from the inside out—which is absolutely true. In one of the central teachings on transformation, Galatians 5, Paul differentiates the works of the flesh from the fruit of the Holy Spirit. It is the Spirit's indwelling presence that transforms us. But for the inner life of the plant to manifest itself in visible fruit, it needs cultivation and care. If the soil is poor, if the plant is not watered, if it never receives sunlight, healthy fruit will be more a dream than a reality. But all those are external to the plant itself and the life within it. We are also changed from the outside in.

The form of worship tills the soil of our hearts so that we can bear fruit for the kingdom. The form isn't sufficient—our hearts and minds need to be animated by the presence of the Holy Spirit. But it will help draw us into the depths of faith, pruning away our consumerism, our emotionalism (though *never* our emotions), and our individualism, and transforming our love and desire to seek God alone.

What's more, formal, corporate worship is how we respond to God as living sacrifices, which is why the repetitiveness of Christian worship does not undermine the possibility of spontaneity or prevent worship from being authentic. Those who practice basketball do so to prepare themselves for the spontaneous events and alterations that happen in a game, and they do so in a way that is conscious of their manner on the court, yet no one considers it "inauthentic." In the same way, practicing the presentation of our bodies as living sacrifices in a corporate context through raising hands, lifting our eyes to the heavens, kneeling, and reciting prayers simply trains us in our whole person, body and soul, to be oriented around the throne of grace.

This repetition within the life of the Spirit as a church does not mean that what we do always takes the same form. Think about when musicians repeat the chorus of a song: they drop an instrument, change keys, slow it down, or speed it up. The chorus is the same as before, except with a very different feeling. But even if it is the exact same musically, the fact that we are singing the chorus again—rather than a verse—changes our awareness of both the words and music. Same stuff, different experience—if only because we're hearing it a second time. The same goes for regular gatherings around Scripture: While the Word of the gospel never changes, the teaching of the church draws our attention to different features every week, even if the form of our response is static.

We should be open to the sort of charismatic, spontaneous movement of the Spirit that causes people to fall to their knees or faces in worship. But the church also has a freedom *as the church* to respond to God's working and presence in ways that individual members may not feel or discern. The practices of the church shape the body—both the body of Christ and the individual Christian body—in ways that we need to be sensitive to.

I'm not ready or qualified to suggest that evangelical churches should install kneelers, nor do I want to unpack every single practice that I think should show up in evangelical churches and how they might be found in Scripture. While I clearly think that saying things repetitively and doing things repetitively is at the heart of presenting our bodies to God and shaping our inner lives, the question of which form Christian worship should take is beyond the scope of this book. My claim is more limited: The form of corporate worship is inextricable from the formation of our inner lives and as such needs to be tied very closely and carefully to Scripture.[3]

MISSIONALITY AND PRAGMATISM

Over the past twenty years, the strong missionary impulse that lies near the heart of the evangelical tradition has been merged with our understanding of the church. While many of these developments have been exciting, they have also presented new challenges and exposed problematic areas of evangelical theology. In particular, they have highlighted how evangelical ecclesiology—our understanding of the church—has depended upon an over-spiritualized anthropology.

This is a generalization, of course, but one of the central features of traditional evangelical gatherings was the "altar call" (noting, of course, the absence of altars). This feature emphasized that the central role of the church was evangelizing the lost, and that it was primarily the pastor's job to do it. As a result, worship and discipleship—which are closely tied together—took a secondary role within the church's corporate gathering. The seeker-sensitive movement continued this tradition, even while it dropped the altar call and looked to frame the gospel in language that folks without prior exposure to Christianity could understand. What we now call the "missional movement" took it one step further by attempting to be the church not primarily in its corporate gathering, but in its diffusion throughout the local community as a way of drawing unbelievers into its life.

The missional model of the church is, in my mind, a good step forward, but churches that seek to incorporate it need to remember that the church has an inner life that is constituted by its worship of the true God—Father, Son, and Holy Spirit. In this way, it does not only act as the bearer of God's good news to the world but also as a model for the life that is to come, a life concentrated on the presence of God, to which we respond in worship. All the ministries of the church that are oriented toward the proclamation of the gospel to a dying world shall someday pass away, leaving the core of self-giving love that marks the presence of God among his people (1 Corinthians 13).

It is the presence of God that animates the church and sends it into the world. As the inner relations of love within the Trinity grounded and energized Jesus' mission in the world, so the inner relationships of love between the church and our Savior ground our mission in the world. Within the church, we know God and are known by God—and in that dynamic of love we are made ambassadors of the reconciliation Christ offers from the cross (2 Corinthians 5:20). The paradox of the church is that the more she focuses on her Head—the person of Jesus Christ—the more her body will conform to his love and pattern in the world and the more the Spirit of Jesus Christ will animate and unify all her members.

I think this missional impulse to participate in the life of the *God who sends* is exactly right. Yet when it neglects the body as our place of personal presence in the world, and when it takes its eyes off the God who died for us, then it devolves into a pragmatism that is more focused on increasing attendance than the work of discipleship. The danger of being inattentive to the body is that we allow the technology horse to pull the church worship cart. I am no Luddite—I have written on a blog for six years, happily check my iPhone "religiously," and even planned the first convention for Christian bloggers. The only reason you are reading this book is because the Internet exists. But the rapid adoption of online church within evangelicalism is a surrender to our culture's view of the body, which undermines the importance of our physical presence within our corporate response to God.

One of the most thorough arguments in favor of online church is Douglas Estes' *SimChurch,* which examines the phenomenon and why it is scripturally permissible.[4] I don't have space to address his whole book, but I read it looking for an answer to one question: Is *presence* possible without our bodies? For Estes, the answer is a definitive yes. His main point is to argue that associating our personal presence with the body is a result of being held captive to a "Western understanding of presence," which he—curiously—traces to Descartes.[5] In a footnote, Estes grants that the Bible never defines *presence.* Yet he argues that the concept of presence is so complex that the modern Western ideal that ties it to the body is insufficient.

I should note up front that I clearly don't think tying the concept of presence to our physical bodies is a result of some sort of "modern Western ideal." The divorce between the person and the body doesn't seem to be present in the original creation of Adam and Eve, as I've already argued. While I suspect the simplified "Jewish versus Greek" dichotomy that is currently popular is an oversimplification, there is nearly unanimous agreement among Old Testament scholars that the Jewish people primarily thought of the human person as essentially embodied.[6] Estes' description of the modern Western ideal may in fact be closer to the ancient Jewish mindset than he seems ready to grant.

Yet Estes is right that the biblical understanding of *presence* is extraordinarily complex—especially within the context of the indwelling presence of the Holy Spirit, which animates and unifies the body of Christ. There are two central passages that raise the possibility of our being "present" in a community even though our bodies are not there. In 1 Corinthians 5:3–5, Paul writes:

> For though absent in body, I am present in spirit; and as
> if present, I have already pronounced judgment on the one
> who did such a thing. When you are assembled in the name
> of the Lord Jesus and my spirit is present, with the power of
> our Lord Jesus, you are to deliver this man to Satan for the

destruction of the flesh, so that his spirit may be saved in the day of the Lord.

Second, Paul writes in Colossians 2:5: "For though I am absent in body, yet I am with you in spirit, rejoicing to see your good order and the firmness of your faith in Christ."

Paul's suggestion that he is with the churches "in spirit" means something more than that his thoughts or prayers are with the respective churches. Scholars generally think that Paul's "spiritual" presence at the churches is specifically a presence that he has by virtue of the mutually indwelling Holy Spirit. In Douglas Moo's phrase, Paul's presence with the Colossians "involves a profound sense of identity, based on and mediated by the Spirit of God."[7] But this sense of identity isn't the same as Paul's personal presence. As James Dunn points out, "In neither case is there any suggestion that the [spirit] is the real person, escaped from the body." Even though Paul is present to the churches, he is so only because the Holy Spirit dwells within his temple, making him a member of the body of Christ.

That's not a trivial point, as it suggests a distinction between various types of presence as a result of the indwelling presence of the Holy Spirit. While Paul can claim to be "present" in the Holy Spirit *to* those who are geographically distant, he also suggests there is a real difference in being bodily present with those who are geographically nearby. Consider the passages I mentioned before:

- For I long to see you, that I may impart to you some spiritual gift to strengthen you. (Romans 1:11)
- But since we were torn away from you, brothers, for a short time, in person not in heart, we endeavored the more eagerly and with great desire to see you face to face. (1 Thessalonians 2:17)
- We pray most earnestly night and day that we may see you face to face and supply what is lacking in your faith. (1 Thessalonians 3:10)

Clearly Paul believes being face-to-face is better. And the same is true of Jesus. While the Holy Spirit is the indwelling presence of God, fulfilling the promise that Jesus made in the Great Commission to be with us until the end of the age, Jesus' bodily presence—which we affirm shall come in glory to judge the living and the dead—is superior even to this. Paul writes, "For now we see in a mirror dimly, but then face to face." And John says, "For when we see him, we shall be like him, for we shall see him as he is."

Two points: First, our presence with other Christians is properly one in the Spirit rather than one mediated by technology. The common argument that Paul writes letters to the churches to proclaim the gospel needs to be set within the broader context of his union with them by virtue of the Spirit's working in their midst. Attempts to draw on accounts of presence that are not grounded in the life of the Spirit risk capitulating to the disembodying tendency of our day. Second, we should not let that understanding of the Holy Spirit overwhelm our understanding of what it means to be human by reducing the body to a tool to communicate. The presence we have with one another in the Spirit is real but incomplete. Treating it as sufficient for the "gathering" of believers undermines the reality of our redeemed, gathered, embodied life before the throne of God—which is precisely the reality to which the church must bear witness.[8]

Online church is the leading edge of evangelicalism's adoption of technology into its worship, but it is an extension of existing trains of thought rather than a creation *ex nihilo*. I think it is an interesting case largely because it highlights the assumptions about the body that have been at work within evangelicalism for some time and that are currently at work in many of the churches that deploy video sermons.

The use of video in the proclamation of the Word rests upon the assumption that the physical presence of the preacher is not necessary for the effective preaching of the gospel. While some who use video sermons have objected to online church in terms of worship and communion (Mark Driscoll, most famously), the grounds on which they do so seem to also undercut the use of video. If the Holy Spirit can use technology to overcome the preacher's bodily absence in proclaiming the Word, then surely he can overcome the congregation's bodily absence in hearing the Word *and* in the partaking of the sacraments.[9]

Video sermons open up two odd possibilities for preaching within the church. First, it means there is nothing preventing a church from adopting an "all-star" lineup of pastors. Why listen to only one celebrity preacher, when you could hear Mark Driscoll one week and John Piper the next? Minor theological differences aside—which could presumably be overcome—such a setup would doubtless draw a larger audience than small-town Pastor Joe. But it might also be the final blow in favor of a celebrity-minded, consumerist evangelicalism. Second, it means that pastors can live on indefinitely in the life of their churches—dying is no hindrance to continuing to play sermons from the archives, especially when pastors starting today will have forty or fifty years of video sermons that can be cycled through indefinitely.

I note these possibilities as "odd" because they are. I am skeptical that they will happen, but it seems the only rule in our technocratic era is that if it can be done, it will.[10] Without an anthropology that affirms not only the body's goodness but also the need for the body's presence within the communal life and corporate worship of the church, there is nothing to hold in check the anti-material thrust of modern technological development.

There are real downsides to the expansion of video venues. Evangelicalism has always had its celebrities, and always will. But never have those celebrities had such widespread dissemination of their content on such a regular basis. George Whitefield would preach to 30,000 people—but then he would go away, leaving behind local pastors to continue his work. Today, with the ease of access and prevalence of content, we border on the edge of cultivating a generation of Christians addicted to what we might call "pastoral porn." While listening to gospel preaching is a good thing, it establishes unrealistic expectations for preaching that have already made it difficult for pastors who are younger or from small towns. To pick a figure at random, I suspect Tim Keller became *Tim Keller* the way anyone gets good at anything—through practicing for hundreds of hours in front of a patient and loving audience. Who knows whether the next generation will have a similar tolerance level, especially if just down the road they're showing Tim Keller archived sermons every Sunday.

WHAT'S DIFFERENT ABOUT BODILY PRESENCE?

Growing up, I was the "overhead projector" boy for my church. In the pre-digital days, I would hold my hand on the transparency and slide it up the projector so people could read the words. The burden was a heavy one, as sometimes there would be multiple transparencies requiring some rather fast and fancy sliding action.

There's clearly a spectrum in terms of technology, and it's wrong to say that just because people adopt one technology they will adopt any technologies.[11] However, it is also wrong to suggest that simply because people want to draw a line in terms of the church's adoption of technologies they are "anti-technology." Not all technology is created equal or with the same values, and some technological developments may be more commensurate with a biblical anthropology than others.[12]

The apostle Paul wrote letters to the churches, a fact that is frequently deployed to justify video sermons. But there are significant differences between a letter and a video sermon. For one, Paul's letters were not "static." Unlike a video sermon, the contents and meaning of a letter change depending on who is reading it and what they are emphasizing. In that sense, the retrograde technology of letter writing would have been a benefit to a small startup church with a young leadership and mostly new believers. Paul's letters would have been read repeatedly within the small community, and the live performances would have helped the community grasp the various nuances and layers of the text. As a result, there is more depth to a letter that is read live by multiple people than to a video sermon that will never change.

Not only that, but as my friend and former professor John Mark Reynolds has pointed out, hearing a letter in community is very different from hearing it alone. In his typically amusing way, he gives this analogy: "Anyone who has attended a Star Trek or Star Wars film on opening day and then gone a few weeks later knows the difference between a piece of art viewed by cult followers and one viewed with casual fans. A film viewed alone is another thing altogether."[13] While online churches provide opportunities for discussion via text and video chat, hearing a sermon in a bedroom rather than seated with friends changes the nature of the experience.

Video sermons also undermine the possibility of spontaneous movements of the Holy Spirit within a congregation's corporate gathering. As any performer—musical or otherwise—knows, the reaction of a crowd has a profound effect on the performance. A tired crowd can make a performance drag, while performers will feed off an energetic crowd. Part of the drama of Christian preaching is that at any point tongues of fire might descend (metaphorically speaking) and the community will be lifted up through the preacher's word. When people are bodily present in preaching, there is a transaction that goes *two* ways. The congregation affects the preaching and vice versa. Because the transaction in video sermons is necessarily one-directional—even our prayers can't impact the preacher, since the sermon already happened—it removes this element of drama.

What's more, bodily presence is essential for authentic community to occur. Tony Steward, an advocate for church online and pastor at *lifechurch.tv*, has acknowledged the difficulties of discipleship in a "permission environment." As he puts it, "For us to be able to connect and reach out to people—and for them to connect with others—they have to give that permission; we can't control it."[14] This is one of the main ways in which technological communication differs from bodily presence. Any time we are bodily present somewhere, we reveal more than we consciously intend. The particular shape of my smile or the hunch of my shoulders can betray more anxiety or joy than I might want at any given moment. Wise, discerning people can detect that—and respond in the freedom of grace that does not wait for people to self-consciously give permission. Communities of care that are genuinely authentic do not wait for permission to get involved.

A GEOGRAPHICAL THEOLOGY

The church is not tied to geography. In John 4:20, Jesus meets a woman at a well whose understanding of God and religion is inextricable from her geography. When Jesus reveals that he knows her sins, she deflects by pointing out, "Our fathers worshiped on this mountain, but you [Jews] say that in Jerusalem is the place where people ought to worship." But Jesus undermines the ties between geography and religion by pointing out that the hour is coming, and is now here, "when the true worshipers will worship the Father in spirit and truth"—rather than at any particular mountain (vv. 22–23).

Such is the basic universal nature of Christianity. While Jesus became incarnate in a specific place and time, the gospel is for all places and all times. And as a people who have been brought together by the gospel, the church is a universal organism that knows no geographical, spatial, or even temporal boundaries.

The question, however, of our late-modern world is what form the invisible, universal church should take in our visible, particular world. The attractiveness of being online is that we can reach any people in any place and—thanks to asynchronicity—anytime. But *any* needs a qualifier depending on the type of media. Reaching people, for instance, with live HD-video streaming might limit our target audience to those wealthy enough to have broadband Internet, which leaves out the poor and homeless.

Additionally, it is easy to choose who we interact with online. Leaving a chat room is a lot easier and quicker than leaving a neighborhood. While we are called to "love our neighbors" regardless of where (or how) we interact with them, this freedom of choice radically reshapes the nature of how communities gather. While the promise of the Internet was that we could interact with people who disagreed with us, it has actually made us more likely to enter homogenous and self-selected cliques, potentially undermining the inclusiveness and catholocity of the church, which have always marked it.

Contrast that with the parable of the good Samaritan. As Jesus relates the incident, he makes a point to mention the coincidental nature of the event: "But a Samaritan, as he journeyed, came to where he was, and when he saw him, he had compassion."[15] In other words, he happened to be traveling one day and the need was thrust upon him. It was, in that sense, an accidental meeting in which the love of God was made manifest. As G. K. Chesterton once put a similar point, "The man who lives in a small community lives in a much larger world. He knows much more of the fierce varieties and uncompromising divergences of men. The reason is obvious. In a large community we can choose our companions. In a small community our companions are chosen for us."[16]

For many of us, "normal life" is increasingly happening online. As a practical matter, I could probably never leave my house again if I didn't want to. But if the church wants to be fully incarnational, to embrace the body with abandon in the way that Jesus did, then we should rethink the way our bodies tie us to the world and how our technologically mediated communities differ. While the church is universal, a church that is incarnational takes shape in the contingent, accidental relationships that arise as a result of our embodied lives, rather than those relationships that we choose based on our online interests.

The Spirit is certainly able to overcome the limits of our physical lives, just like he was able to make Paul "present" to the churches at Corinth and Colossae. But in our creation, fall, redemption, and resurrection, we see that human existence is embodied existence and that the Spirit works in and through the limits associated with human life.

The online church question is a sign of life and vitality in our movement, and an opportunity for greater clarity regarding our understanding of ministry. Just as the early church clarified their understanding of the deity of Christ in the years following the incarnation, and the Protestant church clarified their understanding of Scripture in the Reformation, so we are faced with an opportunity to articulate and clarify our anthropology, our understanding of what it means to be human. Evangelical inattention to the body has left it in a conundrum: Many evangelical churches and leaders are wary of online church, but we've been left without the resources to articulate why. My hope is to play a small role in helping pastors see how and why the body matters for the communal life of the church, even and especially in our corporate worship.[17]

THE COMMUNALLY SHAPED BODY

This section makes me nervous. When I originally conceived of this book, the question of sacraments was the one topic I thoroughly wished to avoid. What is happening in baptism and communion is an exceptionally complex question that requires biblical exegesis, systematic theology, church history, etc., etc. However, baptism and communion are also at the heart of the practices that the church enacts.

In the mainstream evangelical church I grew up in, communion was an important but occasional event, rather than a central moment in the church's life and corporate worship. On the first Sunday of every month, we would take the unleavened wafer and grape juice and remember the death of our Savior. My dad would often make a point of reminding people that there was nothing mystical or magical occurring at the communion table, but that we were gathered in remembrance of Jesus' death.

It's common among many younger evangelicals who have left this way of doing church for the "higher" traditions of Eastern Orthodoxy, Anglicanism, Roman Catholicism, etc., to suggest that understanding communion as "just a symbol" or "just a memorial ceremony" doesn't value the body appropriately. Yet the subtle addition of *just* or *only* inevitably devalues both signs and memory in an unhelpful way. While it's true that something more than a memorial may be going on when we take communion, there is evidence within Scripture to suggest that our contemporary understanding of memory is too centered on the brain and too individualistic. More often than not, it is particular smells, images, or feelings that bring memories to our minds and hearts. When my wife wears the perfume she wore at our wedding, it brings to mind my vision of her walking down the aisle. When the children of Israel crossed the Jordan River, they set up twelve stones as a symbol and memorial that would remind future generations of God's faithfulness (Joshua 4:1–7). Whatever else we think, we should be careful not to undermine the importance of memorials through the language of *just*.[18]

What's more, the central Old Testament word for *memory* can be translated *invoke*, a specifically priestly activity. When God tells

Moses that his name is "to be remembered through all generations" (Exodus 3:15), it could be just as easily translated "invoked through all generations." As Margaret Barker points out, the ambiguity means that if Jesus spoke Hebrew or Aramaic at the Last Supper, he could have also meant, "Do this as my invocation."[19]

The possibility of *invocation* being the correct interpretation raises an inevitable and tricky question of the nature of God's presence—or lack thereof—within the communion elements or ceremony. In short, are they sacraments—places where God gives himself to us in the person of Jesus Christ—or not? Are they, as they are frequently referred to, a "means of grace" where we get "food for the journey"?[20]

If it's possible to wade into these waters without drowning—and it may not be—here's the tentative claim I want to make: Those churches that affirm non-sacramental understandings of communion should still make it the center of their life as a church so that it is a regular part of weekly worship. God in Jesus Christ has set the pattern for our response to his work on the cross, and that pattern is the practice of drinking wine and eating bread within the community of the faithful. For those with a more Baptist theology, communion is still a "eucharist"—a thanksgiving—as it is the appropriate way in which our gratitude as the people of God for Christ's finished work takes shape in the world.

Repeating these practices every week is not the only thing we need for our transformation according to the life of God, but it does provide a context for the formation of "holy attentiveness." It allows participants to become aware of the presence of the Holy Spirit in their own lives and in the life of the community as the Spirit unites the people together in a relationship of love. In that sense, regular communion—even as "only" a memorial of the central event in human history and a proclamation of our distinct identity as the church—gives us the opportunity to increase our awareness of our union with Christ.

I would make a similar point about baptism, which Jesus clearly inaugurates as a necessary response to our salvation in Christ (Matthew 3:13–17). On this account, rather than being a means of God's dispensing his presence to us, baptism is a properly ordered response to the reality of God's regenerative activity that marks someone as a member of the people of God. In that sense, it functions as an identity marker for the community of faith and makes visible our entrance into the household of God. Baptism is not optional—the freedom of the Christian does not mean we can decide what form the Christian life takes. Instead, our freedom as Christians takes shape when we live in the pattern that Christ established for us and for the church, a pattern where we identify with him in his death through baptism as a celebration of our new life.

In that sense, there is nothing in the non-sacramental approaches to baptism and communion that devalues the body. If the gospel—the news that we are set free from our sins through the death and resurrection of Jesus—not only brings us into the Christian life but shapes the Christian's body and soul, then baptism and communion are normative for all Christians to pursue within the visible church.

THE BODY IN WORSHIP

Let's return to the youth group we started this chapter with. Smoke machines, thumping bass, choreographed lights—outside of the lyrics, and the absence of dancers, it was virtually indistinguishable from any rock concert. Our worship needs to be grounded not in preference or even our cultural context but in an anthropology that is informed and guided by the contents of Scripture. God cares about the form our lives take as much as he cares about the motivations by which we live out those forms, just as he cares about our bodies as much as our hearts within them.

Before I proceed, it's important for me to underscore that I have spent many nights working on this book listening to *Explosions in the Sky*, a fully instrumental band that provides much of the music for my favorite television show, *Friday Night Lights*. I think—*think*—I can get away with making the following argument without being called a fundamentalist. But I'll leave it to the reader to decide.

Music shapes the body. It's like an infection that gets into our muscles, the fibers of our hearts, and our neural pathways, affecting our outlook on life and impelling our bodies to move from within—which in my own case is for most people a rather regrettable

224

effect. Music—the sounds, not just the words—is so formative that there is even a subsection of therapy called "Music Therapy," and Colorado State University has established the "Neurologic Music Therapy Training Institute."[21]

Everyone is getting their kicks out of studying how music affects our emotions, our awareness, and our cognitive functioning. But the irony is that science is playing catch-up to a long, distinguished Christian tradition that has known that music is central to our embodied lives. In the twentieth century, both J. R. R. Tolkien and C. S. Lewis wrote stories that included deities singing creation into existence. Go behind them and eventually you'll find yourself somewhere back in the fifth century BC, reading from that proto-gnostic who ostensibly hates the body—Plato.[22] As the hymnist put it, "All nature sings, and round me rings the music of the spheres."[23] The cosmology undergirding the line has been discredited, but the musicality of creation has not.

Music moves us through time as a narrative moves us through a story. It is not a set of random notes on the page. In music, as opposed to noise, one note *leads to* the next. There is directedness to it, where the two notes are connected not just randomly but on purpose (even if that purpose is to confuse and create a sense of chaos). That purpose takes us somewhere, altering our emotions, affecting our heartbeat, giving us a sense of calm, or intensifying our anger.[24]

Yet the developments of music take time. Hearing one note may not alter your emotions (unless that note cuts through a cacophony, in which case it might bring a sense of calm). But hearing "Jesus Loves Me," a beautifully simple song with words that grow more profound the more we understand Scripture, might. As an overly simplistic rule of thumb, the more complex the music, the more delayed the emotional gratification will be. While "Jesus Loves Me" is relatively simple, the emotional payoff to "Be Thou My Vision" comes during the fourth time through the song, as the music builds on itself and the words grow to a climax. Complex music requires more patience to understand, appreciate, and enjoy, for it takes longer for the beauty to unfold—which is true of any musical genre, including rap, rock, or classical.

I am a huge fan of choruses. Such a big fan, in fact, that when I was a worship leader, I sometimes thought about leading a worship set with a single chorus all the way through, structuring it within different musical styles and locating it in the context of various biblical texts to deepen the community's understanding and appreciation of its content. But the danger of an exclusive diet of contemporary choruses is that they train us to pursue instant gratification by putting the emotional release on the bottom shelf. As Jeremy Begbie argues:

> It is worth noting in passing that much of the music currently employed in Christian worship deploys remarkably little in the way of delayed gratification. Admittedly, a congregation must be able to grasp quickly new hymns and songs if music is to enable and release their worship, but as I have argued elsewhere, rather too often goals are reached directly and predictably with a minimum of the kind of delay of which we have been speaking. Could we be witnessing here a musical articulation of the tendency in some quarters of the church to insist on immediate rewards and not to come to terms with the (potentially positive) realities of frustration and disappointment?[25]

Regardless of its merits—and I think *any* music has some merit—most of what we hear on the radio has been industrialized, designed to bring about a certain set of (pleasurable) emotions with very little effort or difficulty. When we feed ourselves on a steady diet of such music in the church, we shape our emotions to expect and want easy gratification. But as Begbie writes, "The Spirit enlarges us in the very waiting, within and through the apparently circuitous, mysterious and painful process of deferred fulfillment."[26]

I'm not arguing that we should replace our choruses with Bach cantatas. Balancing the tensions of cultural context, musical excellence, and theological fittingness—of both the words and the form—is a delicate art. But we should also be wary of the ways we have taken our musical cues from the concert arenas (while simultaneously decrying the derivative nature of Christian music), as the consumeristic nature of most industrialized music depends on an easy gratification of our desires. The body is shaped slowly over time, and learning to wait patiently before our longings are fulfilled is at the heart of what it means to lead Christian lives shaped by grace. When we ignore this in our musical form, we lean toward the easy manipulation of emotions through musical pyrotechnics.

A practical place to start, I think, would be to turn down the volume. I've dubbed the phenomenon "Anderson's Law": the volume of the worship band is inversely proportional to the volume and vitality of the congregational worship. As the band gets louder, the congregational singing gets quieter, and vice versa. Our singing is a part of our embodied response to God's grace as Christians. When the people of God enter Zion, it is with singing, as everlasting joy will crown our heads (Isaiah 51:11). But when we cannot hear each other singing together as the people of God lifting their collective voice in worship to the King, we individualize our faith, undermining our corporate witness as the body of Christ.

CONCLUSION

The body of the Christian belongs in the body of Christ. The reality of the hiddenness of our life in Christ is a social reality, for it knits our lives together with those who have been called out of the darkness into the kingdom of Christ's glorious light. The invisible working of the Spirit in us takes a visible form in the life of the church.

The church is the world where God makes us. The Spirit, the Lord and giver of life, has enabled us to walk according to the pattern we have in Christ out of gratitude for his death and resurrection. The humanity that God created in Adam and revealed to us in Jesus finds its completion and perfection in the communion of saints. Our sanctification as people who have been called into the life of Christ is impossible outside his body, where we are conformed to the pattern of his humanity that he laid down for us. As Paul writes in his magisterial letter to the Ephesians (which I have broken up for emphasis):

And he gave the apostles, the prophets, the evangelists, the shepherds and teachers, to equip the saints for the work of ministry, *for building up the body of Christ . . .*

Until we all attain to the unity of the faith and of the knowledge of the Son of God, *to mature manhood, to the measure of the stature of the fullness of Christ . . .*

So that *we may no longer be children,* tossed to and fro by the waves and carried about by every wind of doctrine, by human cunning, by craftiness in deceitful schemes . . .

Rather, speaking the truth in love, *we are to grow up* in every way into him who is the head, into Christ . . .

From whom the whole body, joined and held together by every joint with which it is equipped, when each part is working properly, makes the body grow so that it builds itself up in love. (4:11–16, emphasis added)

The breath of new life that will revive our faith is found within the people of God who are formed in response to the Word of God, Jesus Christ, the one who took on flesh for us.

SUMMING IT UP

The precious sons of Zion,
worth their weight in fine gold,
how they are regarded as earthen pots,
the work of a potter's hands!

These lines come from Lamentations 4:2, a book of the Bible that I cannot remember ever hearing a sermon on in my twenty-eight years within the evangelical world. Sin treats the precious as though it is worthless, disregarding the intrinsic value of the things around us in favor of our own projected fantasies and dreams.

The passage forms the backdrop for Paul's great inversion in 1 Corinthians. We are earthen vessels that are given the extraordinary privilege and honor of bearing the love of God himself in our eyes, our toes, and all the other members that make us up. That which has been regarded as worthless has become the temple. The body is a beautiful ruin, a tragic glory. It has been stained and broken by the burden of sin, but purchased by the death of Jesus and made new through the indwelling Holy Spirit.

The body is not a task to be completed but a gift that we receive from God himself. And we demonstrate our gratitude by giving it to others in the ways he has ordained. The restoration of our bodies, their redemption and sanctification, is not constituted by the assertion of our will but by the opening of our lives to the presence and power of God himself. Our final restoration will not be through medicine or makeup, but through the resurrection from the dead.

This is a story that affirms the world in all its goodness and glory. It is a story of the excellence of creation, the theater of God's glory, and the dignity of those who bear the image of the Maker of this world. The good news frees us from the monstrous burden of conforming to an impossible beauty, while enabling us to clothe ourselves in the joy and love that make us shine brighter than the stars in the heavens. The good news frees us from the burden of making ourselves by revealing that our lives are not our own; we are made by another for another. In the gospel we find both forgiveness of sins and the reality of our restoration.

But the fundamental *yes* of the promises of God stands with the *no* to our rebellion and sin, just as the same Jesus who affirms man's goodness judges the world ("the world is already judged," he says in John). As long as we have bodies, we will remain in the world. But our calling is to discern the ways in which the structures and institutions that make our world are set up against the knowledge of God. The cross is the shape of a life that is in the world, but not of it. And when we know the power of the resurrection, we shall find ourselves wanting to participate in the sufferings of Christ, to manifest the same love that he poured out for us to a world that is desperate for hope and joy.

We cannot breathe new life into a broken faith. It is not in our power, and it is better that way. We can only open ourselves to the power of God by responding to the work of his son Jesus Christ on our behalf, by cultivating a posture of gratitude and self-giving in response to his love. The power of our lives is not from ourselves, but from God. And the more we live in that power, the more we shall be transformed from glory into glory, from death into his glorious life.

Our Christian lives are barren because we have not cultivated the soil of the body. We have been given an extraordinary gift, one that opens us up to a world of superfluous joys and unimaginable pleasures. And when we realize the extraordinary love and favor that God has given to us in the body, we will want to give it away to those around us in the love of Christ.

> Lord, shall we not bring these gifts to your service?
> Shall we not bring to your service all our powers,
> For life, for dignity, grace and order,
> And intellectual pleasures of the senses?
> The Lord who created must wish us to create
> And employ our creation again in His service,
> Which is already His service in creating.
> For Man is joined in spirit and body,
> And therefore must serve as spirit and body.
> Visible and invisible, two worlds meet in Man;
> Visible and invisible must meet in His Temple;
> You must not deny the body.[1]

WHAT'S NEXT?

My hope in the preceding pages is to have provided something of a starting point for a life of pursuing the kingdom of God that takes seriously the human body as the place of our personal presence in the world.

I realize there are gaps in my presentation, and that you may be left with more questions than answers.

My prayer is that you will join the conversation, that you will pursue your questions and join me in striving to think more deeply about the shape our faith takes in our world. My dream is to see a generation of Christians who are passionately in love with Jesus, who are full of an irrepressible joy, who are committed to serving their neighbors and friends, and who are thinking deeply and hard about the reality of God's goodness to us.

To that end, I encourage you to visit my Web site, *MereOrthodoxy .com*, where I plan to continue writing about this. My e-mail address is also readily available there. Additionally, you can follow me on twitter at *twitter.com/mattleeanderson* or on Facebook at *facebook.com/ matthewleeanderson*.

I look forward to hearing from you.

NOTES

PREFACE: IN WHICH I CLEAR MY THROAT

1. G. K. Chesterton, *Orthodoxy* (New York: Doubleday, 1959, original edition, Dodd & Mead, 1908).
2. Bradley R. E. Wright, *Christians Are Hate-Filled Hypocrites... and Other Lies You've Been Told* (Bethany House) is an interesting counter to the popular narrative.
3. John Keble (Anglican theologian and poet), *The Christian Year,* a collection of hymns and poetry, published in1827.

CHAPTER 1: EARTHEN VESSELS

1. G. K. Chesterton, *Orthodoxy.*
2. Adolph Saphir, *"Mighty in the Scriptures": A Memoir by Adolph Saphir* (London: Shaw and Company, 1893), 350.
3. Daniel Bell, *The Cultural Contradictions of Capitalism* (New York: Basic Books, 1976), 51.
4. See Joan Jacobs Brumberg, *The Body Project* (New York: Vintage Books, 1998).
5. Chris Shilling, *The Body and Social Theory* (London: Sage Publications, 1993), 200.
6. Oliver O'Donovan, *Begotten or Made* (New York: Oxford University Press, 1984), 2. Emphasis mine.
7. Susan Bordo, *Unbearable Weight: Feminism, Western Culture, and the Body* (Berkeley: University of California Press, 1993), 246.
8. Kevin Vanhoozer, *The Drama of Doctrine* (Louisville, KY: Westminster John Knox Press, 2005), 17.
9. See Fred Sanders as well: "The good news that Jesus brings is that God has chosen to accomplish our salvation by being himself for us, by opening up his own life and bringing us into fellowship." Fred Sanders, *The Deep Things of God: How the Trinity Changes Everything* (Wheaton, IL: Crossway Books, 2010), 120. Peter Leithart also takes a similar line in *The Baptized Body* (Moscow, ID: Canon Press, 2007).
10. John 13:35.
11. Oliver O'Donovan, *Resurrection and Moral Order* (Grand Rapids, MI: Eerdmans, 1986), 12.

12. See John Calvin, *Institutes of the Christian Religion*, ed. John T. McNeill, trans. Ford Lewis Battles (Philadelphia: Westminster Press, 1960), III, 1.

13. O'Donovan: "We speak of two *aspects* of the Spirit's work, not two works," *Resurrection and Moral Order*, 104.

14. Christian Smith and Melinda Denton, *Soul Searching* (Oxford: Oxford University Press, 2005), 163–164.

15. O'Donovan's *Resurrection and Moral Order* is the key text here.

16. For Augustine, freedom is inextricable from having properly ordered loves— which are conformed to the order that exists in creation. Among the many places where he unpacks this idea, see *City of God*, 19.14.

17. O'Donovan, *Resurrection and Moral Order*, 25. Emphasis mine.

18. There's more to be said here, of course. In moral deliberation, I affirm something like a medieval fourfold category: the genus of the act (whether it is a properly human action), the act itself, the circumstances, the intention of the agent.

19. This is, of course, in contrast to those like Stanley Hauerwas who treat church practices as determinative of our theology. Practices are important for our formation as Christians, but I think they come somewhere downstream from Scripture.

20. I should note that this does *not* mean that disabilities are necessarily the result of sin.

21. 2 Corinthians 4:7; Philippians 3:21.

22. Matthew 6:25; 4:4.

23. Romans 14:17 NIV.

24. Dallas Willard, *The Spirit of the Disciplines* (San Francisco: HarperCollins, 1988), 67.

25. Katechismus Heidelberd, *The Heidelberg Catechism with Scripture Texts* (Grand Rapids: CRC Publications, 1989), 9.

26. "O Worship the King," Robert Grant. Public domain.

CHAPTER 2: EVANGELICAL INATTENTION AND THE SECULAR BODY

1. Precious Moments History, accessed March 8, 2011: *www.associatepublisher.com/e/p/pr/precious_moments.htm*

2. This is similar to a point that Michael Horton makes in "Precious Moments in American Religion," *Issues, Etc.*, accessed on March 8, 2011, at: *www.mtio.com/articles/bissar116.htm*

3. Chene Heady, "Childish Things," *Touchstone Magazine*, December 2001.

4. See Michael Horton, "Gnostic Worship" in *Modern Reformation* (July/August, vol. 4, 1995):13–21. See *www.modernreformation.org/default.php?page=articledisplay&var1=ArtRead&var2=696&var3=main*.

5. In a footnote, Gregg Allison points to Plato as the problem, as do most critics of evangelicalism. However, no one has yet explained which evangelicals read Plato or how his thought was channeled into evangelicalism. I suspect if they had, they (like Augustine) might affirm the resurrection of the body loudly and unequivocally. See Gregg Allison, "Toward a Theology of Human Embodiment," *Southern Baptist Journal of Theology*, 13/2 (Summer 2009).

6. N. T. Wright, *Surprised by Hope* (New York: HarperCollins, 2008).

7. Brian McLaren, *A New Kind of Christian: A Tale of Two Friends on a Spiritual Journey*, 1st ed. (San Francisco: Jossey-Bass, 2001), 102. Emphasis mine.

8. David Van Drunen doesn't mention the body *per se*, but points out similarities between the four camps with respect to their understanding of culture. See the introduction to *Living in God's Two Kingdoms: a Biblical Vision for Christianity and Culture* (Wheaton, IL: Crossway, 2010).

9. As evangelicalism grew up in America during the period we knew as Victorian, it's easy to simply sneer at their prudish Victorian values and assume that they must have hated sex and the body. The only problem with that is that it probably happens to be false. Victorian women seem to have "had—and enjoyed—sex." See Kara Platoni, "The Sex Scholar," *Stanford Magazine*, accessed March 8, 2011, at: *www.stanfordalumni.org/news/magazine/2010/marapr/features/mosher.html*.

10. Paul Moody and Arthur P. Fitt, *The Shorter Life of D. L. Moody* (Chicago: Bible Institute Colportage Association, 1900), 9. The language of "house" here is a direct echo of Paul in 2 Corinthians 5:1.

11. Dwight L. Moody, *The Gospel Awakening* (Chicago: Revell, 1883), 646.

12. Billy Graham, "The Promise of Heaven," accessed March 8, 2011 at: *http://newsweek.washingtonpost.com/onfaith/guestvoices/2010/03/the_promise_of_heaven.html*

13. See John Wesley, *Primative Physick* (London: 1875).

14. See Clifford Putney, *Muscular Christianity: Manhood and Sports in Protestant America, 1880–1920* (Cambridge, MA: Harvard University Press, 2001).

15. This is obviously a contentious point. But I could find very little careful readings of primary sources on the question of the body. Perhaps an enterprising historian will take up the task.

16. Jean-Paul Sartre, *Being and Nothingness*, trans. Hazel Barnes (New York: Philosophical Library, 1956), 302.

17. See *The Phenomenology of Perception*, for instance. It is no surprise that the leading evangelical thinker on the body's role in spirituality, Dallas Willard, is the leading expert on this tradition of thought. Maurice Merleau-Ponty, *Phenomenology of Perception*, trans. Colin Smith (London: Routledge, 1962).

18. I realize that my reduction of a massive movement to bumper-sticker-style formulations will be deeply unsatisfying, a response which I understand. However, full books have been written about the postmodern world—and this is not one of them. Instead, I would commend James K. A. Smith, *Who's Afraid of Postmodernism?* and Peter J. Leithart, *Solomon Among the Postmoderns*. Both are worth your time.

19. Sarah Coakley, *Powers and Submissions: Spirituality, Philosophy, and Gender* (Oxford, UK: Blackwell Publishers Ltd, 2002), 154–155.

20. One such problematic statement comes from Lisa Isherwood, who remarks that the incarnation she takes very seriously is not "the once and for all Son of God who saved the world through his death but rather the glorious abandonment of the divine into flesh and the passionate dance of the human/divine that ensues." See her essay "F***ing Straight and the Gospel of Radical Equality" in *The Sexual Theologian: Essays on Sex, God, and Politics*, ed. Marcella Althus-Reid (London: T & T Clark International, 2004), 49.

21. See also Stephanie Paulsell, *Honoring the Body: Meditations on a Christian Practice*

(San Francisco: Jossey-Bass, 2002), and Lilian Calles Barger, *Eve's Revenge* (Grand Rapids, MI: Brazos Press, 2003).

22. One helpful exception here is Daniel Heimbach's essay "The Unchangeable Difference: Eternally Fixed Sexual Identity for an Age of Plastic Sexuality" in *Biblical Foundations for Manhood and Womanhood,* Wayne Grudem, ed. (Wheaton, IL: Crossway Books, 2002). Perusing the *Council for Biblical Manhood and Womanhood's* journal over the past decade, many of the contributions are about sexual complementarity—but few seem to go directly into the question of what the body is and why it matters.

23. For this story, see Paul Spears and Steven Loomis, *Education for Human Flourishing* (Downers Grove, IL: InterVarsity Press, 2009).

24. See, among others, William Lane Craig and J.P. Moreland, *Naturalism: A Critical Analysis* (New York: Routledge, 2000).

25. This is most definitely *not* true of J.P. Moreland, whose devotional writings about the body I will draw on later.

26. The lone voice in the wilderness on the relationship has been Glenn Stanton of Focus on the Family. See his pamphlet *A Christian Response to the Sexual Revolution: Discovering the Theology of the Body* (Westchester, PA: Ascension Press, 2010).

27. Dr. Craig Carter, "The Theology of the Body #1," accessed March 8, 2011, at: *http://politicsofthecrossresurrected.blogspot.com/2010/01/theology-of-body-1-teaching-john-paul.html.*

28. Dallas Willard, *Renovation of the Heart* (Colorado Springs: NavPress, 2002), 159.

29. Doug Pagitt, *Reimagining Spiritual Formation: A Week in the Life of an Experimental Church* (Grand Rapids, MI: Zondervan, 2004), 77.

30. See Doug Pagitt and Kathryn Prill, *BodyPrayer: The Posture of Intimacy with God,* 1st ed. (Colorado Springs: WaterBrook Press, 2005).

31. Tony Jones, *The New Christians: Dispatches From the Emergent Frontier,* 1st ed. (San Francisco, Jossey-Bass, 2008), 105.

32. I'm grateful to Matt Jenson for pointing me to Nicholas Healy's article "Practices and the New Ecclesiology: Misplaced Concreteness?" from the *International Journal of Systematic Theology,* 5–3, 2003. He writes, "Diverse intentions and construals alter the action, yet the behavior—the 'practice'—in all these varied cases may well be the same. Within any given congregation, the practice may be performed 'properly' by only a small minority," 295.

33. This critique is made by Reinhard Hutter, "The Christian Life" in *Oxford Handbook of Systematic Theology,* John Webster, Kathryn Tanner, Iain Torrance, eds. (Oxford: Oxford University Press, 2009).

34. If we did, we would reject them and change would be much easier.

35. James K. A. Smith, *Desiring the Kingdom: Worship, Worldview, and Cultural Formation* (Grand Rapids, MI: Baker Academic, 2009), 25. While I agree with him that practices form us, I'm less convinced by Smith's method of deriving our theology from those practices.

36. Two clarifications: (1) our practices as Christians are crucial to our formation but are not a source for our theology, and (2) if the embodied cognition folks are correct, then the contents of "thought" are inextricable from the body and its habits.

37. Sanders, *The Deep Things of God,* 19.

CHAPTER 3: WHAT IS THE BODY?

1. Jim Anderson, "Remembering Grandpa," accessed March 8, 2011, at: *http://decorabilia.blogspot.com/2005/06/remembering-grandpa.html*.

2. For the masochists among us, Isaac Asimov, "Rain, Rain, Go Away," accessed on March 8, 2011, at: *www.kirkwood.k12.mo.us/parent_student/nm/renzali/Rain,%2Rain%20Go%20Away%20Text.pdf*.

3. See his dialogue, *Phaedo*, which is the most critical of the body among Plato's writings. But it needs to be balanced with the *Phaedrus, Symposium,* and the *Timaeus*, where Plato's accounts of the material world are far more sensitive (and more positive). John Mark Reynolds' generous treatment in *When Athens Met Jerusalem* (Downers Grove, IL: InterVarsity Press, 2009) deserves a much broader hearing.

4. See, for instance, *Confessions* Book 7, or *City of God* Book 12.

5. See, for instance, *Institutes* III.9.4.

6. See his *Meditations on First Philosophy.* The notion of the *res extensa* comes from the second meditation, but it's worth pointing out that Descartes seems to give the body a more prominent place in the sixth meditation. Though he is "nothing but a thinking thing," he is "very closely joined and, as it were, intermingled with [the body], so that I and the body form a unit."

7. That would be Gilbert Ryle and a legion of adopters.

8. Noam Chomsky, *On Nature and Language* (Cambridge, UK: Cambridge University Press, 2002), 52.

9. Hans Jonas, *The Phenomenon of Life: Toward a Philosophical Biology* (New York: Harper & Row, 1966), 10.

10. I owe this point to Isaac Wiegman.

11. O'Donovan, *Begotten or Made,* 63. O'Donovan goes on to object to the dubious status of embryos in our culture, suggesting that our desire to experiment on them takes place in the context of this program of self-transcendence, where we make ourselves the objects of inquiry.

12. Ibid., 62. See also my discussion of *technique* in chapter 1.

13. Shaun Gallagher's notion of "body schema" is primarily what I have in mind here. See his *How the Body Shapes the Mind* (New York: Oxford University Press, 2005), 73.

14. There are resources, of course, within the phenomenological tradition of philosophy for such a conception, especially the work of Merleau-Ponty. See also the work of Brent Waters, who seems to be overcoming this divide in interesting ways.

15. Alasdair MacIntyre, "What Is the Body?" *Selected Essays* (Cambridge, UK: Cambridge University Press, 2006), 102–103.

16. This would be, I think, J.P. Moreland and Scott Rae's position. See their book, *Body and Soul* (Downers Grove, IL: InterVarsity Press, 2000).

17. See Nancey Murphy, *Bodies and Souls, or Spirited Bodies?* (Cambridge, UK: Cambridge University Press, 2006), 70. As best I can tell, the central divide comes down to this: Moreland affirms the existence of the substantial soul as a means of explaining the human person's higher functions of rationality, intentionality, self-direction, etc. Nancey Murphy deploys something approaching systems theory to argue that non-substantial arrangements of material things can have "top-down causation." For Murphy, full explanation

of these capabilities requires "attention to human social relations, to cultural factors, and, most importantly, to our relationship with God."

18. Calvin Schrag, *The Self after Postmodernity* (New Haven, CT: Yale University Press, 1997), 47. He goes on: "The human body, it is presumed, is but an instance of physical bodies in general, existing alongside other bodies that make up the corporeal furniture of the universe, defined through the properties of extension, figure, mass, and motion. Hence, the solution to the problem at issue, it is claimed, requires a theory that is able to explain the correlations and connections between supposed mental states and supposed physical properties." Schrag turns, not surprisingly, to phenomenology to help navigate the mess.

19. John Cooper, *Body, Soul, and Life Everlasting* (Grand Rapids, MI; Eerdmans, 1989), 106.

20. Cooper's book is very helpful, as is Hans Walter Wolff's *Anthropology of the Old Testament* (Mifflintown, PA: Sigler Press, reprint 1996).

21. I leave aside the intractably difficult relationship between evolution and Genesis.

22. Gordon Wenham, *Word Biblical Commentary: Genesis 1–15* (Nashville: Word, 1987), 59. Philosophically, John Oderberg puts the point this way: "More precisely, the idea that an entity can organize itself into existence . . . is deeply suspicious. For if an entity—any entity—is to organize itself into *existence*, it has to exist before it can do any organizing, let alone organizing its own existence; so it has to exist before it exists, which is absurd. This means that self-organizing systems are really systems that are organized into existence *from without*, as a convection cell is organized into existence by its environment, albeit with apparent spontaneity and unpredictability." See David Oderberg, *Real Essentialism* (New York: Routledge, 2007), 199.

23. The original creation of humans as having the "breath of life" is clearly not what differentiates humans from animals, as the same phrase is later associated with animals (Genesis 6:17; 7:15). But it is clear that bodies cannot be properly human without being animated by God. In his vision of the valley of dry bones, Ezekiel records that it is the "breath of life" that makes them alive.

24. I owe this point to Matt Jenson.

25. As referenced in Janet Martin Soskice, *The Kindness of God* (Oxford, UK: Oxford University Press, 2008), 39.

26. From the profound essay "Homosexuality in Christian Perspective," accessed March 8, 2011, at: *www.lcms.org/graphics/assets/media/WRHC/183_Homosexuality %20in%20Christian%20Perspective.PDF.*

27. Patrick Lee and Robert George, *Body-Self Dualism in Contemporary Ethics and Politics* (Cambridge, UK: Cambridge University Press, 2008).

28. Regarding early Christianity's understanding of the body, Peter Brown's *The Body and Society* (New York: Columbia University Press, 1988) is authoritative.

29. Rodney Clapp, *Tortured Wonders: Christian Spirituality for People, Not Angels* (Grand Rapids, MI: Brazos Press, 2006), 46.

30. N. T. Wright, *The Resurrection of the Son of God Vol 3: Christian Origins and the Question of God* (Minneapolis, MN: Fortress Press, 2003), 477.

31. James K. A. Smith suggests something similar in *Desiring the Kingdom,* 58.

32. J.P. Moreland and Klaus Issler, *The Lost Virtue of Happiness* (Colorado Springs: NavPress, 2006), 43. I highly recommend the whole book.
33. Willard, *Renovation of the Heart*, 166–167.
34. Murphy, *Bodies and Souls, or Spirited Bodies?* 28–29. As a matter of clarification, Murphy does not say who among the early church thought that souls were saved out of this world.
35. See Hans Walter Wolff, *Anthropology of the Old Testament*, 28.
36. One other point here worth mentioning is that an inner life is helpful for avoiding what I might call social determinism, or the idea that we are simply products of our social circumstances.
37. See Matt Jenson, *The Gravity of Sin* (London: T&T Clark, 2006).
38. Willard, *Renovation of the Heart*, 165–166.
39. Everyone has different limits, of course, and some people's bodily limitations are—like my grandfather's—tied to disabilities. While I have reservations about some features of her work, Deborah Creamer's *Disability and Christian Theology: Embodied Limits and Constructive Possibilities* (Oxford, UK: Oxford University Press, 2009) is an interesting examination of how limits and disabilities intersect.
40. Doug Pagitt, "The Emerging Church and Embodied Theology" in *Listening to the Beliefs of Emerging Churches: Five Perspectives,* Robert Webber, gen. ed. (Grand Rapids, MI: Zondervan, 2007), 124–125. I suspect this notion also undergirds Pagitt's understanding of the time-bound nature of theology. See also the section from Brian McLaren, which I quoted previously on this theme (page 38).
41. This is not to minimize the hermeneutic question, or to claim certainty or totality of knowledge. But the hermeneutic task is to discern the ways in which the witness to the unrepeatable events of Jesus Christ is authoritative over our lives and context here and now. That this task is possible, even if difficult, points to the universality of the revelation of God to man, and man to man.
42. Sanders, *The Deep Things of God*, 125.

CHAPTER 4: THE BODY TOWARD OTHERS

1. David Edelstein, "Jack Abramoff and Other Trolls," accessed on March 8, 2011, at: *http://nymag.com/movies/reviews/65900/.*
2. Gallagher, *How the Body Shapes the Mind*, 83.
3. W. H. Auden, "W. H. Tonight at Seven-Thirty," *Selected Poems*, Edward Mendelson, ed. (New York: Vintage Books, 2007), 280–281.
4. From an interview accessed March 8, 2011, at: *www.homileticsonline.com/subscriber/interviews/stevenson.asp.* Tyler Wigg Stevenson's book *Brand Jesus: Christianity in a Consumerist Age* (New York: Seabury Books, 2007) is a careful critique of consumerism that explores how Christians can live in a consumerist society. See also Skye Jethanie, *The Divine Commodity* (Grand Rapids, MI: Zondervan, 2009).
5. Jethanie, *The Divine Commodity*, 36.
6. Clapp is referring to what he calls capitalism. However, I am wary of his (and many other people's) conflations of consumerism as an ideology and capitalism as an economic theory. Is a capitalist system possible that does not depend on a consumerist mentality? If we get the anthropology right, I think that it is. Clapp, *Tortured Wonders*, 79.

7. *The Stanford Encyclopedia of Philosophy* has a helpful overview. Accessed March 8, 2011, at: *http://plato.stanford.edu/entries/liberalism/*.

8. Gilbert Meilaender, *Neither Beast Nor God: The Dignity of the Human Person*, 1st ed. (New York: Encounter Books, 2009), 27.

9. Psalm 24:1–2.

10. Wenham, *Genesis 1–15*, 38.

11. Genesis 1:28.

12. The language of *center* is, perhaps, not ideal, as it presupposes a static ordering. However, creation can be ordered in multiple ways at the same time. When I love my wife, I am ordered toward her and pursuing her good. But I am simultaneously ordered toward God and my love for him. Who is in the center?

13. Matthew 6:26. Emphasis mine.

14. A theocentric understanding of creation, then, is not sufficient for creation care. We need a Christocentric account of the created order.

15. Steven Bouma-Prediger, *For the Beauty of the Earth* (Grand Rapids, MI: Baker Academic, 2001).

16. Wenham, *Genesis 1–15*, 33.

17. Andy Crouch, *Culture Making: Recovering Our Creative Calling* (Dowers Grove, IL: InterVarsity Press, 2008). See chapter 6 (though the whole book really must be read).

18. Wenham, *Genesis 1–15*, 67.

19. Augustine, *Confessions*, trans. Henry Chadwick (Oxford, UK: Oxford University Press, 1998), 204.

20. As a phrase, this is preferable to *ecological ethics* or *environmentalism*, as it includes the specific referent to God's creative activity.

21. Accessed March 8, 2011, the statement is available at: *www.baptistcreationcare.org*

22. Jonathan Merritt's book *Green Like God: Unlocking the Divine Plan for Our Planet* (New York: FaithWords, 2010) is a good representative of the new class of evangelical leaders.

23. See Lauren Feldman, "The Climate Change Generation?" Accessed March 8, 2011, at: *http://scienceblogs.com/framing-science/The_Climate_Change_Generation_2010.pdf*.

24. Buster Smith and Byron Johnson, "The Liberalization of Young Evangelicals: A Research Note," *Journal for the Scientific Study of Religion*, 49–2 (June 2010).

25. Thom Rainer and Jess Rainer, *The Millennials* (Nashville: B&H Publishing Group, 2011), 43.

26. In abortion, the causal forces at work in the killing are easy to identify. In environmental issues, however, the system is so incredibly complex that we should be careful before too hastily assigning responsibility for future generations.

27. John 12:32.

28. David Van Drunen, *Living in God's Two Kingdoms: A Biblical Vision for Christianity and Culture* (Wheaton, IL: Crossway, 2010), 66. Van Drunen's suggestion is that humanity's original home was the *new* creation. As he puts it, "Creation is not seeking an improvement of its present existence but the attainment of its original destiny."

CHAPTER 5: THE BODY AS SHAPED BY THE WORLD

1. Winston Churchill, Speech to House of Commons on December 28, 1943. Accessed on March 8, 2011, at: *http://hansard.millbanksystems.com/commons/1943/oct/28/house-of-commons-rebuilding.*
2. Available at my blog, Mere Orthodoxy: *http://mereorthodoxy.com/?p=2425.*
3. There is a pragmatic intuition that suggests we should give all our money to the poor; that is important to guard against, lest we start making the same arguments Judas did.
4. Shaun Gallagher defines a body image as a "system of perceptions, attitudes, and beliefs pertaining to one's own body." See *How the Body Shapes the Mind,* 24.
5. From the National Eating Disorder Association, accessed on March 8, 2011, at:. *www.nationaleatingdisorders.org/uploads/file/Statistics%20%20Updated%20Feb %2010,%202008%20B.pdf.*
6. See Courtney Martin, *Perfect Girls, Starving Daughters* (New York: Free Press, 2007), chapter 7.
7. Michael Levine, "Why I Hate Beauty," accessed on March 8, 2011, at: *www. psychologytoday.com/articles/200107/why-i-hate-beauty.*
8. There is more to say, of course, about the social problem of beauty. Space considerations prevent me from the sort of treatment the topic deserves.
9. The problem of pornography versus art is one with a long history, and I don't have time to explore it in detail here. I commend Pope John Paul II's thoughts in his book *Theology of the Body: Human Love in the Divine Plan.* I also hope to address this in more detail in my blog.
10. There is more to be said here, of course, especially about how the sexualization of American culture is affecting younger girls.
11. Taken from R. Marie Griffith, *Born Again Bodies* (Berkeley, CA: University of California Press, 2004), 167.
12. Neva Coyle, *Loved on a Grander Scale* (Ann Arbor, MI: Servant Publications, 1998). See also, Lauren Winner, "The Weigh and the Truth," *Christianity Today,* accessed on March 8, 2011, at: *www.christianitytoday.com/ct/article_print .html?id=15907.*
13. See again R. Marie Griffith's brilliant book *Born Again Bodies.*
14. Ibid., 183.
15. 1 Timothy 4:8.
16. John Dyer, *From the Garden to the City* (Grand Rapids, MI: Kregel Publications, forthcoming), chapter 2. This was taken from an advance copy and may not reflect his final wording.
17. John Borland, "Transcending the Human, DIY Style," *Wired* Magazine. Accessed March 8, 2011, at: *www.wired.com/threatlevel/2010/12/transcending-the-human -diy-style/.*
18. Mark Driscoll, accessed March 8, 2011, at: *www.youtube.com/watch?v=9cT5GxM4f50*
19. Roger Scruton, "Hiding Behind the Screen," *The New Atlantis,* Number 28 (Summer 2010): 48–60.
20. I am grateful to Ben Simpson for pointing me to this study. Accessed March 8, 2011, at: *http://espn.go.com/blog/truehoop/post/_/id/13761/study-good-players -arent-afraid-to-touch-teammates.*
21. The point is similar to John Paul II's: "It can be supposed that, in its original and deeper meaning, communication was and is directly connected with

subjects. They communicate precisely on the basis of the common union that exists between them." See *Theology of the Body*, December 19, 1979.

22. See also my contribution to *The New Media Frontier*, John Mark Reynolds & Roger Overton, eds. (Wheaton, IL: Crossway Books, 2008) for more on bodily presence.

23. I will address some questions regarding the church's use of the Internet in chapter 11.

24. See also 1 Thessalonians 2:12; Colossians 1:10; Philippians 1:27.

25. From "The Old Rugged Cross," George Bennard, 1913. Public domain.

26. Thomas Staubli and Silvia Schroer, *Body Symbolism in the Bible* (Collegeville, MN: The Liturgical Press, 2001), 24. They overstate, I think, the difference in Hebraic and Greek ways of thinking. And there is some evidence that the Jewish people knew of beautiful form as well—see Genesis 6:1–4; 12:11–14.

27. By contemporary standards, he almost certainly would not have been. See Mike Fillon, "The Real Face of Jesus," *Popular Mechanics*, accessed on March 8, 2011, at: *www.popularmechanics.com/science/health/forensics/1282186*.

28. John Piper, "Let Christians Vote as Though They Were Not Voting," accessed March 8, 2011, at: *www.desiringgod.org/resource-library/taste-see-articles/let-christians-vote-as-though-they-were-not-voting*.

29. C. S. Lewis, *Reflections on the Psalms* (Orlando, FL: Harcourt, Inc., 1958), 95.

30. G. K. Chesterton, *Orthodoxy* (San Francisco: Ignatius Press, 1908), 70. Whatever you make of the morality of consuming alcohol, Chesterton's point is a prudent one.

31. O'Donovan's point that compassion is "a virtue that circumvents thought" needs to be attended to. Compassion as a virtue needs to be set within a context of rational deliberation and a normative order of goods. O'Donovan, *Begotten or Made?* 10–11.

32. Taken from Stratford Caldecott, "Chesterton Alive Today: Reviving the Moral and Social Imagination." Available at *www.secondspring.co.uk/spring/beaconsfield.htm*.

CHAPTER 6: TATTOOS AND THE MEANING OF OUR BODIES

1. Chuck Colson, "Would Jesus Get a Tattoo?" Accessed March 9, 2011, at: *www.christianpost.com/news/would-jesus-get-a-tattoo-45376/*.

2. Pew Research Center, accessed March 9, 2011, at: *http://pewresearch.org/millennials/*.

3. Lauren Sandler, *Righteous: Dispatches from the Evangelical Youth Movement* (New York: Viking Penguin, 2006), 6.

4. Much of this history is taken from Margo DeMello, *Bodies of Inscription: A Cultural History of the Modern Tattoo Community* (Durham, NC: Duke University Press, 2000).

5. A "stigma" is, of course, a social disgrace. But in its original Greek form, it's also a mark on the body. More on this later.

6. See Alan Grovener, "The Changing Image of Tattooing in American Culture, 1846–1966" in *Written on the Body: The Tattoo in European and American History*, Jane Caplan, ed. (London: Reaktion Books, 2000), 212–233.

7. See Margo DeMello, *Bodies of Inscription* (Durham, NC: Duke University Press, 2000), 71–96.

8. Ibid., 34–37.
9. Brett McCracken's *Hipster Christianity* (Grand Rapids, MI: Baker Books, 2010) describes the phenomenon well.
10. See *Written on the Body: The Tattoo in European and American History,* Jane Caplan, ed.
11. Victoria Pitts-Taylor, *In the Flesh: The Cultural Politics of Body Modification* (New York: Palgrave Macmillan, 2003). I lean on her description of the movement for much of what follows.
12. DeMello, *Bodies of Inscription,* 73–96.
13. Ibid., 90.
14. Susan Benson in *Written on the Body,* 245. See also DeMello, 161–162.
15. Terry Eagleton, *After Theory* (New York: Basic Books, 2003), 165. His thoughts on the body on the surrounding pages are worth reading.
16. To reiterate, tattoos are about the least significant issue that this attenuated notion of ethics undermines. More significant issues in bioethics are frequently shaped by the same impulses and intuitions, yet far more hangs on them.
17. Oliver O'Donovan, *Desire of the Nations* (Cambridge, UK: Cambridge University Press, 1996), 248.
18. 1 Thessalonians 2:13.
19. See Lorne Zelyck, "Under the Needle: An Ethical Evaluation of Tattoos and Body Piercings," *Christian Research Journal* 28 (6), 2005.
20. See Mark Gustafson's excellent essay "The Tattoo in the Later Roman Empire and Beyond" in *Written on the Body,* 17–31.
21. Exodus 26:1, 31; 28:6, 15; 39:29; Numbers 15:38.
22. Jacob Milgrom, *Leviticus* (Minneapolis: Augsburg Fortress, 2004), 236–238.
23. Genesis 24:47; Isaiah 3:21; Ezekiel 16:12; Isaiah 3:19–20.
24. Exodus 21:6; Deuteronomy 15:17.
25. Milgrom, *Leviticus,* 242.
26. See C. P. Jones, "Stigma and Tattoo," and Mark Gustafson, "The Tattoo in the Later Roman Empire and Beyond" in *Written on the Body.*
27. Grant Osborne, *Revelation* (Grand Rapids, MI: Baker Books, 2002), 686.
28. This is true not only in the modern era, but throughout church history. See Steve Gilbert, *Tattoo History: A Source Book* (Berkeley, CA: Juno Books, 2000), 17.
29. Terry Mattingly, "Missing the Point of Coptic Tattoos," GetReligion, accessed March 9, 2011, at: *www.getreligion.org/2009/10/missing-the-point-of-coptic-tattoos/.*

CHAPTER 7: THE BODY AND ITS PLEASURE

1. See Mark Oppenheimer, "In the Biblical Sense," *Slate,* accessed March 9, 2011, at: *www.slate.com/id/56724/.* See also the discussion of the sexualization of evangelicalism in Janice Irvine, *Talk About Sex* (Berkeley, CA: University of California Press, 2002), 81ff.
2. See Richard Kyle, *Evangelicalism: An Americanized Christianity* (New Brunswick: Transaction, 2006), 194.
3. See Lionel Lewis and Daniel Brissett, "Sex As God's Work," *Society,* 23–33, 1986.
4. See the following, among others: Brian Alexander, "One Preacher's Message: Have Hotter Sex," MSNBC, accessed March 9, 2011, at: *www.msnbc.msn.com/id/13834042/ns/health-sexual_health/,* and "Pastor Issues 30-Day Sex

Challenge," at: *www.cbsnews.com/stories/2008/02/20/earlyshow/living/relationships/ main3850842.shtml*, and "Pastor's Sex Challenge to Congregation," at: *www. cbsnews.com/stories/2008/11/13/earlyshow/living/relationships/main4598299.shtml*.

5. See sociologist Bradley Wright's discussion "Christianity and the Frequency of Orgasms," accessed March 9, 2011, at: *http://brewright.blogspot.com/2007/06/ do-christians-have-orgasms-more-often.html*, or *The Social Organization of Sexuality: Sexual Practices in the United States* (Chicago: University of Chicago, 1994), 115ff.

6. See Diane Richard, "Christian Women Have More Fun," *Contemporary Sexuality*, June 2000, Vol. 34, Issue 6.

7. "It is indeed the case that the New Testament reaches back behind the Old, revealing and disclosing the secret presupposed but nowhere revealed or disclosed in the Old, and thus proving what the Old in itself and as such can never prove—that in all its parts it is right and speaks the truth in a way which is normative for us." Karl Barth, *Church Dogmatics 3.2* (Edinburgh: T&T Clark, 1960), 299.

8. Robert Jenson, *Song of Songs* (Louisville, KY: Westminster Press, 2005), 14.

9. Ephesians 5:31.

10. My favorite is Isaiah 62:2–5, which was read at our wedding.

11. See also Wenham, *Genesis 1:15*, 70.

12. See John Paul II, *Theology of the Body* (Boston: Pauline Books and Media, 1997). General audience of January 2, 1980.

13. See ibid., January 9, 1980.

14. Douglas Rosenau, *A Celebration of Sex* (Nashville: Thomas Nelson, 2002), 6.

15. Daniel Heimbach, *True Sexual Morality* (Wheaton: Crossway Books, 2004), 140.

16. There is much more to say here, but space prevents me from fully exploring this aspect of our sexuality.

17. The definitive treatment on 1 Corinthians 6, in my mind, is Alistair May's careful and thorough *The Body for the Lord: Sex and Identity in 1 Corinthians 5–7.* (London: T & T Clark, 2004). Highly recommended.

18. See Pope John Paul II, *Theology of the Body*, November 14, 1979. While the pope identifies this communion of persons as the "image of God," I am not (yet) convinced that is the case. Man might have a relational dimension with another human being that is necessary for human flourishing without that dimension constituting the *imago dei*.

19. On the grounds that 1 Timothy 3:2 et al. should be translated "one-woman man," which I take it single men can be.

20. Matthew 22:30. Most of the Christian tradition has resisted the notion that we are androgynous in heaven, including its most Platonic expositors, such as Augustine.

21. Matthew 19:12. This is another point where Jesus and Paul speak with one voice. See 1 Corinthians 7.

22. O'Donovan, *Resurrection and Moral Order*, 70.

23. See as additional evidence the statements relativizing the natural family in Matthew (10:34–39 and elsewhere).

24. Rosenau, *A Celebration of Sex*, 5.

25. Heimbach, *True Sexual Morality*, 284. Heimbach's discussion of sexual issues is quite helpful.

26. The role of singleness in sexual ethics has been acknowledged at an aca-

demic level within evangelicalism for some time. Stanley Grenz's *Sexual Ethics: An Evangelical Perspective* has a good chapter on it, as does the more recent volume by Andreas Kostenberger, *God, Marriage, and Family*. However, this teaching has (by and large) not trickled down to popular preaching and teaching about sexuality. Barry Danylak's contribution *Redeeming Singleness* is a notable exception.

27. Charlie Fidelman, "Study Spoiled by Scarcity of 'Porn Virgins,' " *Montreal Gazette*, accessed March 9, 2011, at: *www.vancouversun.com/life/Study+spoiled+scarcity +porn+virgins/2298048/story.html*.

28. Bradley R. E. Wright points out that only 10 percent of evangelical men attending church every week looked at an X-rated film last year. However, he says nothing about Web sites. See his book *Christians Are Hate-Filled Hypocrites . . . and Other Lies You've Been Told* (Minneapolis: Bethany House, 2010), 140.

29. Wendell Berry, "Feminism, the Body, and the Machine," *What Are People For?* (New York: Northpoint Press, 1990), 191.

30. My goal is simply to make the case as hard as possible to ensure that evangelical rhetoric against pornography doesn't depend upon current realities, but actually gets to the heart of the matter.

31. C. S. Lewis, *Weight of Glory*, 26.

32. Ibid., 45.

CHAPTER 8: HOMOSEXUALITY AND THE CHRISTIAN BODY

1. Eugene Rogers, *Theology and Sexuality: Classic and Contemporary Readings* (Oxford, UK; Malden MA: Blackwell Publishers, 2002), 318–319. Pew Forum, "Religion Among the Millennials," accessed March 9, 2011, at: *http://pewforum.org/Age/ Religion-Among-the-Millennials.aspx*.

2. Mark Moring, "Jennifer Knapp Comes Out," *Christianity Today*, accessed March 9, 2011, at: *www.christianitytoday.com/ct/music/interviews/2010/jenniferknapp -apr10.html;* See also Mark Moring, "Radio, Retail React to Jennifer Knapp, *Christianity Today*, accessed March 9, 2011, at: *www.christianitytoday.com/ct/ music/news/2010/knappmedia.html*.

3. Phyllis Tickle, *The Great Emergence* (Grand Rapids: Baker Books, 2008), 101. Tickle later suggests that the Protestant notion of *sola Scriptura* is that Scripture is the "sole authority." That, of course, is *not* the Protestant doctrine of *sola Scriptura* but rather a weak and problematic imitation of it. See James Payton's excellent chapter on the subject in *Getting the Reformation Wrong* (Downers Grove, IL: InterVarsity Press, 2010).

4. James Nelson, *Embodiment: An Approach to Sexuality and Christian Theology* (Minneapolis: Augsburg Publishing House, 1978), 199. Brian McLaren writes, "If a Christian today experiences gay friends, neighbors, colleagues, or relatives as healthy, sincere, and morally equal, she or he must similarly marginalize and discredit this experience. . . ." McLaren, *A New Kind of Christianity* (New York: HarperCollins, 2010), 177.

5. Wright, *Christians Are Hate-Filled Hypocrites*, 172.

6. John 12:32.

7. McLaren, *A New Kind of Christianity*, 181–182.

8. *Judgment* has negative connotations, as it has become an emotionally laden term. But law courts tend to be given more to moral discernment than anything else, and that concept is lurking behind the Bible's use of the term.

9. This also means that we cannot be more inclusive than the gospel without subverting it. And a Christian ethic does draw lines around the community—see, for instance, 1 Corinthians 5:9–13; Matthew 18:17.

10. I cannot recommend Wesley Hill's book *Washed and Waiting* (Grand Rapids, MI: Zondervan, 2010) highly enough on this score. Hill has same-sex attraction, but has chosen celibacy because of his reading of Scripture. Additionally, I might have made the same point about listening to those disciplines that study the human experience—sociology, psychology, anthropology, biology, genetics, etc. None of those provide *normative* categories for moral deliberation—they do not tell us *how* to live in the world. But they do provide the raw material for discerning how the authority of Scripture should shape our experience, and in that context need to be heard.

11. Richard Hays, *The Moral Vision of the New Testament: Community, Cross, New Creation* (San Francisco: HarperSanFrancisco, 1996), 389. This does not entail, of course, that Paul is sanctioning what he critiques in Romans 1, or eliminating the possibility of making moral judgments from within the gospel's confines. See Robert Gagnon, *The Bible and Homosexual Practice* (Nashville: Abingdon Press, 2001), 277–283.

12. This is not a point about any particular participant in the public dialogue but rather how such dialogues operate in the public square. I presume no maliciousness on either side of the issue.

13. Colossians 3:3.

14. Mark Yarhouse, *Homosexuality and the Christian* (Minneapolis: Bethany House, 2010), 48. See also his work with Lori Burkett in *Sexual Identity: A Guide to Living in the Time Between the Times* (Lanham, MD: University Press of America, 2003).

15. Andrew Marin, *Love Is an Orientation* (Downers Grove, IL: InterVarsity Press, 2009), 38.

16. I take it that everyone in the debate wants to conform sexual desires to some sort of normative account, as "liberal" Eugene Rogers argues in *Sexuality and the Christian Body* (Oxford: Blackwell, 1999).

17. See Augustine, *Confessions*, Book II, chapters 4–10.

18. This is not simply to say that same-sex attractions are entirely environmental in nature. The relationship between our body and the world is far more complex.

19. For a broader account of this, I recommend James Smith's book *Desiring the Kingdom.*

20. Smith, *Desiring the Kingdom.* Buy it and read it!

21. In other words, while social environments may shape us, we ought not to be social determinists—a temptation, I think, of sociologies of the body that deconstruct the human person into the various social forces that compose us.

22. This is a point that Albert Mohler makes in his essay "Homosexual Marriage as a Challenge to the Church" in *Sex and the Supremacy of Christ* (Wheaton, IL: Crossway Books, 2005), 121–122.

23. From Oliver O'Donovan, "Good News for Gay Christians," available at: *www.fulcrum-anglican.org.uk/news/2007/20070108odonovan7.cfm?doc=179.*

24. Hill, *Washed and Waiting*, 15.

25. See Mark Yarhouse and Stanton Jones, *Homosexuality: The Use of Scientific Research in the Church's Moral Debate* (Downers Grove, IL: InterVarsity Press, 2000).

26. Norman Doidge writes of "sexual plasticity" with respect to the brain in *The Brain that Changes Itself* (New York: Viking Books, 2007). While I have some reservations with his account, the basic point of biological plasticity undermines the moral case based on nature. The pertinent question is what mold the plastic is conformed to. Regarding alcoholism, the notion of its being a source of therapy floats about. See for example, Hal Kibbey's write-up of the research being conducted at Indiana University, accessed March 9, 2011, at: *www.indiana.edu/~rcapub/v17n3/p18.html*. There is also a helpful roundup of the news stories pertaining to the question at the About.com page, accessed March 9, 2011, at: *http://alcoholism.about.com/od/genetics/Genetics_of_Alcoholism.htm*.

27. Rowan Williams, "The Body's Grace," in *Theology and Sexuality: Classic and Contemporary Readings*, Eugene Rogers, ed. (Oxford, UK: Blackwell Publishers, 2002), 318–319.

28. See Robert George and Patrick Lee's discussion in *Body-Self Dualism in Contemporary Ethics and Politics*, 186–187.

29. The frequent use of "crude," "narrow," etc., to refer to sexual complementarity strikes me as something like hand-waving. It dismisses the position without addressing it. In Genesis 1–3, for instance, it's hard to see how sexual differentiation is "non-scriptural" considering that the first commandment Adam and Eve are given is "Be fruitful and multiply" (1:28). I would be curious to hear from Williams or others how this command could be fulfilled on *any* account of human origins except through something like a "crude" sexual complementarity.

30. Williams, "The Body's Grace," 320.

31. Gerard Loughlin, "God's Sex" in *Radical Orthodoxy: A New Theology*, John Milbank, ed. (London: Routledge, 1999), 158. I could list five or six more similar claims, but I will limit myself to one more: "Reducing what is going on here to a crude theology of 'parts that fit' will simply not do," William Stacy Johnson in his book *A Time to Embrace* (Grand Rapids: Eerdmans, 2006), 120.

32. The notion of sexual complementarity has slowly been overwhelmed by the conclusions of contemporary science, which have pointed to a range of sexualities. We speak, for instance, of those who have both male and female sexual organs at birth (called "intersex"). My case here is one regarding what is normative as revealed in Scripture.

33. Meilaender, "Homosexuality in Christian Perspective," accessed March 9, 2011, at: *www.lcms.org/graphics/assets/media/WRHC/183_Homosexuality%20in%20 Christian%20Perspective.PDF*.

34. The insight comes from Oliver O'Donovan's essay "Transsexualism and Christian Marriage," *Journal of Religious Ethics*, 11–1 (Spring 1983): 135–162.

35. Hays, *Moral Vision of the New Testament*, 381.

36. Walter Wink, "Homosexuality and the Bible" in *Homosexuality and Christian Faith* (Minneapolis, MN: Augsburg Fortress, 1999), 47. Wink at one point intimates that traditional Christian morality is built on "the basis of bad science," 46. Yet that seems to misunderstand the nature and source for the dogmatic claims of Christian moral teaching.

37. The phrase "created order" is controversial, as critics associate it with abuses throughout church history. Such abuses are tragic failures of the church's moral deliberation. But abuse does not invalidate proper use.

38. Hays, *Moral Vision of the New Testament*, 385. In that sense, if desires are formed

in and through our social environments at all, Wesley Hill's line that homosexuality is a "tragic sign" is exactly right. Robert Gagnon modifies Hays'
argument here in *The Bible and Homosexuality Practice* based on Romans 2:3–5.
But the "coming judgment" that he points to does not seem specifically tied to
the particular manifestations of sin in Romans 1, but rather the universality
of the judgment in 2:1.

39. Hays, *Moral Vision of the New Testament*, 386.
40. See Robin Scroggs, *The New Testament and Homosexuality* (Minneapolis, MN:
Fortress Press, 1983), 126. Contra Scroggs, if Paul had wanted to refer to
pederasts, he had the word at hand.
41. Mark Smith, "Ancient Bisexuality and the Interpretation of Romans 1:26–27"
in *Journal of the American Academy of Religion* 64, no. 22 (1996): 244. Much
of the emphasis on pederasty has to do with (ironically) making Plato's *Symposium* a stand-in for all Greco-Roman views of sex rather than one strand.
Contra Brian McLaren and others, it is not Hellenism that was pushing for
male-female relationships as normative.
42. See John Piper's two essays on this in *Sex and the Supremacy of Christ*.
43. See Eugene Rogers, *Sexuality and the Christian Body*, 61–66.
44. Ibid., 65.
45. If I understand Rogers correctly, I *think* his point rests upon the supposition
that sexuality is socially constructed for Paul in the same way that Jew/Gentile
relationships might be, and hence the same rules of inclusion apply. Paul,
however, seems to draw a line between inclusion based on dietary laws (1
Corinthians 10) and on sexuality (1 Corinthians 5).
46. Alistair May, *The Body for the Lord* (UK: Continuum International Publishing
Group Ltd, 2004), 58. The point is also made by Stephen Barton in his entry
on 1 Corinthians in *Eerdman's Commentary on the Bible*, James Dunn and John
Rogerson, eds. (Grand Rapids, MI: Eerdmans, 2003), 1324. As he puts it,
"incest threatens the boundary between the church and the world."
47. Stanley Hauerwas, "Sex in Public," *The Hauerwas Reader* (Durham, NC: Duke
University Press, 2001), 496.
48. Alistair May, who makes this case, also points out that Paul warns against
Christians being married to non-Christians for this reason. See 1 Corinthians
7:39, where he says that a widow can be free to marry whom she wishes,
"only in the Lord."
49. Given that we are members of each other within the church, this unique
corrosiveness explains the strength of Paul's commandment in 1 Corinthians
5:9–13 that believers should separate from those who are sinning sexually
and are unrepentant.
50. Oliver O'Donovan, *Church in Crisis: The Gay Controversy and the Anglican Communion* (Eugene, OR: Cascade Books, 2008), 99. The attentive reader will
note that I say nothing about the terminological debates regarding 1 Corinthians 9:9, etc. I will simply affirm that I think Paul's practical invention of
"arsenokoities" is a melding of "arsenos koiten," which the Septuagint uses
to refer to Leviticus 20:13. Here, a "Jewish" reading of the New Testament
actually reinforces the reading that Paul is incorporating Jewish teaching about
sexuality into Christianity and grounding it in the person of Jesus Christ.

51. Psalm 19:12. See also Psalm 90:8, where Moses affirms that God sees our "secret sins."

CHAPTER 9: THE MORTAL BODY

1. G. K. Chesterton, *Orthodoxy*, 110.
2. Elizabeth Lucas, "Popularity of Cremation Heats Up in America," Scripps News Service, accessed March 9, 2011, at: *www.scrippsnews.com/content/popularity-cremation-heats-america.*
3. See the mildly dizzying articles at *www.greenendings.co.uk/press.htm.*
4. See Ben Peays' discussion on fantasy funerals in *Everyday Theology*, Kevin Vanhoozer, ed. (Grand Rapids: Baker, 2007), 209–228. Some of the services he mentions have gone out of business.
5. Tasnim Shamma, "Options for Green Burials on the Rise," *Newsweek*, accessed March 9, 2011, at: *www.newsweek.com/2010/08/26/green-burial-options-increase.html.*
6. This is inextricable from the industrialization of death. Many of the arguments for cemeteries outside the city limits were made on grounds of health and sanitation. See Stephen Prothero's *Purified by Fire.*
7. Urban sprawl has swallowed up many of those gravesites.
8. San Francisco actually moved all of theirs outside the city. See the discussion at: *www.sfgenealogy.com/sf/history/hcmcpr.htm* (accessed March 9, 2011).
9. From their Web site: *www.bellefontainecemetery.org/history/narrative/.*
10. See Brent Waters, *From Human to Post-Human: Christian Theology and Technology in a Postmodern World* (Burlington: Ashgate, 2006), 60–67.
11. Arthur McGill, *Death and Life: An American Theology* (Minneapolis: Fortress Press, 1987), 19.
12. Personal Care Products Council, 2010 Annual Meeting Notes, accessed March 9, 2011, at: *www.perfumerflavorist.com/events/coverage/85521417.html.*
13. Ignatius, in particular, at times sounds just a little too willing to seek out martyrdom. Paul stayed on in this life, though he almost certainly could have stirred things up to the point of being martyred sooner had he wanted.
14. The preceding is taken from Peter Brown, *The Body and Society*, 5, 33.
15. McGill, *Death and Life: An American Theology*, 11.
16. 1 Corinthians 15:52–53.
17. C. S. Lewis, "Transposition," *The Weight of Glory* (New York: HarperCollins, 1976), 111. This, I think, is Paul's basic point in Philippians 3:21. Also, I'd note that *permanence* does not mean the same thing as *static*, nor does *transitory* simply mean "change."
18. Phillip Cushman, "Why the Self Is Empty," *American Psychologist*, Vol. 45 (5) (May 1990): 599–611.
19. John Paul II, *Theology of the Body*, November 7, 1979.
20. C. S. Lewis, *That Hideous Strength* (New York: Scribner, 1996), 171.
21. Philippians 3:17, among other places.
22. Philippians 2:29–30.
23. Hebrews 12:1–2.
24. See the aforementioned discussion at: *www.scrippsnews.com/content/popularity-cremation-heats-america.* Stephen Prothero apparently claims in the article

that evangelicals engage in cremation less than other traditions. He cites no source for this, nor could I find one.

25. The National Association of Evangelicals, "Evangelical Leaders Prefer Traditional Burial," accessed March 9, 2011, at: *www.nae.net/news-and-events/359 -evangelical-leaders-prefer-traditional-burial.* The correlation between cremation rates and the level of church attendance is worth noting, as is Anderson's distinction between "preference" and "mandate." That says more about evangelical ethical reflection than the statistics.

26. David Jones, "To Bury or Burn: Toward an Ethic of Cremation," *Journal of the Evangelical Theological Society* (June 2010): 347.

27. Fr. Roger Landry, "The Church's Earnest Recommendation and Clear Preference," accessed March 9, 2011, at: *www.catholicpreaching.com/index.php?content=articles &articles=20080815anchor.*

28. Stephen Prothero's *Purified by Fire* (Berkeley, CA: University of California Press, 2001) is a fantastic read on this issue.

29. Personal correspondence.

30. G. K. Chesterton, *Orthodoxy*, 141.

CHAPTER 10: SPIRITUAL DISCIPLINES: THE BODY SHAPED BY GRACE AND GRATITUDE

1. My point is that Abraham's approach to the stone shares certain similarities to the work of sanctification in us.

2. See 1 Corinthians 2:16; 2 Corinthians 6:16–18.

3. I have leaned on the individualistic interpretation. But in our formation, there can be no opposition between the individual and community. For a good discussion of the nature of the temple in Scripture that focuses on the corporate aspect, see Gary Badcock, *The House Where God Lives: The Doctrine of the Church* (Grand Rapids, MI: Eerdmans, 2009), 110–133. I should note as well that I think the notion of the physical body as a temple stands behind much of Romans 1–8.

4. Ingolf Dalferth, *Becoming Present* (Leuven, Belgium: Peeters, 2006), 36, 30, respectively.

5. Eugene Peterson, *Practice Resurrection* (Grand Rapids, MI: Eerdmans, 2010), 8.

6. I think Paul's moral psychology here is world-class. Shaun Gallagher, a leading philosopher, confirms Paul's point in *How the Body Shapes the Mind* (New York: Oxford University Press Inc., 2005), a sensitive integration of neuroscience and philosophy. He writes on page 29: "Further, as one's conscious attention is directed toward one's body, there usually takes place a discrimination or isolation of the outstanding bodily feature defined by the circumstance. In such experience the body becomes consciously articulated into parts, although the isolated bodily feature or part continues to function only in relation to the rest of the body, which may not be the object of conscious attention."

7. See Hans Walter Wolff's *Anthropology of the Old Testament,* where he writes: "The individual part of the body is frequently seen [in the Old Testament] with its activities and capacities," 67. Calling this attentive awareness "mental" might not be quite right. When I attend to the moving of my fingers, my mind is certainly involved. But my awareness is of a different kind than when I am reasoning or not attending to the body.

8. Job 31:1.

9. Sometimes trees are just trees.
10. Doug Pagitt, *Church Re-Imagined: The Spiritual Formation of People in Communities of Faith* (Grand Rapids, MI: Zondervan, 2005), 85.
11. Albert Mohler, "The Subtle Body: Should Christians Practice Yoga?" accessed on March 9, 2011, at: *www.albertmohler.com/2010/09/20/the-subtle-body-should-christians-practice-yoga/*.
12. Albert Mohler, "Yahoo, Yoga, and Yours Truly," accessed March 9, 2011, at: *www.albertmohler.com/2010/10/07/yahoo-yoga-and-yours-truly/*.
13. The fact that most people in the rest of the world practice yoga to connect with the divine does not presuppose that anyone who practices it is doing likewise. Practices require intentions to validate their meaning.
14. 1 Timothy 4:7–8.
15. I suspect—though I am by no means certain—that there could be situations where the two goods would be incommensurate. If we are on the way to the gym, for instance, and meet a homeless man who is injured, we are presented with a choice between pursuing our physical health and pursuing an act of service and love to another.
16. See Nicholas Healy's article "Practices and the New Ecclesiology: Misplaced Concreteness?" *International Journal of Systematic Theology,* 5–3, 2000.
17. Barth, *Church Dogmatics* 3.2, 57.
18. Does pursuing health and fitness allow us to give ourselves away to others? Yes, but it is a different way of shaping the body than presenting it *to God,* which those who want to include yoga in the spiritual disciplines seem to want to do.
19. See Matthew 16:24; Philippians 3:10.
20. Emphasis added. The "innermost parts" are literally the physical insides of man, which the Old Testament does not necessarily differentiate much beyond the "heart." That the lamp of God searches our hearts points to the depths to which his presence shapes our embodied lives.
21. Colossians 2:20–23.
22. John Piper's book *A Hunger for God* (Wheaton, IL: Crossway Books, 1997) is a classic on the topic.
23. Scot McKnight, *Fasting: The Ancient Practices* (Nashville: Thomas Nelson, 2010), xxiii. His book is great and should be read in full.
24. This differentiates food and sexual ethics for Paul. What holds in one arena may not hold in the other.
25. Piper, *A Hunger for God,* 61.
26. Matthew 6:16–18.
27. 1 Thessalonians 5:16–18.
28. Philippians 2:9–10.
29. James 3:5–9.
30. Matthew 12:36–37.
31. See Geoffrey Hughes, *An Encyclopedia of Swearing: The Social History of Oaths, Profanity, Foul Language, and Ethnic Slurs in the English-Speaking World* (Oxford, UK: Blackwell, 1991), which is (as you might expect) full of swearing, but fascinating nonetheless.

32. I'm grateful to Matt Jenson for pointing out that extemporaneous prayers can also be grounded in anxieties.
33. See Sanders, *The Deep Things of God*.
34. Blaise Pascal, *Pensees*, A. J. Krailsheimer, trans. (New York: Penguin, 1995), 44–45.
35. Willard, *Spirit of the Disciplines*, 160.
36. 1 Corinthians 6:11
37. 1 Corinthians 6:20

CHAPTER 11: THE BODY AND THE CHURCH

1. Brett McCracken details this in his book *Hipster Christianity*.
2. Bob Kauflin points to several passages in the Old Testament where God rejects those who simply perform the actions with no interest in the heart, including Amos 5:23–24 and Isaiah 1:15. See "How Do We Grow in Physical Expressiveness? Part 2," accessed March 9, 2011, at: *www.worshipmatters. com/2006/05/24/how-do-we-grow-in-physical-expressiveness-in-worship-part-2/*.
3. For those interested in reading further, I have some methodological reservations about James Smith's *Desiring the Kingdom*, but his analysis of how the practices of the church body shape us is worth reading and wrestling with.
4. The most famous iteration is *lifechurch.tv*, though it was the baptism at Flamingo Road that first brought the issue to the forefront of the evangelical consciousness.
5. Estes' reading of Descartes is simply a novelty. He suggests that for Descartes, we can only know things that we can touch in the world. It is the first time I have ever encountered anyone who turned Descartes into an empiricist. In the *Meditations*, Descartes' method depends upon the apprehension of "clear and distinct ideas," which do not come to him through sensory verification. Whatever else we say about Descartes, he both thinks that God is not physical and that we can know him. In fact, the standard reading of Descartes—which I think there is some reason to question—is that he is *overly* suspicious of sensory data and too rationalistic. Whatever else we make of Estes' claims that identifying presence with the body is a result of our Western worldview, Descartes is the wrong person to blame. See Douglas Estes, *SimChurch* (Grand Rapids, MI: Zondervan, 2009), 60ff.
6. Even John Cooper's *Body, Soul, and Life Everlasting: Biblical Anthropology and the Monism-Dualism Debate*, which is a sensitive defense of the existence of the soul, argues for a "functional holism" that treats the body as essential to our humanity.
7. Douglas Moo, *The Letters to the Colossians and Philemon* (Grand Rapids, MI: Eerdmans, 2008), 173. See also Gordon Fee, *The Epistle to the Corinthians* (Grand Rapids, MI: Eerdmans, 1987), 205.
8. The missionary impulse behind online church is very real. I see no reason to cast doubt on the validity of the conversions and religious experiences that are happening. However, the anthropology of our life in Christ needs to drive our ecclesiology as well. While I am open to online church being a supplement to brick and mortar churches, I also know that the direction of technology is always toward expansion. We should be wary of turning missions into a "technique."
9. Unless, of course, there's something to the particularities of being *that* bread

in *that* place and *that* time—but I don't see how we could emphasize the importance of those particularities without simultaneously doing the same for the sermon.

10. Jacques Ellul makes this point in *The Technological Society*, John Wilkinson, trans. (New York: Vintage Books, 1964).

11. Though identifying a criterion for which technologies to adopt is a difficult task.

12. Is technology neutral? No. See John Dyer's excellent book *From the Garden to the City*.

13. John Mark Reynolds, "Not a Book: A Bad Argument for Church Online," *Evangel*, accessed March 9, 2011, at: *http://firstthings.com/blogs/evangel/2009/10/not-a-book-a-bad-argument-for-church-on-line/*.

14. Tony Steward, "Responses to Concerns about Church Online," accessed March 9, 2011, at: *www.catalystspace.com/content/read/concerns_about_church_online/*.

15. I'm indebted in this reading to Oliver O'Donovan, whose essay on place in *The Bonds of Imperfection* (Grand Rapids, MI: Eerdmans, 2004), 296ff. is a must-read.

16. G. K. Chesterton, *Heretics* (New York: John Lane, 1912), 180.

17. See also Chad Hall's excellent discussion of online church in "Church . . . Virtually," *LeadershipJournal.net*, accessed on March 9, 2011, at: *www.christianitytoday.com/le/communitylife/evangelism/churchvirtually.html?start=1*. Mark Roberts' discussion on his blog is also helpful, accessed March 9, 2011, at: *www.markdroberts.com/htmfiles/resources/onlinechurch.htm*.

18. Peter Leithart makes a similar argument regarding the language of symbols in *The Baptized Body*.

19. Margaret Barker, *Temple Theology* (London: SPCK Publishing, 2004), 38.

20. Like Leithart, I'm troubled by the language of "means of grace," as though grace were some quantifiable substance that could be injected into the soul like an infusion of caffeine into the bloodstream. Grace is God's self-giving, and if sacraments really are sacraments, they are places where God gives himself in a unique way. See *The Baptized Body*, 15ff.

21. See the American Music Therapy Association's Web site, accessed March 9, 2011, at: *www.musictherapy.org/* and *www.colostate.edu/Dept/cbrm/institute.htm*.

22. See, for instance, *Timaeus* or *Republic*.

23. "This Is My Father's World," Maltbie Davenport Babcock, 1901. Public domain.

24. See Roger Scruton, "Soul Music," *The American*, accessed March 9, 2011, at: *www.american.com/archive/2010/february/soul-music*.

25. Jeremy Begbie, *Theology, Music, and Time* (Cambridge, UK: Cambridge University Press, 2000), 305. The whole book is a must-read.

26. Ibid.

EPILOGUE: SUMMING IT UP
1. T. S. Eliot, "Chorus from the Rock," 1934.

MATTHEW LEE ANDERSON writes at *Mere Orthodoxy* and *Evangel*. He has contributed to various volumes, including *Proud to Be Right* and *The New Media Frontier*. He is a perpetual member of the Torrey Honors Institute and a graduate of Biola University. Matthew lives with his wife in St. Louis, where he works at The Journey.